Susan J. Douglas is a Professor of Media and American Studies at Hampshire College, Massachusetts, and the media critic for *Progressive* magazine. She has also written for the *Village Voice*, the *Nation* and *In These Times* and is the author of *Inventing American Broadcasting: 1899–1922*. She lives in Amherst, Massachusetts.

SUSAN J. DOUGLAS

Where the Girls Are

*Growing Up Female
with the Mass Media*

PENGUIN BOOKS

PENGUIN BOOKS

Published by the Penguin Group
Penguin Books Ltd, 27 Wrights Lane, London W8 5TZ, England
Penguin Books USA Inc., 375 Hudson Street, New York, New York 10014, USA
Penguin Books Australia Ltd, Ringwood, Victoria, Australia
Penguin Books Canada Ltd, 10 Alcorn Avenue, Toronto, Ontario, Canada M4V 3B2
Penguin Books (NZ) Ltd, 182–190 Wairau Road, Auckland 10, New Zealand

Penguin Books Ltd, Registered Offices: Harmondsworth, Middlesex, England

First published in the USA by Times Books, a division of Random House 1994
Published in Penguin Books 1995
10 9 8 7 6 5 4 3 2 1

Grateful acknowledgment is made to the following for permission
to reprint previously published material:
EMI Music Publishing: Excerpt from "Sweet Talkin' Guy" by Douglas Morris, Elliot
Greenberg, Barbara Baer and Robert Schwartz. Copyright © 1966 and renewed 1994 by
Screen Gems–EMI Music, Inc. and Ronzique Music, Inc.. All rights controlled and
administered by Screen Gems–EMI Music, Inc. (BMI). Excerpt from "Chains" by
Gerry Goffin and Carole King. Copyright © 1962 and renewed 1990 by Screen
Gems–EMI Music, Inc. (BMI). All rights reserved. International Copyright Secured.
Reprinted by permission.
Stone Agate Music: Excerpt from "Nowhere to Run" by Holland/Dozier/Holland.
Copyright © 1965 by Stone Agate Music. Excerpt from "Too Many Fish in the Sea" by
Norman Whitfield and Edward Holland, Jr. Copyright © 1964 by Stone Agate Music.
Reprinted by permission.

Printed in England by Clays Ltd, St Ives plc

For my incandescent colleagues,
Joan Braderman, Meredith Michaels, and Mary Russo,
and for T. R. Durham, the Leader of the Pack

Contents

Where
the
Girls
Are

Introduction

I am a woman of the baby boom, which means my history is filled with embarrassment, littered with images I'd just as soon forget. Old photos of my friends and me in platform shoes or, worse, hot pants, our hair freshly ironed, arm-in-arm with some neanderthal yet highly self-satisfied boyfriend in a surplus army jacket, serve as unforgiving reprimands of how naive and pliable we seemed in our youth. Reading the diary I kept as a teenager is now excruciating, so mortifying that, if anyone else were to find it, I think I would blind myself with hot coals or simply commit hara-kiri. I look back at my former self, her hair mottled like tortoise shell after an unfortunate encounter with a box of Summer Blonde in the upstairs bathroom, the words she wrote in her spiral notebooks obsessed with two topics—boys and sex—and I wonder: Who are you? How could you have been so insipid? Are you related to me? How did you become me?

I don't know where you were in, say, 1964, but I divided my time between screaming wildly for the Beatles, wearing a cheerleading uniform, scrubbing my face ten times a day with Noxzema, and putting my hair up in rollers the size of Foster's lager cans. (This was when I and all my friends learned how to sleep on our faces.) I memorized the lyrics to every Shirelles hit and rarely missed watching *Shindig* or *Hootenanny*. My friends and I were slaves to fashion, and slaves of the mass media, getting weak-kneed over the likes of Edd "Kookie" Byrnes and Troy Donahue, flagellating ourselves because we didn't look like Natalie Wood or Sandra Dee or Jean Shrimpton.

Only a few years later, I had thrown out my bras, and certainly all my hair rollers, had friends who refused to shave their legs (I wasn't that brave), talked back to men in power, learned how to curse, hurled my slippers, or whatever else was handy, at the TV set during Nixon press conferences, *Kojak,* or *The Brady Bunch,* and subscribed to *Ms.* Yet, behind closed doors, I still applied blush-on and read *Glamour* magazine. I regarded that girl I had been in 1964 as some preconscious pupa, whose shell I had adamantly left behind and whose "I Will Follow Him" mind-set I had repudiated. An eruption had occurred, the Red Sea had parted, and there was no connection whatsoever—except, perhaps, the blush-on—between the young girl who chased boys and the young woman who embraced feminism. Never look back—that was my motto—or I might have to remember my earlier false consciousness, when I had sung along passionately with Little Peggy March and when one of my highest ambitions was to be just like Gidget, popular, cute, and perky.

But today, with the proliferation of oldies stations, cable TV with its endless reruns of *I Dream of Jeannie* and *Get Smart,* blockbuster movie remakes of sixties TV shows, and the election of the first president to have had a favorite Beatle (Paul, I regret to report), it has become impossible not to look back. Baby boom culture is everywhere, in all of its naive and preposterous excesses. Often it crowds out the cultural memories and icons of other generations, so that kids not even born when *Bewitched* premiered in 1964 nonetheless grew up with Darrin and Sam, just like I did, although they viewed them under very different circumstances. Nostalgic and often embarrassing images wash over us as pundits, newscasters, and pop psychologists pontificate about what Elvis, *Route 66,* and teach-ins signify about the huge generation of 76 million people born between 1946 and 1964.

As a grown-up baby boomer with a family, a job, eye bags the size of George Shultz's, thighs the fashion magazines suggest belong in a burnoose, and what used to be called in junior high school an attitude problem, I've been watching all this with an increasingly curious—and jaundiced—eye. For what gets looked back on and celebrated as pathbreaking—James Dean, Elvis, the Beatles—are the boys. Don't get me wrong, I like looking back at these boys too, but doing so requires a great deal of self-abnegation. Because what film and TV recorded girls doing during these years—teasing our hair, chasing the Beatles, and doing the watusi in bikinis—was silly, mindless, and irrelevant to history. No wonder looking back produces for women an overwhelming reaction: the urge to disown these past images, these past associations, as having nothing to do with who we are today.

We wince at women's cultural history and seek to amputate ourselves from this pop culture past, to place as much distance as possible between our present selves and Gidget, and for good reason. Girls and women come across as the kitsch of the 1960s—flying nuns, witches, genies, twig-thin models, and go-go-boot-clad dancers in cages. None of our teen girl culture, none of what we did, apparently had any redeeming value at all. According to the prevailing cultural history of our times, the impact of the boys was serious, lasting, and authentic. They were the thoughtful, dedicated rebels, the counterculture leaders, the ones who made history. The impact of the girls was fleeting, superficial, trivial. The supposedly serious cultural documents of teenage rebellion, like *Rebel Without a Cause, The Wild One,* or *Blackboard Jungle,* emphasized male alienation and malaise. Histories of the sixties still focus on the boys, their music and their politics, while we appear as nothing more than mindless, hysterical, out-of-control bimbos who shrieked and fainted while watching the Beatles or jiggled our bare breasts at Woodstock. Idiots, hysterics, dumbos—empty vessels.

Just think about it. Male rock 'n' rollers, no matter how lewd, drug-besotted, paunchy, or short-lived, have become canonized. Elvis is a saint, a legend, immortalized now on a stamp, while Jerry Lee Lewis, who had a habit of marrying his thirteen-year-old cousins and having wives who died mysteriously, was portrayed by box office star Dennis Quaid in *Great Balls of Fire!* There have been movie bios of Buddy Holly and Ritchie Valens, and forty-seven made-for-TV movies about the King. Pledge drives for PBS are built around documentaries celebrating the genius of Paul Simon, Elton John, and James Taylor. I'm a fan of all these guys, but I can't help noticing that no comparable celebratory tributes have been made to Laura Nyro, Joni Mitchell, or Aretha Franklin. Must a female singer have the crap beat out of her—as Tina Turner did—to merit a film? Where's the movie about the Shirelles, or Grace Slick? Apparently, they didn't matter, and had no impact on social change in America. We hear little about the beehived, satin-sheathed girl groups whose music we danced to and sang along with as we tried to figure out whether to "Tell Him" or not.

What we do get to see plenty of from our collective past is blank-eyed blondes in shirtwaist dresses and crinolines and, later, miniskirts and hip huggers, who served others, who wore high heels and smiles while they vacuumed, who had breasts the size of medicine balls and thighs the size of Tweety Pie's, and who never knew as much as Dad, or even Mr. Ed. Unlike popular culture featuring boys, the major impact of kitsch for girls was supposedly reactionary, not subversive: it urged us to be as domestic as June Cleaver, as buxom and dumb as Elly May Clampett, and as removed from politics as Lily Munster. There is a crucial contradiction here: baby boom culture for girls didn't matter at all, yet it mattered very much. It was laughable and historically insignificant, but at the same time, it was a dangerous and all too powerful enforcer of suffocating sex-role stereotypes.

What's more, neither of these premises helps explain the rise, and persistence, of one of the most important social revolutions since World War II: the women's liberation movement. The common wisdom about the unremitting sexism of popular culture, and our lemminglike acquiescence to it, can't be quite right. For somehow, millions of girls went from singing "I Want to Be Bobby's Girl" to chanting "I Am Woman (Hear Me Roar)." Girls like me, who gorged ourselves on all these pop culture pastries, evolved from cheerleaders, experts at the Bristol stomp, and *Seventeen* magazine junkies to women impatient with our continued second-class status, committed to equality and change, and determined to hold our own in a man's world. Millions of us—even women who today claim not to be feminists—jumped across that great divide between prefeminism and feminism, and once we did, there was no going back. But in our haste to deny our own history, to repudiate what we now regard as our preconscious selves, we've lost sight of the fact that these selves weren't quite so preconscious, frivolous, or passive, and that there is an important connection betwen them and us.

The truth is that growing up female with the mass media helped make me a feminist, and it helped make millions of other women feminists too, whether they take on that label or not. I'm not supposed to admit I'm a feminist, and neither are you, for this portion of our history evokes as much derision as what preceded it. The moment the women's movement emerged in 1970, feminism once again became a dirty word, with considerable help from the mainstream news media. News reports and opinion columnists created a new stereotype, of fanatics, "braless bubbleheads," Amazons, "the angries," and "a band of wild lesbians." The result is that we all know what feminists are. They are shrill, overly aggressive, man-hating, ball-busting, selfish, hairy, extremist, deliberately unattractive women with absolutely no sense of humor who see sexism at every turn. They make men's testicles shrivel up to the size of peas, they detest the family and think all children should be deported or drowned. Feminists are relentless, unforgiving, and unwilling to bend or compromise; they are singlehandedly responsible for the high divorce rate, the shortage of decent men, and the unfortunate proliferation of Birkenstocks in America.

Given all this baggage, it's best to say, "I'm not a feminist, but . . ." before putting forward a feminist position. As recently as 1989, *Time* announced that "hairy legs haunt the feminist movement" and concluded that the women's movement was "hopelessly dated."[1] We all saw what happened to Hillary Clinton in the 1992 campaign, a full ten years *after* she changed her name to Bill's so voters wouldn't think she was too independent or anything. Excoriated by the Republicans as a "feminazi" because she has only one child and has argued (in print, no less) that children have a right to be protected against abusive parents, Hillary was forced to prove she could operate a hand mixer and impersonate a deaf-mute. When, as first lady, she testified before Congress about health care, congressmen and pundits alike expressed dumbfounded shock that a woman like this—you know, assertive, independent, brainy—could be witty and charming. (Once the mikes were off, you could see them saying to each other, "Sheeit, Bob, I didn't know them fem-nist bitches knew how to laugh!") This is what happens to you in America if you dare to identify yourself with the F word.

Yet in a culture saturated by representations of happy brides and contented moms, and then by representations of feminists as deranged, karate-chopping, man-repelling witches, a women's movement did burst on the scene and continues, against great odds, to flourish. Girls who were anything but feminists in their youth have grown up to become women who (whether they embrace the F word or not) endorse many feminist goals and values, and this despite Marilyn Monroe, *Beach Blanket Bingo,* and the Paul Anka hit "You're Having My Baby."[2]

Although many of us have undergone this transformation in consciousness, we'd still rather have a root canal than appear in public in a bathing suit. As we consider the metamorphosis that millions of women, and men, for that matter, experienced over the past three decades, we immediately confront the well-known female yin and yang of solid confidence and abject insecurity. In a variety of ways the mass media helped make us the cultural schizophrenics we are today, women who rebel against yet submit to prevailing images about what a desirable, worthwhile woman should be. Our collective history of interacting with and being shaped by the mass media has engendered in many women a kind of cultural identity crisis. We are ambivalent toward femininity on the one hand and feminism on the other. Pulled in opposite directions—told we were equal, yet told we were subordinate; told we could change history, yet told we were trapped by history—we got the bends at an early age, and we've never gotten rid of them.

When I open *Vogue,* for example, I am simultaneously infuriated and seduced, grateful to escape temporarily into a narcissistic paradise where I'm the center of the universe, outraged that completely unattainable standards of wealth and beauty exclude me and most women I know from the promised land. I adore the materialism; I despise the materialism. I yearn for the self-indulgence; I think the self-indulgence is repellent. I want to look beautiful; I think wanting to look beautiful is about the most dumb-ass goal you could have. The magazine stokes my desire; the magazine triggers my bile. And this doesn't only happen when I'm reading *Vogue;* it happens all the time. The TV grilling of Anita Hill made many of us shake our fists in rage; Special K ads make most of us hide our thighs in shame. On the one hand, on the other hand—that's not just me—that's what it means to be a woman in America.[3]

To explain this schizophrenia, we must reject the notion that popular culture for girls and women didn't matter, or that it consisted only of retrograde images. American women today are a bundle of contradictions because much of the media imagery we grew up with was itself filled with mixed messages about what women should and should not do, what women could and could not be. This was true in the 1960s, and it is true today. The media, of course, urged us to be pliant, cute, sexually available, thin, blond, poreless, wrinkle-free, and deferential to men. But it is easy to forget that the media also suggested we could be rebellious, tough, enterprising, and shrewd. And much of what we watched was porous, allowing us to accept *and* rebel against what we saw and how it was presented.[4] The jigsaw pieces of our inner selves have moved around in relation to the jigsaw imagery of the media, and it is the ongoing rearrangement of these shards on the public screens of America, and the private screens of our minds, that is the forgotten story of American culture over the past thirty-five years. The mass consumption of that culture, the ways in which the shards got reassembled, actually encouraged many of us to embrace feminism in some form. For throughout this process, we have found ourselves pinioned between two voices, one insisting we were equal, the other insisting we were subordinate. After a while, the tension became unbearable, and millions of women found they were no longer willing to tolerate the gap between the promises of equality and the reality of inequality.[5]

At first blush it might seem that "He's So Fine" or *A Summer Place* had absolutely nothing to do with feminism, except that they contributed to an ideology many of us would eventually react against. Those who regard much of 1960s pop culture as sexist trash, and who remember all too well how the network news dismissively covered the women's movement in the 1970s, may be loath to regard the mass media as agents of feminism. But here's the contradiction we confront: the news media, TV shows, magazines, and films of the past four decades may have turned *feminism* into a dirty word, but they also made feminism inevitable.

To appreciate the mass media's often inadvertent role in this transformation, we must head down a memory lane that has been blockaded for far too long. We must rewatch and relisten, but with a new mission: to go where the girls are. And, as we consider the rise of feminism, we must move beyond the standard political histories of a handful of feminist leaders and explore the cultural history of the millions who became their followers. It's time to reclaim a past too frequently ignored, hooted at, and dismissed, because it is in these images of women that we find the roots of who we are now. This is a different sort of archeology of the 1950s, '60s, and '70s than we're used to, because it excavates and holds to the light remnants of a collective female past not usually thought of as making serious history.

What are my credentials for writing such a book? Allow me to introduce myself. I am one of those people *The Wall Street Journal*, CBS News, and *Spy* magazine love to make fun of: I am a professor of media studies. You know what that means. I probably teach entire courses on the films of Connie Francis, go to academic conferences where the main intellectual exchange is trading comic books, never make my students read books, and insist that Gary Lewis and the Playboys were more important than Hegel, John Dos Passos, or Frances Perkins. All I do now, of course, is study Madonna. The reason I chose the media over, say, the Renaissance or quantum mechanics is that I don't like to read, don't know much about history, and needed desperately to find a way to watch television for a living.

This, anyway, is the caricature of people like me. See, if enough people think studying the media is a waste of time, then the media themselves can seem less influential than they really are. Then they get off the hook for doing what they do best: promoting a white, upper-middle-class, male view of the world that urges the rest of us to sit passively on our sofas and fantasize about consumer goods while they handle the important stuff, like the economy, the environment, or child care.[6] If it was important enough to them to spend hundreds of thousands of dollars to bring us *Mr. Ed,* Enjoli perfume ("I can bring home the bacon, fry it up in the pan, and never, ever let you forget you're a man"), and *Dallas,* then it's important enough for us to figure out why.

Now, there has been ample documentation in the past few years that the mass media are hardly a girl's best friend. It seems as if every time we turn on the TV or open a magazine advertisers try to make those of us born before 1970 feel like over-the-hill lumps of hideous cellulite in desperate need of a scalpel and a lifetime supply of Retin-A. Women like me are not too happy with the seeming insistence of those selling hair dye or skin cream that unless we all look like Christie Brinkley, act like Krystle Carrington, and shut up already about equal rights, we're worthless. Women *are* angry at the media, because a full twenty years after the women's movement, diet soda companies, women's magazines, and the *Sports Illustrated* "swimsuit issue" still bombard us with smiling, air-brushed, anorexic, and compliant women whose message seems to be "Shut up, get a face-lift, and stop eating." One of the things we are angriest about, because the strategy has been so successful, is the way we have become alienated from our own bodies. We have learned to despise the curves, bulges, stretch marks, and wrinkles that mean we've probably worked hard in and out of our homes, produced some fabulous children, enjoyed a good meal or two, tossed back a few drinks, laughed, cried, gotten sunburned more than once, endured countless indignities, and, in general, led pretty full and varied lives. The mass media often trivialize our lives and our achievements, narrowing the litmus test of female worth to one question: Does she have dimpled thighs or crow's-feet? If so, onto the trash heap of history. No wonder we want to throw our TV sets out the window whenever an ad for Oil of Olay or Ultra Slim-Fast comes on.

But our relationship to the mass media isn't quite this simple. If we are honest, we have to admit that we have loved the media as much as we have hated them—and often at exactly the same time. After all, the mass media did give us The Four Tops, Bette Midler, *The Avengers,* Aretha Franklin, *Saturday Night Live,* Johnny Carson, and *Cagney & Lacey.* And even though I spend an inordinate amount of time yelling back at my television set and muttering expletives as I survey the ads in *Glamour* or the covers of *Vanity Fair,* I don't always hate the media, or think the media are—or have been—always bad. We all have our guilty media pleasures, the ones that comfort us at the end of a rotten day or allow us to escape into a fantasy world where we really do get to soak in a bubble bath whenever we want. No, the point here is that we love *and* hate the media, at exactly the same time, in no small part because the media, simultaneously, love *and* hate women. (Here I depart from the argument in *Backlash,* Susan Faludi's important polemic on how the media have mounted a major war against women since the mid-1980s. While Faludi is extremely convincing about the breadth and depth of the backlash against feminism, she casts the media as all bad, and she suggests that this kind of backlash is relatively recent. Neither point is true. The war that has been raging in the media is not a simplistic war against women but a complex struggle between feminism and antifeminism that has reflected, reinforced, and exaggerated our culture's ambivalence about women's roles for over thirty-five years.)

Since the 1950s, women growing up in America have been indelibly imprinted by movies, television, ads, magazines, and popular music. Now it's true that, when we're born, we come with this twisted coil of DNA inside us that determines whether we'll be shy or gregarious, athletic or klutzy, cautious or daring. And we have our parents, who, for better or worse, twist that coil around in certain ways so that some kinks we can never get out, no matter how much we spend on psychotherapy or channeling—and some kinks we wouldn't want to. But we're hardly born complete, and our parents, as they will quickly attest, rarely got the last word, or even the first. Little kids have all these cracks and crevices in their puttylike psychological edifices, and one relentless dispenser of psychic Spackle is the mass media. They help fill in those holes marked "What does it mean to be a girl?" or "What is an American?" or "What is happiness?"

Along with our parents, the mass media raised us, socialized us, entertained us, comforted us, deceived us, disciplined us, told us what we could do and told us what we couldn't. And they played a key role in turning each of us into not one woman but many women—a pastiche of all the good women and bad women that came to us through the printing presses, projectors, and airwaves of America. This has been one of the mass media's most important legacies for female consciousness: the erosion of anything resembling a unified self. Presented with an array of media archetypes, and given morality tales in which we identify first with one type, then another, confronted by quizzes in women's magazines so we can gauge whether we're romantic, assertive, in need of changing our perfume, or ready to marry, women have grown accustomed to compartmentalizing ourselves into a whole host of personas, which we occupy simultaneously.

For kids born after World War II, the media's influence was unprecedented. The living rooms, dens, and bedrooms of America became places where people's primary activity was consuming the mass media in some form or other, and much of this media was geared to the fastest-growing market segment, baby boomers. Media executives knew if they were going to succeed with this group, already known for its rising rebellion against fifties conformity, they would have to produce songs or movies or TV shows that spoke to that rebellion. They would have to create products specifically for teens and definitely not for adults. And they would have to heighten the sense of distance between "cool," alienated teenagers and fuddy-duddy, stick-in-the-mud parents who yelled at us to turn the lights out when we weren't using them and often counseled fiscal restraint. Spending without guilt, and with abandon, in defiance of our parents, was "with it" and "hip." "Hey you—yeah, *you*," yelled the advertisers, record producers, magazine publishers, and TV networks of America, "we've got something special just for you girls."

We were the first generation of preteen and teenage girls to be so relentlessly isolated as a distinct market segment.[7] Advertisers and their clients wanted to convey a sense of entitlement, and a sense of generational power, because those attitudes on our part meant profits for them. So at the same time that the makers of Pixie Bands, Maybelline eyeliner, Breck shampoo, and *Beach Blanket Bingo* reinforced our roles as cute, airheaded girls, the mass media produced a teen girl popular culture of songs, movies, TV shows, and magazines that cultivated in us a highly self-conscious sense of importance, difference, and even rebellion. Because young women became critically important economically, as a market, the suspicion began to percolate among them, over time, that they might be important culturally, and then politically, as a generation.[8] Instead of co-opting rebellion, the media actually helped promote it.

Historians will argue, and rightly so, that American women have been surrounded by contradictory expectations since at least the nineteenth century.[9] My point is that this situation intensified with the particular array of media technology and outlets that interlocked in people's homes after World War II. It wasn't simply the sheer size

and ubiquity of the media, although these, of course, were important. It was also the fact that the media themselves were going
through a major transformation in how they regarded and marketed
to their audiences that heightened, dramatically, the contradictions in
the images and messages they produced. Radio, TV, magazines, popular music, film—these were the *mass* media, predicated on the
notion of a national, unified market, and their raison d'être was to
reach as many people as possible. To appeal to the "lowest common
denominator," TV and advertisers offered homogenized, romanti-
cized images of America, which, especially under the influence of
the cold war and McCarthyism, eschewed controversy and reinforced
middle-class, sexually repressed, white-bread norms and values.

Even in the 1950s, however, there was rebellion against these
sappy representations of American life, as indicated by the rising popularity of rock 'n' roll, FM radio, "beat" poetry and literature, and
foreign films. These cultural insurgencies drove home the fact that
the media market was not national and unified but divided—especially, but not solely, by age. Even so, media executives tried to please
simultaneously the "lowest common denominator" and the more
rebellious sectors of the audience, often in the same song, TV show,
or film. By the 1960s, the contradictions grew wider and more
obvious, and the images and messages of this period were obsessed
with shifting gender codes, riven with generational antagonisms,
schizophrenic about female sexuality, relentless in their assaults on the
imperfections of the female face and body, and determined to straddle the widening gap between traditional womanhood and the
young, hip, modern "chick."

These contradictions still exist, and the mass media continue to
provide us with stories, images, and whopping rationalizations that
shape how we make sense of the roles we assume in our families, our
workplaces, our society. These stories and images don't come from
Pluto: our deepest aspirations and anxieties are carefully, relentlessly
researched. Then they're repackaged and sold back to us as something
we can get simply by watching or buying. Despite what TV execu-

tives like to say, the mass media are not simple mirrors, reflecting "reality" to us. The news, sitcoms, or ads are not reflections of the world; they are very careful, deliberate constructions. To borrow Todd Gitlin's metaphor, they are more like fun-house mirrors that distort and warp "reality" by exaggerating and magnifying some features of American life and values while collapsing, ignoring, and demonizing others.[10] Certainly there is a symbiotic relationship between the media executives, who think we're morons, and the audience, many of whom think media executives are cognitively challenged. But let's remember that they have the cameras, the production facilities, and the money, and we don't.

This doesn't mean that the media are all-powerful, or that audiences are just helpless masses of inarticulate protoplasm, lying there ready to believe whatever they see or hear. Hardly anyone with any sense believes that six rich, jowly, white guys in pin-striped suits sit together in some skyscraper and gleefully conspire to inundate all of us with the message that scrubbing the mildew off bathroom tiles is, for women, akin to a religious epiphany. Viewers *do* resist the homogenizing pull of TV, by ignoring it when it's on, yelling "Bullshit!" at the commercials, channel clicking, or deconstructing the news.[11] We might not buy into Dan Rather's newscast, Folgers ads that pretend that having an infant is romantic, or a Rambo movie's proposals for international diplomacy. We also live real lives apart from the media, and our everyday experiences all too frequently contradict the version of reality put out by Lorimar Productions, Joan Lunden, or AT&T.

But some images and messages are harder to resist than others, like the one that insists that a forty-year-old woman should have thighs like a twelve-year-old boy's, and that no self-respecting woman should ever have wrinkles. This is because women, much more than men, have learned from ads, movies, and TV shows that they must constantly put themselves under surveillance. In standard Hollywood movies, men act—they solve crimes, engage in sword fights, right social injustice, and swing from vines—while women are on screen to be looked at. Constantly positioned on staircases, stages, rugs, beds, beaches, even tables, their bodies exposed while men are covered by sheets, robes, boxer shorts, or jungle gear, women are primarily physical specimens to be surveyed intently by the camera, the male characters in the film, and, of course, the audience.[12] Print ads in particular reinforce this, with their endless images of pouty-lipped, beautiful women looking at themselves in the mirror, being gazed at adoringly by men and by other women consumed with envy. Women learn to turn themselves into objects to be scrutinized; they learn they must continually watch themselves being watched by others, whether they're walking on the beach, drinking a beer, entering a restaurant, or rocking a baby.[13]

the male gaze

In part because they got us when we were so young, and in part because the mass media have been obsessed with defining—and exaggerating—codes of masculinity and femininity, they have ensnared us in an endless struggle for gender self-definition. With the recent heavy promotion of baldness remedies, bodies by Soloflex, and macho cosmetics lines, men, too, may learn the pleasures of such relentless self-consciousness. But certainly advertising, movies, and TV shows have also taught men how to look at, assess, and treat women, so this media imagery comes back at us in our own interpersonal relationships, and rarely in ways we find helpful.

Throughout our lives we have been getting profoundly contradictory messages about what it means to be an American woman. Our national mythology teaches us that Americans are supposed to be independent, rugged individuals who are achievement-oriented, competitive, active, shrewd, and assertive go-getters, like Benjamin Franklin, Thomas Edison, or Ross Perot. Women, however, are supposed to be dependent, passive, nurturing types, uninterested in competition, achievement, or success, who should conform to the wishes of the men in their lives.[14] It doesn't take a rocket scientist to see that these two lists of behavioral traits are mutually exclusive, and that women are stuck right in the middle. What a woman has to do, on her own, is cobble together some compromise between these traits that is appropriate to her class, race, and interpersonal relations with her family, friends, co-workers, and lovers.

Women also stand at the intersection of another major cultural contradiction: the war between what academics call the "producer" ethos and the "consumer" ethos.[15] The work ethic, with its emphasis on industriousness, thrift, deferred gratification, and self-denial, was crucial to establishing the United States as an economic giant by the late nineteenth and early twentieth centuries. But then this problem arose. Someone had to buy all the stuff the country's factories were producing. And much of what was getting produced wasn't necessities, it was conveniences and little luxuries. People who had had the virtues of the work ethic beaten into them by hickory branches and McGuffey's readers weren't going to buy all these things, especially on credit. So advertisers had to start convincing people to reverse their value systems completely, to spend, to be self-indulgent, to gratify themselves immediately, and to feel entitled to plenty of leisure time. Since this consumer ethos is extremely seductive, but the producer ethos still holds us in its unforgiving and guilt-inducing grip, we oscillate uneasily between the two. This has been especially true for women, traditionally the primary consumers in America, who were also expected to be models of productivity and efficiency, not to mention self-sacrifice, when running their households. The American woman has thus emerged as a bundle of contradictions, seeking to be simultaneously passive and active, outspoken and quiet, selfish and selfless, thrifty and profligate, daring and scared, and who had better know which persona to assume when.

My generation grew up internalizing an endless film loop of fairy-tale princesses, beach bunnies, witches, flying nuns, bionic women, and beauty queens, a series of flickering images that urged us, since childhood, to be all these things all the time. We grew up in different places, with different parents, and with wildly varying class and ethnic backgrounds. There is much that women my age don't have in common. Yet we do have a shared history of listening to the Chiffons, watching *Bewitched,* wearing miniskirts, idolizing Diana

Ross, singing "I Am Woman," watching *Charlie's Angels,* being converted by Gloria Steinem, Germaine Greer, and Betty Friedan, hooting over *Dallas* and *Dynasty* (but not missing a single week), and, as a result, becoming women with a profound love-hate relationship with the mass media, and with the cultural values the mass media convey.

Like all histories, my account of our relationship with this popular culture is neither objective nor exhaustive; rather, it is idiosyncratic, and replete with the sorts of biases that come from my having been raised in a particular place and time. I am a white, middle-class woman—now a wife and mother—who grew up in a place that was something between a small town and a suburb, who went to college and then to graduate school, who has always lived in the Northeast, and who has a proven track record of consuming vast amounts of media imagery. I write this book not from the perspective of someone who was ever a feminist leader or a political activist but rather from the perspective of someone who, like most women, watched from the sidelines, yet who found being a spectator an increasingly political and politicizing act.

Because of who I am, this history cannot speak for everyone. Every woman has her own story. Some of us were smiling baton twirlers, or domesticated members of the Junior Homemakers of America, or gum-popping, leather-clad hair hoppers who hung out at the Laundromat. Some of us were quiet and shy, members of none of these stereotypically female groups. But because we were all culturally united, in an often sick and twisted way, by Walt Disney, the nightly news, Mark Eden Bust Developers, *The Mary Tyler Moore Show,* Cyndi Lauper, and ads for skin creams with "advanced delivery systems," we recognize this history as a shared history. Although I can hardly speak for women of color, working-class women, or lesbians, we often experienced the same very narrow, parochial kind of imagery that made white, upper-middle-class lives the norm and everything else deviant.

In my tour through the images of the past four decades, my goal is to expose, review, and, at times, make fun of the media-induced schizophrenia so many of us feel, while showing how it has produced tension, anger, and uncertainty in everyday women. Most women take for granted their own conflicted relationships to the mass media. They assume they are the only ones who love and hate *Vogue* at the same time, the only ones riddled with internal contradictions about whether to be assertive or diplomatic, gentle or tough. And too many assume that such contradictory feelings are unusual, abnormal. They aren't. Most women feel this because they've been socialized by the mass media, and women should know that feeling these contradictions on a daily basis is what it means to be an American woman. And, contrary to media stereotypes, such contradictions and ambivalence are also at the heart of what it means to be a feminist.

Our pop culture past isn't *all* embarrassing, and it's not irrelevant to how we feel or what we face today. Some of it was pretty goofy— I mean, identical cousins, get real—but much of it requires a second look. History, including this history, matters. It may help to explain why American women are both mad as hell and yet resigned, at times even happy, to leave things the way they are. This history also helps to explain why so many women are ambivalent about feminism, shunning the label but embracing so many of the precepts. And in the end it reveals why the mass media are both our best allies and our most lethal enemies.

CHAPTER 1
Fractured Fairy Tales

In the fall of 1957, the kids of America were castigated by political leaders, newspaper columnists, their teachers, and, worst of all, their *Weekly Readers*. It turned out that while we were running around in our coonskin caps (yes, girls did *too* wear them), learning to twirl hula hoops, and rotting our brains on Twinkies and the Mickey Mouse Club, the Soviets were taking education seriously. The proof: On October 4, they sent the first rocket-powered satellite into orbit before the United States did, terrifying the country that we were no longer number one in advanced technology. Only a month later, the Ruskies sent a female husky named Kudryavka (Curly, in English) into orbit. On November 10, one week after "Muttnik," as the press called her, went up, the U.S. Office of Education published a study confirming cold warriors' worst fears. The Soviet Union outranked the United States in every aspect of scientific and technical education. Their kids weren't making Pilgrim hats out of construction paper; they were learning calculus, chemistry, and quantum mechanics.

As Walter Lippmann wrote in the *New York Herald Tribune*, *Sputnik* didn't result from "some kind of lucky guess in inventing a gadget." This cosmic humiliation occurred because the Soviets were systematically and rigorously educating their students in science and technology and training them to become relentlessly competitive engineers. And so the worst had happened. We were "falling behind in the progress of science and technology," warned Lippmann, and if we continued to lose momentum, added *Newsweek,* "Russia will be ahead of the West in almost all fields in a few years. Unless the West steps up its scientific development, it will become technologically inferior to Russia within ten years."[1] The only hope was to reinvigorate American education, to add more discipline, to place more emphasis on science, and to use *Sputnik,* and the threat of thermonuclear war, to get American kids to switch their priorities from spitball hurling to titration analysis.

Between 1946 and 1951, a record 22 million kids had been born in the United States, forming the first bulge of that demographic goiter in the population known as the baby boom. In 1957, those children, between the ages of six and eleven, glutted the overcrowded, antiquated classrooms of America. Nothing less than the survival of the free world rested on our puny, puff-sleeved shoulders. As we earnestly studied our *Weekly Reader*s and heard how if we didn't shape up fast we'd all be living on borscht, sharing an apartment the size of a refrigerator carton with all our relatives, and genuflecting to Nikita Khrushchev, one thing was clear: no one said, "Just boys—just you boys study hard." This was on everyone's heads, girls too, and we were not let off the hook, especially in grammar school—we had to get A's as well, to fend off the red peril and save our country and ourselves.

Now, on the other hand, no one painted seductive pictures of us girls growing up to become engineers. The Russians had lots of women engineers, doctors too, and we all knew what they looked like: Broderick Crawford in drag. It was because all their women were dead ringers for Mr. Potato Head that we knew their society was, at its heart, joyless, regimented, and bankrupt. No one was going to let that happen here. But it might if they took over. Our girls were going to stay feminine, but they were also going to roll up their sleeves and make America number one again. So when we were kids, and many of our elders were fighting for an improved educational system, including greater access to a college education, the understanding was that they were pushing these reforms not just for boys but for all kids—well, white kids, anyway. This activism, stoked by the *Sputnik* scare, led to the construction of hundreds of new schools, and Congress passed the National Defense Education Act of 1958, which authorized low-interest, long-term tuition loans to college and graduate students. Again, not just boy students—girls too.

Just three years later, this very young, handsome, and eloquent man became president, and he breathed energy into our aspirations. In January 1961 he delivered an inaugural address that still has the capacity to choke up even the most hardened cynics who were young and idealistic back then. (Remember, this was before we knew that his dad had bought him the election or that it was impossible for him to keep his fly zipped within a fifty-mile radius of rustling pettipants.) In addition to the "ask not what you can do for your country" part, there was the stirring sentence "Let the word go forth . . . that the torch has been passed to a new generation of Americans." Less than two months later, he established the Peace Corps to encourage young Americans to work on behalf of those less fortunate than they. Now Kennedy didn't say "a new generation of men," even if that was what he was thinking. Nor was the Peace Corps restricted to males: on the contrary, young women flocked to serve, often as a direct result of Kennedy's inspiration. Never for one minute did I think JFK was talking only to boys. He was talking to me as well. The spirit of the times invited, even urged, girls to try to change the world too.

Thus did the political climate of the late 1950s and early 1960s begin disrupting, if ever so imperceptibly, comfortable assumptions about girls' aspirations. Economic circumstances, most notably the postwar boom and the triumphal enthronement of American consumer culture, also began to dislodge assumptions about who was important and who wasn't. And the ones who were becoming more important every day were us—the kids.

Many of our parents, of course, survivors of the Great Depression and of World War II, were determined that their kids have a more secure and carefree youth. Because there were so damn many of us— don't forget that the birthrate in 1950s America exceeded that in

India—we created special pressures on the society, and we saw new buildings, from ranch houses to libraries to schools, going up just for us. But precisely because there were so many of us, we, as kids, became one of the most important things any group can become in America: a market. Once you're a market, you're really, truly special. Once you're a market—especially a really big market—you can change history.

Advertisers magnified the national gestalt, insisting we were a new and different generation, blessed as no other had been, riding a seemingly never-ending crest of prosperity and progress. We would be better educated, healthier, more affluent, and certainly more sophisticated than any generation before us, especially if we bought the right products. There we were, surrounded as never before by a blinding and deafening array of images from television, magazines, and newspapers, increasing amounts of it promoting consumer goods from Kool-Aid to Revlon dolls, trying to imagine our futures. As we did so, many of us, boys and girls alike, got this almost transcendent sense of historical destiny. We got this idea that we really were the chosen ones.

Coonskin caps may have been the first important clue. Their success proved that eight-year-olds had such economic clout that they could make the manufacturer of a rather ratty hunk of fur a millionaire—a lesson not lost on enterprising types. Imagine sitting at your kitchen table, trying to figure out how to make a fast fortune, coming up with Silly Putty, and being *right*! Whoever invented Barbie, a toy that today makes a feminist mom apoplectic, must have become a gazillionaire. So did the manufacturers of Colorforms, Magic Markers, Clue, and Trix (with the telling slogan "Trix are for kids"). Just as we became isolated as a market, the television industry partitioned the broadcast schedule into slots just for us—early morning, late afternoon, and at least half the day on Saturday. All of this because we were important—meaning the fastest-growing market segment in the country. When we turned the corner from kid to teenager, the marketing blitz was even more intense. By 1960 there were approximately 11.7 million girls between the ages of twelve and eighteen in the United States, and their average allowance of four dollars a week was spent on lipstick, Phisohex, size 30AA stretch bras, *'Teen* magazine, Ben Casey shirts, and forty-fives like "Big Bad John." By pitching so many things to us all the time that were only and specifically for us, the mass media insisted that *we* mattered. They told us that we were a force to be reckoned with. And we girls came to believe that we were freer from constraints than our mothers; that we were modern, riding a wave of progress, less old-fashioned; that, for us, anything was possible.

So this, maybe, is where my confusion began. While exhortations to study hard, make something of myself, and extend democracy throughout the world were going in one ear, resonating with sales pitches that reaffirmed that, as a girl, I had indeed been born into the very best of times, retrograde messages about traditional femininity were going in the other. Saturday morning, after all, dominated as it was by opera-singing supermice and other male heroes constantly rescuing female victims tied to railroad tracks and conveyor belts in sawmills, intermixed with ads for the Barbie game ("You Are Not Ready When He Calls—Miss One Turn" and "He Criticizes Your Hairdo—Go to the Beauty Shop") was a bastion of sexist assumptions.

Like millions of girls of my generation, I was told I was a member of a new, privileged generation whose destiny was more open and exciting than that of my parents. But, at the exact same time, I was told that I couldn't really expect much more than to end up like my mother. Was I supposed to be an American—individualistic, competitive, aggressive, achievement-oriented, tough, independent? This was the kind of person who would help us triumph over *Sputnik*. Or was I supposed to be a girl—nurturing, self-abnegating, passive, dependent, primarily concerned with the well-being of others, and completely indifferent to personal success? By the late 1950s and early 1960s, the answer was starting to become less clear. All too often it seemed that being a real American and a real girl at the same time required the skills of a top-notch contortionist.

These warring messages—"be an American"; "no, no, be a girl"—one softer and occasional, one louder and insistent, were amplified, repeated, and dramatized in the electronic hothouse we grew up in. We were the first television generation, and being raised with the box gave us psychological mutations all our own. The black-and-white images emanating from our sets began to illuminate our vision of who we were and what we might become. But even as television gave shape to our most precious and private dreams, our hopes and our fears, cracks and fissures appeared, for the medium's messages were so often at odds with one another.

The major split we began to see on TV in the late 1950s and early 1960s, and to experience in our own lives, even as kids, was the gap between current events and entertainment programming. Although before 1963 TV news was still only fifteen minutes long, television brought politics into our living rooms through its coverage of the civil rights movement, the Kennedy–Nixon debates, President Kennedy's live press conferences, and the televised rocket launches from Cape Canaveral. What we saw revealed a larger world of conflict, inequality, and insecurity. At the same time, entertainment programming got more removed from reality. The so-called golden age of television, with its hard-hitting, socially conscious teleplays, was over, replaced by *Sing Along with Mitch* and *Wagon Train*. The grittiness of shows like *The Honeymooners, The Goldbergs,* and *I Love Lucy*— with their emphasis on domestic friction, particularly the war between the sexes, and their reliance on female characters who looked like someone you might see in real life—gave way by the late fifties and early sixties to the pabulum of *Leave It to Beaver, The Jetsons,* and *My Favorite Martian.* Now we saw harmonious nuclear families and wasp-waisted, perfectly coiffed moms who never lost their tempers, and we were subjected to the most nauseating innovation to hit the airwaves, the laugh track. News cameras showed us sit-ins protesting segregation; the networks gave us *Dennis the Menace, The Flintstones, Hazel,* and *Mr. Ed,* inhabitants of a bizarre cartoon world hermetically sealed off from politics and history. These were the poles that we, as kids, oscillated between.

While John Kennedy and *My Weekly Reader* suggested that even we girls had a larger historical destiny, I was still coming home after school and rotting my brain with TV. Most of the shows I watched then were not telling me that I, some dumb girl, could change the world. No, these shows had a different message. I would not change the world; I'd watch my boyfriend or husband do that. I did not have my own destiny; my fate, my life, would be dependent on my man's. Since I would be nothing without a man—especially a cute, strong, successful one—I'd better learn how to be cute and popular, how to stand out from the herd, and how to get my hair to go into the most preposterous style yet invented, the flip. And here came the rub, one of the earliest contortion acts. For embedded in the rather unforgiving gender ideology of the late 1950s was the following contradiction: I was supposed to be, simultaneously, a narcissist and a masochist. To be a success as a girl and then as a woman, I learned early that I was supposed to be obsessively self-centered, scrutinizing every pore, every gesture, every stray eyebrow hair, eradicating every flaw, enhancing every asset, yet never, ever letting anybody see me doing this. No matter what girls did behind closed doors, in front of their mirrors, they were never supposed to act self-absorbed in public. We were supposed to be as self-abnegating, and as cheerful about it, as Cinderella or Snow White. The message to women and girls in the 1950s wasn't just "Be passive, be dumb, keep your mouth shut, and learn how to make Spam-and-Velveeta croquettes." It was worse. It was "To really have it all, be a martyr."

No one more powerfully or more regularly reaffirmed the importance of the doormat as a role model for little girls than Walt Disney. When I was a kid, Disney was a demigod, the personification of America's generosity of spirit, its trusting innocence, its sense of good-natured, harmless fun. When I got older, however, I saw the

dark side of Disney, the right-wing reactionary who supported Barry
Goldwater for president in 1964 and denied entry to Disneyland to
over 500 teenagers in the summer of 1966 because they had beards or
their hair was too long.[2] The fantasy worlds he created were as ster-
ilized and white as an operating room in Switzerland, populated by
boys instructed to look and dress like Pat Boone and girls forced to
look and dress like Tricia Nixon. As we look back on this much-
revered national icon, we see that Disney was obsessed with order
and tradition, and there were few traditions he spent more time buttressing than suffocating sex-role stereotypes for boys and girls. For
girls, Disney's fairy tales were not harmless.

Let's take another look at these stories, some of which we first
saw in the movies or on the longest-running prime-time series in
network television, the Walt Disney show, variously titled *Disneyland,
Walt Disney Presents,* and *The Wonderful World of Disney.* Today, as a
mother with the single most important—and insidious—aid to child
rearing, the VCR, I have gotten to see with my daughter these
female morality plays hundreds of times. (I know, some of you are
thinking, "What kind of a mother is she?" Answer: One who needs
to cook dinner, take a shower, and read a newspaper headline once in
a while.) I remember their effect on me, and I see, with regret, their
effect on her.

Cinderella, Sleeping Beauty, Peter Pan, Lady and the Tramp, and *Snow
White* got us baby boomers during the Paleozoic era of psyche for-
mation, when the most basic features of our psychological landscape
were oozing into place. And what got laid down? Primal images
about good girls and bad girls, and about which kind of boys were
the most irresistible.

First, there were the good and wonderful girls, the true princesses, the ones we were supposed to emulate. They were beautiful,
of course, usually much more beautiful than anyone else, but completely unself-conscious about it—you never saw Snow White or
Cinderella preening in front of some mirror. They were so virtuous,
so warm and welcoming, so in tune with nature, that bluebirds

couldn't resist alighting on their heads or shoulders and surrounding them with birdsong. (I remember playing in the woods as a kid and feeling completely rejected when birds would only run away from me.) These girls were extremely hardworking, always scrubbing cement floors and serving food to others, and, despite the fact that they never heard one word of thanks, and instead just got more unfair abuse, they smiled happily, sang throughout their chores, and never, ever, ever, complained.

Because they were so beautiful and kind and young, they were detested by older, vindictive, murderous stepmothers or queens wearing too much eyeliner and eyeshadow, usually blue or purple. These women had way too much power for their own good, embodying the age-old truism that any power at all completely corrupted women and turned them into monsters. In their hands, power was lethal: it was used only to bolster their own overweening vanity, and to destroy what was pure and good in the world. In the ensuing battle between the innocent, deserving, self-sacrificing girl and the vain, black-hearted, covetous woman, the girl won in the end, rescued from female power run amok by some handsome prince she had met only once. She lay there, in a coma, or was locked in some garret, waiting, powerlessly, for some cipher of a guy she barely knew to give her her life back through a kiss so powerful it could raise Lazarus from the grave.

The only good women besides the princess were the chubby, postmenopausal fairy godmothers, asexual grandmas well beyond the age of successfully competing in the contest over "who's the fairest of them all." Except for them, all the females were in competition, over who was prettiest, who was most appealing to men, who the birds and dogs liked best, or who had the smallest feet. With the advantage of hindsight, and the VCR, it becomes clear that Disney Studios, in films from *The Parent Trap* to *Mary Poppins,* was obsessed with female competition and seemed determined to offer us only two choices: the powerless but beloved masochist or the powerful but detested narcissist.

Take *Peter Pan,* for example. I loved it as a kid because I thought flying would be real neat. As a mother with a more jaundiced eye, I have a somewhat less charitable take. In the Disney version, one of the central themes is female competition over the attentions of a boy. Tinker Bell is a scheming, overly possessive, vain little chorus girl constantly admiring her reflection in mirrors or any available body of water. These scenes tell us right away she's a no-good little bitch. Wendy is a kind-hearted, servile, masochistic wimp who only wants to wait on boys. She is in awe of Peter from the moment she meets him, silently accepting the dismissive remarks he makes to her in the nursery about girls talking too much and so forth. When Wendy gets to Neverland, the vain and catty mermaids splash her with water and try to drive her away so they can have the happily self-absorbed Peter all to themselves.

In James Barrie's original version, Tinker Bell is indeed jealous of Wendy and does whatever she can to have her eliminated with extreme prejudice. But since she's mainly a flash of light, and described by Barrie as "slightly inclined to embonpoint"—plumpness—we don't get beat over the head with the relentless Disney equation: vanity means a girl is probably evil and deserves to die. And Barrie's Wendy has a mouth on her. From the moment she meets Peter she's pretty patronizing, telling him he's ignorant and conceited. The mermaids in this version splash everyone, male and female alike, because they don't like people, not because they constitute some harem competing with Wendy for Peter.

These differences may seem minor, but with the special license that animation allows, Disney was able to emphasize that girls do primarily two things—stare at themselves in the mirror and fight over boys—while the boys are more outward-looking and doing more important things. And what about Peter, this boy so irresistible to every female he meets? He is cocky, self-absorbed, egocentric, aloof, and indifferent to the feelings of the females around him. (The Tramp in *Lady and the Tramp,* also held up as a real charmer, has the same MO.) Peter likes playing the girls off one another and takes special delight in the Wendy-mermaid catfight. He refuses to grow up and thus is supposed to be especially charming. Sound like any boyfriends or husbands you ever had?

Now the argument can be made that Disney, just like the other purveyors of pop culture to kids in the late 1950s and early 1960s, was simply reflecting the times, including all the taken-for-granted "truths" about jealousy, vanity, passivity, and a terror of mice being biologically mapped onto the genetic structure of girls. But Disney wasn't passively or innocently reflecting anything; he was actively emphasizing and exaggerating certain assumptions about women and girls while clearly ignoring others. All we have to do is compare his *Peter Pan* with the one starring Mary Martin (which ran on Broadway during the same decade) to see that the story worked fine, if not better, without Wendy being a helpless, fawning twit and Tinker Bell a narcissistic bimbo. But to too many men, or at least male cartoonists, the ongoing catfight between girls, especially beautiful girls, over some boy, any boy, was irresistible; they had to play it over and over—Betty versus Veronica, Lois Lane versus Lana Lang, and so on.

These cartoon dramas put that little voice in our heads, the one always warning us to beware of other girls, especially pretty ones or ones with too much makeup, and installed the little surveillance camera in there too, the one incessantly scanning others—and ourselves—to scrutinize who *was* the fairest of them all.[3] For, in truth, we were damned if we were vain and damned if we weren't. We learned, through these fairy tales, and certainly later through advertising, that we *had* to scrutinize ourselves all the time, identify our many imperfections, and learn to eliminate or disguise them, otherwise no one would ever love us. But we also learned that we had to be highly secretive about doing this: we couldn't appear to be obsessed with our appearance, for then no one would love us either.

No discussion of Walt Disney's influence on our tender psyches is complete without mentioning *The Mickey Mouse Club,* which ran from 1955 to 1959, featuring Karen and Cubby and, of course, Annette.[4] Annette stood out because she was clearly favored by Disney as the prettiest, and because she was getting "them." You could see them, just a suggestion at first, then getting bigger each season, shaming the more flat-chested, freckle-faced girls, making Annette more enviable but also more of a joke. Annette's emerging breasts made many of the boys I knew lust after her, but they also allowed these boys to snicker at her. So here was an uneasy early lesson. Girls were defined by their bodies, by whether their breasts were too big or too small, by whether they came in too fast or too slow, by the fact that these breasts simultaneously attracted and terrified boys. Girls were damned if they had big ones and damned if they had little ones, and were vulnerable, open, and exposed because they had them at all. This is what Annette, through no fault of her own, taught us. Shows like *The Mickey Mouse Club* influenced more than just my own self-image and my notions of how I should look and behave. They also shaped how real boys I knew sized up and treated me and my girlfriends.

Disney's notions about the ennobling effects of female masochism were echoed by adult programming. *Queen for a Day,* which aired from 1956 to 1964 and was the number one daytime show in America, also became emblazoned on my plastic little psyche. Thirteen million of us were completely hooked on this game show–cum-psychodrama, a monument to the glories of female martyrdom and victimization.[5] Here was the premise. Four contestants were interviewed, one after the other, by Jack Bailey, one of the most condescending, smarmiest game show hosts ever. Each woman sheepishly recounted a really heart-tugging sob story and made a request for a prize she felt would lighten her load, or, more likely, someone else's. Maybe she had six children, all under the age of seven, and had just been told she had to go to the hospital for a lifesaving operation. She would be laid up for several weeks. Her request: someone to take care of the kids while she was recuperating. Or maybe her husband and child suffered from severe asthma and could barely breathe without a vaporizer, but they couldn't afford one unless *Queen for a Day* helped. They were always stories like these, about financial deprivation and physical and emotional loss, about the isolation and sense of helplessness of many bereft housewives. One purpose of the show was to dramatize that there was no problem, no catastrophe that couldn't be fixed by a new dishwasher or some costume jewelry.

Of the four women chosen for any show, there was always one who was much more pathetic. After all four had spilled their guts on national television, they sat side by side at a table, an applause meter superimposed on the screen under each one, their eyes darting like caged rabbits, waiting to be judged. Who was the most pathetic? As Bailey called out "contestant number one, contestant number two, contestant number three," the audience was meant to clap the loudest and the longest for whichever woman was most pitiable, and she became Queen for a Day. She almost always burst into tears as she was handed a dozen roses, draped with a fake ermine–trimmed robe, and, of course, crowned. Then began the parade of consumer goods—the washers, dryers, knit dresses, Jell-O molds, Naugahyde recliners, year's supply of Rice-a-Roni, matched luggage, cases of car wax, wristwatches, swing sets, and gift certificates to the Spiegel catalog—that would solve her problems. These fetish objects, the witch doctor–host suggested, would obliterate any suspicion that the Queen for a Day and other women like her were trapped because economically, politically, and socially they were, in America, second-class citizens.

The message in *Queen for a Day* was that nothing was more glorious or elevating in a woman than masochism. The woman who suffered in silence, who worked liked a dog and put everyone else's needs before her own, who washed men's feet with her hair (like in all those 1950s Bible movies) and, when given the chance, asked nothing for herself—this was the deserving woman, the noble woman, the saint. There was a hint of immortality about all this, that these women would be remembered tearfully, living forever in the grateful hearts of those who knew, guiltily, they could never be as selfless or as noble.

If you've ever subjected yourself to the Douglas Sirk melodrama *Imitation of Life,* the number four box office hit in 1959, you know what I mean. Here we have Lana Turner as Laura, a selfish, blond bitch who is always primping in front of a mirror and is obsessed with her career. She is Marilyn Quayle's worst nightmare, the mother who, once she gets a taste of professional success, callously relegates her child to the care of others so she can claw her way to the top. The word *sacrifice* means nothing to this bloodsucker. She "takes in" a black woman, Annie (Juanita Moore), and her daughter, Sarah Jane (Susan Kohner), and they all live together for the next fifteen years or so. Annie, who is more beatific, good, and holy than the Virgin herself, raises Susie (Sandra Dee), Laura's daughter, while Laura becomes a famous actress.

To make a really long story short, the fair-skinned Sarah Jane keeps trying to pass for white, and since Annie, who's obviously black, kinda makes this hard to do, the Judas Sarah Jane treats her saintly mother like a leper, denying her in public and running away to dance half naked in strip joints. But no matter how spiteful and hideous Sarah Jane is, Annie never gets fed up or even a bit peeved. Annie just keeps loving her, and all she wants out of life is to give Sarah Jane money and get an occasional, begrudging hug. At the same time, Annie selflessly waits on Laura, runs her house, and becomes the real mother figure for Susie. The thanks she gets is that Sarah Jane runs away from home for good and says she never wants to see her mother again.

At the end of the movie, worn out from self-neglect and a broken heart, Annie dies, and, boy, is Sarah Jane sorry then. *Everybody's* sorry. The death and funeral scenes are some of the most effective tear-wrenching moments ever filmed. On her deathbed, with the violins and chorus of angelic soprano voices virtually pumping the water out of our tear ducts, Annie sets a new standard of female self-sacrifice. This is genuine "Forgive them, Lord, for they know not what they do" material. As Laura kneels at her bedside, her chin quivering and her eyes widened as if she's watching the Virgin speak at Lourdes, Annie says, "I want everything that's left to go to Sarah Jane . . . tell her I know I was selfish and if I loved her too much I'm sorry." By now Sirk has us where he wants us: we in the audience are slobbering indignantly to ourselves, *"Selfish!? You?!?!* Why, that little ingrate . . ."

Annie keeps laying it on: "My pearl necklace—I want you to give it to Susie." She turns to the black minister who's come to the house. "Reverend, I want your wife to have my fur scarf." Then she tells Laura that every Christmas for the past fifteen years or so, she's been sending money to their old milkman from the first cold-water flat they all lived in because he had been so tolerant about their being late with their bills. And here's the kicker—she's selflessly sent the money in Laura's name as well, even though the now filthy rich Laura would have never, ever thought of such a gesture. Yet Annie made sure her self-centered boss would be warmly remembered as an altruist. Annie's final request is to send the former milkman a fifty-dollar bill. As she begins to fade, with Laura, self-absorbed to the end, screaming at her, "You can't leave me—I won't let you," Annie mumbles, "Our wedding day . . . and the day we die are the great events of life."

After we're all given time to bawl our eyes out over this death scene, the camera cuts to a funeral service fit for a head of state, where none other than Mahalia Jackson is belting out a spiritual about redemption and relief in the afterlife. The church is packed with mourners and bleachers of flowers, and Annie's casket is covered with a blanket of lilies. Just after the casket is loaded into the hearse, Sarah Jane appears, hurling herself onto the casket and sobbing, "Mama, I didn't mean it, I didn't mean it, can you hear me? I *did* love you, I *did* love you." Now there's barely a dry eye in the house; even some men are blubbering. As Laura pries Sarah Jane off the casket, Sarah Jane yells, "I killed my mother!" The funeral procession begins, headed by mounted police, who are followed by a brass band and dozens of friends marching, row upon row. Then comes the hearse. Covered with gilt ornamentation and drawn by four white horses, the carriage is right out of a fairy tale, and not unlike the hearses favored by the royal families of Europe.

As the choral music swells, and hundreds of bystanders mourn Annie's passing, we see that, in death, she has finally gotten the attention, the praise, the credit, and the glory she deserves. Through her martyrdom, she has become larger than life, eternal, a legend. All are desperately sorry that they didn't appreciate her more when she was alive. Everyone, especially her wretched daughter, is sorry she's gone; no one will forget her now, for she has achieved immortality. No wonder my mother used to say with some regularity, "You'll be sorry when I'm dead and gone." If you want never to be forgotten as a woman, if you want to live on in the hearts and minds of legions, be a doormat your entire life. Sure, there's some deferred gratification involved, but the payoff in the end is really big. When you're feeling down and as if no one appreciates all you do for others, just imagine your own death and how much they'll all cry, and you'll feel better.

What's especially interesting here is the reversal Sirk does: the fair, blond woman is self-centered and bad, the darker woman is Christ-like and good. Usually in popular culture it was the other way around, although black women, when they got movie or TV roles at all, could only be selfless earth mothers who spoke in malapropisms and loved white children more than their own. We see here how black women and white women were used against each other in American popular culture, the white woman embodying standards of beauty impossible for the black woman to achieve, but the black woman serving as a powerful moral rebuke to the self-indulgent narcissism of the white woman who dares to think of herself. *Imitation of Life* was simply one of the more over-the-top parables, resonating with the sacrificial rituals of *Queen for a Day,* about women learning the importance of behaving like flagellants.

At night on TV in the age of *Sputnik* there were the infamous family sitcoms, like *Father Knows Best, Leave It to Beaver, The Adventures of Ozzie and Harriet,* and *The Donna Reed Show,* with their smiling, benevolent, self-effacing, pearl-clad moms who loved to vacuum in high heels. Their messages about a woman's proper place were sometimes surprisingly bald. In a 1959 episode of *Father Knows Best,* entitled "Kathy Becomes a Girl," Kathy, a.k.a. Kitten, has entered junior high, but because she's a tomboy, she's having trouble making friends. She still likes to climb trees and wrestle with boys, while the other girls like to wear frilly dresses and wash their hands a lot. Even though Kathy protests, "Who wants to be like those silly girls?" her mom and older sister, Betty, know she needs and wants to become a real girl. Mom says she was a tomboy once too, but she knew when to "put down the baseball bat and pick up the lipstick." Betty shoves her into a bubble bath and then puts makeup on her, advising, "Nothing will make a boy sit up and take notice like a little glamour." But, of course, it's the talk with Dad that clinches her transformation. "You can become a queen to some man," advises Dad, who then describes the "cute tricks" Mom uses. "Being dependent—a little helpless now and then" is an excellent strategy, because men like to be gallant, "the big protectors." This is a revelation to Kathy. "We girls have got it made—all we do is sit back!" she exclaims. Then she gets her final piece of advice from Dad: "The worst thing you can do is to try to beat a man at his own game. You just beat the women at theirs."

A year later, we witnessed "Betty's Career Problem." Betty finds herself in constant competition for scholastic honors and class offices with a young man named Cliff Bowman. Then a job opens up at a local department store for an assistant merchandise buyer, and Betty and Cliff find themselves in the personnel office both applying for it. Cliff tells Betty not to waste her time, since no firm will hire pretty girls for career jobs. "They know from experience that pretty girls usually get married and chuck the job." The interviewer, who hires Cliff right away, reaffirms this position. Even though Betty insists that she's "dead serious about this job," he replies, "I don't know what to say to you, Miss Anderson. We find that training pretty girls for career jobs doesn't pay off." He does offer her a modeling job in an upcoming fashion show but advises, "Miss Anderson, take inventory of yourself—are you after a job or a man? You can't have both." It turns out that Betty has to model a wedding gown, and Cliff has been hired to model the groom's suit. As they stand there in their costumes, Betty announces she won't pursue a career with the department store after all. "I've found something that you could never do better than I can—be a bride," she says, and the sound track bursts into applause. So much for Betty's delusions about working outside the home.

Television shows were filled with such predictable swill. But they kept butting up against real life. In the world of politics and culture, a new kind of woman emerged on the scene in 1961. Our new, thirty-one-year-old first lady, Jacqueline Kennedy, was a one-woman revolution, and an extremely important symbol for baby boom girls just entering adolescence. Only one first lady had been younger than Jackie, but that was back in 1886, much too long ago to count. Jackie personified a generation of women, who, in a variety of quiet but significant ways, represented a departure from 1950s stuffiness, conformity, and confinement. No Mamie Eisenhower sausage-link bangs or crinolined skirts for her. Jackie's smooth, glamorous bouffant hairdo seemed to symbolize a new, relaxed style, an uncoiling of the constraints that had hemmed in other, older first ladies. Jackie was tradition and modernity, the old femininity and new womanhood, seemingly sustained in a perfect suspension. She was a wife and mother, but she had also worked outside the home. She deferred to her husband, but at times outshone him. The week of JFK's inauguration, it was Jackie's picture, not Jack's, that appeared on the cover of *Time.* She was young, beautiful, slim, stylish, and rich—a true princess, it seemed—who, it turned out, read voraciously, loved sports, and had feet the size of pontoons. Jackie Kennedy, in the early 1960s, was the most charismatic woman in America, possibly in the world, and she was critically important to baby boom culture because of the way she fractured the old fairy tales.

The press couldn't get enough of Jackie. And it wasn't just *Time* or *Newsweek.* She found herself on the covers of all those trashy movie magazines I used to gorge on, like *Motion Picture, Modern Screen, Movie Stars,* and *TV Radio Mirror,* that ran stories like "Is Bur-

ton Jealous of Liz's Children?" or "I Was Vince Edwards' First Wife."
By December 1962, a picture of Jackie or some screaming headline
about her had appeared on the cover of *Photoplay* in ten of the previous seventeen issues. She couldn't be on all of them because there had
to be room for that cuckolding home wrecker Liz Taylor. They did
share the *Photoplay* cover once, with a headline that pronounced
them "America's 2 Queens!" The other Jackie headlines were great,
like "Jackie Turned Her Back on Hollywood" or "The Illness That's
Breaking Jackie's Heart." The entire magazine industry—from *Redbook* to *U.S. News and World Report* to *The New York Times Magazine*—was obsessed with her.

Certain images were ubiquitous, such as the shot of her working
as an "inquiring photographer" for the Washington *Times-Herald* in
the early 1950s. She made this look like a fun job for a young
woman. After all, she got to interview politicians and socialites, and
she covered, under her own byline, the coronation of Queen Elizabeth.[6] And we constantly saw her horseback riding, even falling off
her horse, as well as swimming and waterskiing, prompting *U.S.
News and World Report* to gush that she was "the most athletic wife of
a president in memory."[7] She also dared to wear slacks in public, some
of them "shocking pink," all of them "tapered," enraging old farts
who favored midcalf shirtwaist dresses and hats with veils as the only
appropriate first lady attire.

Much was made of the fact that she was smart—a "certifiable
egghead," said *Newsweek*[8]—and painted; spoke French, Italian, and
Spanish; loved literature, art, classical music, and the opera; and had
attended Vassar, George Washington University, and the Sorbonne.
"Once," reported *Time,* "when Jack lost some notes from Tennyson's
Ulysses that he wanted to use in a speech, Jackie obligingly quoted
excerpts, from childhood recollection."[9] In another widely publicized story, reporters seemed amazed that she knew the ancient
Greek origin of the word *ostracize*. I remember vividly the time she
went to France with the president and did something he couldn't do
at all: addressed the crowds who flocked to see them in French. The

adulation she received—hordes who yelled "Vive Jackie! Vive Jackie!"—prompted one of her husband's famous quips, "I am the man who accompanied Jacqueline Kennedy to Paris." The same thing happened when they went to Latin America in 1961. *U.S. News and World Report* headlined its story about the trip this way: "First Lady Gives a Lesson in Diplomacy." "Breaking the language barrier for the President" by addressing the crowds in Spanish, Jackie stole the spotlight as "a new kind of ambassador of good will for the U.S."[10] When she went to India a few months later, she was hailed as the *Amriki Rani,* Queen of America. After a visit to England, one Fleet Street reporter summed up her influence this way: "Jacqueline Kennedy has given the American people from this day on one thing they had always lacked—majesty."[11]

Jackie even added the egghead's touch to decorating in her highly publicized restoration of the White House. She was appalled, when she first toured the White House, that it reflected so little of the history of the presidency. "It looks like a house where nothing has ever taken place," she observed. "There is no trace of the past."[12] She made it clear that she was not assuming the simply female role of redecorating. She was directing a historically informed and accurate restoration. This required (the press was quick to note) knowledge, brains, and organizational skill. She took on the role of curator, persuading Congress to designate the White House a national museum and insisting that its furnishings should represent the full sweep of American history. Yet after watching her assume such a commanding role as first lady, after hearing about what a well-educated intellect she was, it was a shock to watch her conduct that TV tour of the White House in February 1962. She had such a whispery, soft, little girl's voice, a voice like, well, Marilyn Monroe's. (Only later would we appreciate the full irony of this.) The little girl voice just didn't seem to match the eggheaded, accomplished woman. In an October 1962 Gallup poll, people said one of the things they liked least about Jackie was her voice.[13]

But the big story, aside from her fabulous wardrobe, was her feet. This was a media obsession—were they only size 9AA, as had been speculated, or were they really 10, or 10½, or even, as some had whispered, 11? When she was on her tour of India, Jackie had to take off her shoes and put on violet velvet slippers to visit the memorial to Mahatma Gandhi. When she did, Keyes Beech, an enterprising correspondent for the *Chicago Daily News,* looked in her shoes and immediately cabled home with this scoop of the year: "I can state with absolute authority that she wears 10A and not 10AA."[14] Why did anyone care, and what did it mean? The fact that Jackie Kennedy's foot would never have fit into Cinderella's size 4½ glass slipper seemed highly symbolic at this moment in history. For me, it was a personal vindication and a relief, since my feet were edging toward size 9 and I desperately needed to believe you could still be thought of as a girl if your feet were as big as your brother's.

But that was exactly the point. Jackie had these traditionally "masculine" qualities—she was smart and loved intellectual pursuits, she was knowledgeable about history and the arts, she wore pants, and she had big feet—yet she was still completely feminine, a princess, a queen. She knew how to take charge, and she also knew how to be gracious and ornamental. For those of us raised on Cinderella and Snow White, she suggested new possibilities for the princess role. Being educated, having some knowledge your husband didn't have, was glamorous, even enviable. This was important because women's magazines were still telling girls that the way to land a man was to pretend you were dumber than he was. Jackie Kennedy told us all kinds of subterfuges and compromises were possible (as long as you looked like Jackie Kennedy, of course).

Poised on the brink of the 1960s, facing the abyss of the teen and preteen years, the girls of America already had their heads jammed with images and fantasies about how their lives might proceed. We had learned how to put ourselves under surveillance, and learned about the importance of female masochism. Then, in August 1962, we heard that the greatest living sex symbol in America, Marilyn Monroe, had died of an overdose of pills. Is this, we wondered, what too much beauty, too much sex appeal, and what appeared at the time like too little brains got you—an early, tawdry death? Too much has been written about Marilyn Monroe, and I won't add to the output. But her suicide did represent the death of a certain kind of femininity, and a certain kind of female victimization. When she died, it seemed to me, even back then, that an era had passed, and that the seemingly dumb-blond, busty bombshell would no longer exert the cultural or sexual pull that she once did. For while all these twisted lessons about being nice no matter what, never complaining, and being a doormat were well threaded into my psyche, Marilyn Monroe, Sleeping Beauty, and all those pathetic women on *Queen for a Day* made me realize I wanted something else too. I wanted more control than they had. And, one way or another, I was going to get it.

As I watched all these martyrs on the large and small screens, I also watched a woman in real life: my mother. She didn't seem to have much more control over her life than they did, and, as a result, she was what you might call testy much of the time. So it wasn't just that I wanted to avoid ending up as *Queen for a Day*. I especially wanted to avoid ending up like Mom.

CHAPTER 2

Mama Said

The most popular prime-time shows in the late 1950s and early 1960s were westerns, and those of us glued to the tube back then can still identify, upon hearing the first five notes, the themes to *Sugarfoot, The Rifleman, Rawhide, Maverick,* or *Have Gun Will Travel.* Of the top twenty-five prime-time shows in the 1959–60 season, eleven were about cowboys with shiny metal oblongs of various sizes strapped to their thighs, and their oblongs were bigger and faster than anyone else's. Or they had long, sinewy, powerful ropes that they twirled masterfully to render someone else helpless. They were often astride muscular, thrusting, panting steeds, the horses themselves equipped with guns and lassos, all the various phalluses between, on, and around the cowboy's legs rushing, galloping, stiffening toward a showdown. Because females didn't have any of these cylindrical accessories, they had to stay to home and take care of the youngins, bake corn bread, and darn the cowboys' smelly socks. I watched all these shows that extolled male adventurism and naturalized female drudgery with someone who was extremely pissed off on pretty much a daily basis, my mother.

Unlike June Cleaver, Donna Reed, or Harriet Nelson, my mother worked outside the home—as well as inside it—once my brother and I were established in school. She was not alone—in 1960, one out of five women with children age six and younger was in the labor force, and nearly 38 percent of women over the age of sixteen had a job. Their median income was only 60 percent of what men made, in part because they were restricted to low-paying jobs like schoolteacher, beautician, waitress, nurse, and secretary, and were paid less than men for doing exactly the same work. Then they came home and had to be totally responsible for the children and do everything around the house, and I mean everything, with the possible exception of taking out the garbage once in a while or mowing the lawn. (Some things, of course, haven't changed much.) And this was at a time when the standards for household cleanliness, not to mention for the laundry, had been raised to a psychotically obsessive level by advertisers who had read "The Whiteness of the Whale" in *Moby-Dick* one too many times.

Plus, unlike Ozzie or Dr. Stone or Ward, who were always hanging around the house in their cardigans, eager to help Mom reason with the kids, my father, and most fathers I knew, were not around the house much, and when they were, they stayed far away from the metal cylinders Mom *did* get to deploy, Pledge cans and vacuum cleaner hoses. No wonder so many of our mothers were pissed. They worked all the time with little or no acknowledgment, while their ingrate kids watched TV shows that insisted that good mothers, like true princesses, never complained, smiled a real lot, were constantly good-natured, and never expected anything from anyone. When our mothers sat back to relax in front of the TV after a twelve- to fifteen-hour day, they were surrounded by allegories about masculine heroism and the sanctity of male gonads. Rarely, if ever, did they see any suggestion that the incessant, mundane, and often painful contortions of a woman's daily life might, in fact, be heroic too. They didn't even see any representations of working mothers on a regular basis, and, when they did, all they saw and heard was that working mothers were, by definition, bad mothers. Plus they were harangued by white tornadoes and white knights with long lances to get up off their butts and make their already spotless houses even cleaner.

But there were other, historically rooted reasons why many of our mothers had an attitude problem, reasons few of us understood when we were kids. All too many of us witnessed the tensions and the resentments in our mothers, and these shaped, quite powerfully, how we negotiated our way through the media dreams before us. We saw major contradictions about women and work: TV moms didn't work, many real moms we knew did. These moms worked because they had to or wanted to, or both, and they seemed, simultaneously, proud of the work they did and completely stressed out by it. My confusion about what I would be when I grew up stemmed from the disparity between glowing media images of happy, fulfilled moms and my mother's daily indications that her life was one no sane girl would ever want to aspire to. We got it, even as kids, that there was a big difference between June Cleaver's attitude toward life and Mom's. June was never harried, and my mother was always harried. At first, of course, I blamed Mom—what was the matter with her, anyhow? Little did I know what she and her generation had already been through. All I knew was that there was a resistance there—powerful, indignant, and defiant—and you don't live with that resistance without internalizing it. If my memory serves me correctly, I didn't learn to yell back at the TV set on my own; I learned it, in part, from Mom.

We must remind ourselves of the ideological roller-coaster ride our mothers took to understand how their tensions and struggles in relation to the mass media eventually became our own. Born in the 1920s and '30s, our mothers had been whipsawed first by the Depression, then by World War II, and finally by the postwar recovery, each of which was accompanied by dramatically different cultural messages about proper female behavior, messages with all the subtlety of a sledgehammer.[1] My mother was twenty years old and single when the United States entered World War II, and she was a prime target for the Rosie the Riveter sell job, the most concerted propaganda campaign up to that time aimed specifically at women. In the 1930s, the message to women had been "Don't steal a job from a man," and twenty-six states had laws prohibiting the employment of married women.[2] Single, white women could find work as salesgirls, beauticians, schoolteachers, secretaries, and nurses; women of color were much more restricted, consigned to jobs like maid, cook, or laundress. Although over three-fourths of the women who worked did so because they had to, the common wisdom was that most women worked for a more frivolous reason—because they wanted something called "pin money."

When the Japanese bombed Pearl Harbor, they also blew apart all this accepted wisdom about American women and work. With thousands of men leaving their jobs every week to go fight in the war, there was no one to manufacture the planes, ships, and ammo they would need—well, no one except women. The campaign orchestrated by the Office of War Information, in collaboration with ad agencies, women's magazines, radio producers, and filmmakers, tried, overnight, to make wearing overalls and wielding a welding torch glamorous. Here's a sampling of what the OWI-sponsored newsreels, ads, and radio shows told our mothers.[3] The newsreel "Glamour Girls of 1943," with its bevy of female riveters and assembly-line workers, was narrated by a stentorian male baritone who bellowed about "women on an equal footing with men, earning the same pay" and proclaimed, "With industrial advances, there's practically no limit to the types of jobs women can do." The radio show *Womanpower,* with a similar male baritone, explained its title at the beginning of each broadcast: "the power to create and sustain life; the power to construct in the midst of destruction; an unlimited source of moral and physical energy working to win the war." Magazine ads were filled with images of determined women workers and had headlines like "Women Teach Industry Recipe for Protection" or showed a smiling riveter captioned "Miss America, 1943." The campaign worked—over 6 million women joined the workforce during the war, 2 million of them in heavy industry. One-third of the home-front jobs were held by women. Others, like my mother, joined the WACs and the WAVES.

By the end of the war, most of these women had discovered that they liked working outside the home—they liked the money, the sense of purpose, the autonomy. Polls showed that 80 percent wanted to continue working after the war. Women also wanted to be reunited with their husbands or sweethearts, and they wanted to start families. This was a very real desire, but they didn't want to give up everything for it. Poor, deluded souls—they wanted it all, and they didn't quite get it. The war was over, and they were supposed to sashay back to the kitchen and learn how to make green beans baked with Campbell's cream of mushroom soup.

The backlash against our mothers, which began nine seconds after Japan surrendered, makes the backlash of the 1980s look flaccid. Fueled by the fear that there wouldn't be enough jobs for returning servicemen and that depression conditions might return, the campaign to get women out of the workforce began immediately: in 1946, 4 million women were fired from their jobs.[4] But there was an ideological component as well, stemming from the postwar hysteria over Communism. If the United States was going to fight off contamination from this scourge—and the disease/infestation metaphor was rampant—then *our* women had to be very different from *their* women. Their women worked in masculine jobs and had their kids raised outside the home in state-run child-care centers that brainwashed kids to become good little comrades. Therefore, our kids had to be raised at home by their moms if we were going to remain democratic and free. There actually were politicians and newspapers that proclaimed day care a "Communist plot."

As if fears of a new depression and subversion by the reds weren't enough to convince Mom to stay home, pop psychologists added another reason—women who wanted to continue working outside the home were nuts. In 1947, Marynia Farnham and Ferdinand Lundberg, a shrink and a sociologist, published the best-seller *Modern Woman: The Lost Sex*. The hypocrisy of Farnham, herself a career woman, having the chutzpah to order other women to stay home didn't seem to compromise the book's influence. In fact, it was even better that this drivel came from a woman. Feminists—meaning any women who thought there might be more to life than baking cookies and administering rectal thermometers—were "neurotically disturbed women" afflicted with the much-dreaded "penis envy."

Feminism was "at its core a deep illness." Lundberg and Farnham asserted that the only healthy woman was one who followed her biological destiny and procreated on a regular basis, learned to crochet, avoided higher education at all costs because it would make her frigid, and, in general, embraced a "feminine way of life." Women who wanted to step out of the confines of the kitchen and the bedroom were sick, sick, sick, and if this kind of woman had children, she turned them into "delinquents," "criminals," and "confirmed alcoholics."

A classic example of such a woman was Mildred Pierce, the character Joan Crawford portrayed in her 1945 comeback film, for which she won an Oscar. Mildred, a working mom, turns her daughter, Veda, into a monster. Mildred works hard to build up a restaurant business, and, as a result, she is able to give Veda everything she wants—everything except time and mother love, that is. Mildred's financial power and independence ruin Veda, who ends up, in sequence, a spoiled brat, a tramp, and a murderer. The story in *Mildred Pierce* is a simple one: to save themselves, their children, and, indeed, the very social fabric of America, women needed to return the workplace to its rightful inhabitants, men.[5]

The desire to work outside the home, so healthy and welcome in 1944, was, just three years later, prima facie evidence that you were a neurotic, castrating hysteric. Resonating with this message were the women of film noir, the black widow spiders, seductresses, and gun-crazy bitches whose appetites for money and sex drove men to ruin in *The Postman Always Rings Twice* (1946), *Double Indemnity* (on the cutting edge in 1944), *They Live by Night* (1949), *Gun Crazy/Deadly Is the Female,* (1949), and, later, *Kiss Me Deadly* (1955).[6] In "crime" comics, quite popular in the postwar years, the breasts of women were as large as the *Enola Gay;* as a result, the genre became known as "headlight comics," and the women were villains, victims, or both.

Gone were the ads telling women they could do anything a man could do. Instead, ads like one for the Penn Mutual Life Insurance Company showed a bride under the headline "Lady, Do *You* Have a

Job!" reciting, "I promise to love, honor, obey, cook meals, make beds, sort laundry, take care of babies, etc. . . ." Even more horrifying and repressive was the now infamous Johnson & Johnson campaign, which, through trick photography, featured gargantuan babies imprisoning their Tinker Bell–sized moms in cribs, playpens, high chairs, and toddler leashes and castigating, "Whoa, Mom! Can't you *take* it? Shame, Mom! You said you'd like to have a baby's easy life— but now that we've changed places, you *fuss.*" After listening to everything she's done wrong, Mom concedes, "I haven't been a careful mother, have I? Watch me *reform!*" Moms, in other words, were always wrong, never doing things quite right, and in constant need of improvement that could come only from listening to expert advice.

But backlash of this intensity is a sign of struggle, of men's sense of being under siege, a sign that women have made important gains they will not relinquish easily, or ever.[7] Because the contrast between the Rosie the Riveter campaign and the virulent antifeminism that followed it was so stark, it is easy to paint a black-and-white, before-and-after portrait of this period. It is common to think of the postwar backlash as beginning with a vengeance in 1946 and reigning in a monolithic and uncontested form until the late 1960s. But this was not the case.

The ideology that Betty Friedan would label in 1963 "the feminine mystique" had not really consolidated until sometime between 1952 and 1955. The years before this were more turbulent than we think, the messages about motherhood and working outside the home more ambiguous. In the late 1940s and early 1950s, the period when our mothers were getting their adult lives and their households started, America went back into the trenches, this time over women's proper roles, a battle played out in movies, TV shows, and ads. The antifeminism was so vehement, even vicious, at times, that the feminism of the period has been too frequently eclipsed. But it was there, in movies like *Adam's Rib* and *Pat and Mike,* in Ashley Montagu's 1953 best-seller *The Natural Superiority of Women* (which maintained that men had "womb and breast envy"), in numerous magazine articles, and, of course, in Simone de Beauvoir's *The Second Sex,* also published in 1952. And it was there on the new invention in the home, television.

On television in the late 1940s and early 1950s, various female characters often defied the compliant, womb-centered, housewife stereotype. The most famous, of course, was Lucy, but there were others, including Alice Kramden of *The Honeymooners,* Imogene Coca of *Your Show of Shows,* Gracie Allen of *The Burns and Allen Show,* Mama and Katrin in *Mama,* and Molly Goldberg of *The Goldbergs.* Either physically or verbally, or both, these women refused to stay in their place, and broke the stays of corseted demureness. These were transgressive women, trespassers who delighted in violating the boundaries of femininity. Some of them, like Lucille Ball and Imogene Coca, were physically mutinous, brilliantly using their faces and bodies in slapstick enactments of the battle of the sexes. These women and their bodies refused to be contained in the home or limited by the prevailing orthodoxy about appropriate female comportment. Their voices mattered too; often they were loud, they weren't afraid to yell, and they didn't back away from verbal combat.

Gracie Allen was the master of linguistic slapstick, using puns, malapropisms, and a willful misunderstanding of language to turn male logic on its head. She refused to be contained by the conventions of male language that seemed to leave women no position from which to speak honestly about their lives. Gracie the character was supposed to be addled and ditzy, but viewers knew that Gracie the comedienne knew exactly what she was doing and why. Alice Kramden gave as good as she got, never backed down, and emerged as the repository of reason and sensibility in each episode of *The Honeymooners,* despite her husband's size and temper, and his weekly threats to sock her so hard she'd go right to the moon. And Molly Goldberg—"Yoo-hoo, Mrs. Bloom"—was anything but contained and demure. There were also single working women in *Private Secretary, Our Miss Brooks, How to Marry a Millionaire,* and *Oh! Susanna,* and while they labored in stereotypical jobs and were often obsessed with men, at least there was an acknowledgment of women's participation in the workforce with women holding the leading roles in such shows. This, too, would soon change.

Through one kind of slapstick or another, these shows gave expression to the deep anxieties over who would wear the pants in postwar America. And while it is true that the shows' narratives tended to manage and resolve these anxieties so that the woman was happily tamed at the end of each episode, our mothers could nonetheless see, on television, women resisting and making fun of the credo that "real" women found fulfillment in diaper pails and macaroni recipes, or that they thought obeying their husbands made much sense. By the late 1950s, when these shows were replaced by *Father Knows Best, The Donna Reed Show,* and *Leave It to Beaver,* with their cookie-cutter moms, television's physical and linguistic containment of women was complete. Gags and slapstick were replaced by laugh track–buttressed comedies about the process of raising children, in which fathers came into their own as authorities. June Cleaver, for example, often came to Ward in a befuddled state for advice, asking, "Ward, did boys do this when you were their age?"[8] The ironic thing was, however, that this media containment was achieved at the very moment that more and more real-life moms were leaving the domestic sphere and going back to work.

Nowhere was the postwar schizophrenia about women's proper roles more evident than in the *Ladies' Home Journal.* In between ads for Pond's cleansing cream ("She's Engaged! She's Lovely! She Uses Pond's!") and Ivory Flakes ("How to Bring Out the Wolf in a Man") were earnest articles about why women ought to get involved in national and international politics, and the need for a feminist revolution. In her highly popular monthly advice column, "If You Ask Me," Eleanor Roosevelt routinely wrote things like "I think girls should have exactly the same opportunities as boys" and advocated establishing nurseries for the children of working mothers.[9] Profiles of successful career women emphasized that such women did not regard their jobs as "a mere stopgap to marriage" and that they often had to be "twice as good" as the men around them to succeed.[10] Ads such as those for Ipana toothpaste featured models who were also mothers with text like "Can a MODEL mother be a model MOTHER? Judging by little Jojo's bursting health, cover-girl Natalie Reid does *two* jobs well." A poll commissioned by the magazine in 1946 reported that 75 percent of men and 80 percent of women supported equal pay for equal work.[11]

In the immediate postwar era, our mothers were told that they were inferior to men and, at the same time, that they were vastly superior. Equality rarely entered into the equation. In the *Ladies' Home Journal* article "Queens Did Better Than Kings," the author argued that "queens love peace because women love peace . . . the male instinct for fighting and killing contrasts at its very root with the female instinct for giving, raising and protecting life," thus women needed to take over political leadership.[12] But such assertions often played into the hands of those seeking to keep women in their "proper" place, as did the postwar insistence that men were weaker and had much harder lives than women.[13] Article after article, with titles like "Proof That She Is the Stronger Sex" and "Women May Control U.S.," noted that women were healthier and lived longer than men. "The American woman does less and less, lives longer and longer, while her husband, a drone, 'a social eunuch,' his insurance paid up, dies of a heart attack before he's 50," wrote George Lawton in *The New York Times* in 1948. What should women do? "The next time you meet a man be kind to him."[14] Compared with women, men were fragile and self-destructive, and needed coddling and protection.

At the same time, the tone in the *Ladies' Home Journal* steadily became less enlightened. Ipana, for example, revised its message, with its model mother now announcing, "It's more fun being a Mother than a Model." The change was especially notable in columns like "Making Marriage Work" by Clifford R. Adams, Ph.D. (predecessor to "Can This Marriage Be Saved?" which should have been titled,

"Will This Wife Eat Shit?"). Here my mother's generation learned that women should not "argue about politics and religion," or be "good at cracking wise and making pointed remarks." Every column, month in and month out, drilled into its readers that "the happiness of the marriage and the home depends primarily on her"—the wife. Women should not even consider the thought that men "subtly evade their responsibilities" or that husbands are "inclined to overlook the rights of wives." Nor should wives "overreact to a husband who answers sharply," the number one complaint men had against their spouses.[15] In "What Sends People to Reno," Dr. James F. Bender advised that "bad housekeeping" and "poor cooking" are each a "direct cause of divorce" and that "underweight women make poor marital risks" because they are "usually jittery."[16] Some readers caught on to the trend; one irate woman wrote, "*Ladies' Home Journal* blames women for bad marriages and makes them solely responsible for marital success . . . all marriages hinge on whether we keep beautiful, are good cooks, understanding helpmates, etc. . . . On the other hand, masculine magazines inflate the male ego and also blame the weaker sex for every known marriage failure. Really, this is going too far."[17] Hers, however, was an unheeded voice.

The antifeminist onslaught intensified in other mass circulation magazines. In "What's Wrong with American Women?" first published in *Esquire* and reprinted in *Reader's Digest* in 1949, the author unburdened himself of the opinion that the American woman is "the most spoiled and self-centered woman in the world," and he complained about America's loathsome "near-matriarchy."[18] In a subsequent issue, the magazine summed up the "chief charges commonly leveled against women": "They reach their decisions emotionally instead of logically; they are unpredictable; they usually don't like each other much; they have a genuine fondness for trouble and if there isn't any real trouble they will cook up some out of boredom. Finally, they must have the last word and a disproportionate percentage of the other words."[19] In "Women Aren't Men," also in *Reader's Digest,* our mothers could read that the "egotistic desires of women . . . for equal rights" were responsible for the high divorce rate and escalating juvenile delinquency in America. Especially vile were working mothers. But they paid a price. "The neglected child" realizes right away that his mother works because she loves her job more than she loves him, thus he "often hates her with a passionate intensity."[20]

By the early 1950s, the battle lines hardened, and, within a few years, it appeared that the antifeminists had won. In the ten-year period from 1940 to 1950, our mothers had been told, first, that they shouldn't work outside the home, especially once they were married, then that there was no job they couldn't do and that it was exciting and patriotic to work outside the home, and, finally, that their real job was to wash diapers, make meat loaf, and obey their husbands no matter how brutish, dumb, or unreasonable they were. While endless movies in the 1950s and '60s glorified male heroism during World War II, our mothers' roles in helping win the war were repressed, and they appeared primarily as the sweethearts left behind, not as the welders and riveters who built the ships and planes. It was as if their experiences—including the nascent feminism of the time—had never really happened. But repressing public memories doesn't mean that private ones are forgotten.

We watched our mothers react in a variety of ways. Between cleaning, making Jell-O molds, being den mothers, chauffeuring, running the nation's PTAs, and ironing Dad's boxers, housewives in this period averaged a ninety-nine-hour workweek.[21] Yet ads for household appliances, like Maytag's, which showed an ecstatic woman gushing, "Look . . . no work!" or the one for an electric mixer that instructed, "You Dial It!—Dormeyer Does It!" suggested that women led a life of leisure. Our mothers saw themselves simultaneously revered and loathed. They were childlike nincompoops who would never learn how to drive a car or balance a checkbook, but they were domineering, unreasonable Amazons who controlled the nation's wealth and from whom men needed to escape as often as possible. But it wasn't just our mothers who took in these messages.

We daughters absorbed them as well, and they encouraged us to respect Dad and to resist and ridicule Mom.

To cope with the misogyny of American culture, many of our mothers smoked, or drank, or took Miltowns, or saw a shrink, or yelled a lot at us. And an increasing number of them did one other thing: despite all the propaganda casting working women as neurotic freaks, they got jobs. By 1955, there were more women with jobs than at any point in the nation's previous history.[22] At the very time when the feminine mystique imagery was most ironclad, women began flocking to the job market. Women whose husbands made too much money to justify their having jobs of their own did volunteer work with charities or, significantly, with political campaigns. Other mothers I knew, in the midst of raising several kids, went back to college. Whether they were beauticians, nurses, B.A. candidates, or envelope stuffers for the Democratic party, our mothers accentuated the inconsistencies of American womanhood even more. Just because the feminine mystique had become the official ideology by the late 1950s doesn't mean that all women bought into it. But it divided many of our mothers against themselves, pulled between idealized images and the more gritty reality of their own lives, pulled between defiance and self-abnegation.

So while we kids were beginning to reverberate between the lessons of *Sputnik* and the lessons of Snow White, our mothers, too, were ensnared in the historical contradictions of the moment. Economic forces and opportunities pulled them one way, cultural ideology pulled them another. My mother had worked since she was a teenager, and she looked back fondly on the fun and sense of purpose she had had during World War II. By the mid-1950s, with a national need for more teachers, nurses, and secretaries, there was an implicit call to women like my mother to reenter the workforce. And my mother wanted the extra money, to help buy the vast array of consumer goods and services that defined the good life for her and her children. So she went back to work, and here's where she and millions like her got nailed.

A burgeoning consumer culture needs one big thing—consumers. Consumers, of course, need money. But America's consumer culture was predicated on the notion that women were the major consumers of most goods—that was their job, after all—and that, to sell to them, you had to emphasize their roles as wives and mothers, because it was in these capacities, not in their capacities as secretaries or nurses, that women bought. So, to buy more things, many of our mothers had to work. To sell to them, advertisers erased and diminished this fact, and stressed how many more products they needed, and how many more tasks they had to undertake with those products, to be genuinely good wives and moms. No wonder Mom was often a bit testy. Here she was, part of a system that insisted it needed her to consume inside the home but adamantly refused to admit it also needed her to produce outside the home. She was supposed to deny a central fact of her life, and she was damned for doing the very things that were keeping not just the family but the entire U.S. economy financially healthy.

The delusion, or the insistence, that all women identified themselves primarily as wives and mothers seems to have gripped the consciousness of pretty much everyone in advertising. A 1958 how-to text, *What Makes Women Buy,* offers the perfectly preserved, fossilized remains of the stereotypes about women that triumphed between 1953 and 1963. Advertisers had some pretty fixed ideas about our mothers and which immutable female traits had to be taken into account when selling to them. Having the intelligence, common sense, and strength to manage a household, let alone a household and a job, wasn't among those traits. Women, the book intoned, "have a strong tendency toward irrational beliefs" and are "highly intuitive." The conviction that a woman "lives in two worlds—her real world and an imaginary world she creates" led advertisers to invent guys like the shiny-headed, bullet-shaped, cartoon genie Mr. Clean to really reach our childlike, daydream-believin' moms.

Slaves to their reproductive systems, "at least half of all women are turned into 'witches' of varying degrees once a month."

"Woman's bone structure and bodily proportions overwhelmingly lead her toward more passive interests and an inward life," which I guess explains why American moms always sat on their asses, drinking beer and watching ball games, while our naturally more active dads chased the kids around the house and drove them to scout meetings and Little League. "The instability of woman's bodily functions and nervous system makes her a more emotional customer than a man," which is why my mother systematically hunted for bargains while my dad would come home with ten of something if it had a great new package. Women "tire more easily than men," and "the average woman would be more interested in reading about sewing than about swimming." (Who'd want to *read* about either?) Instead, "home decorating is a high natural interest," wired, presumably, into one (or both) of the X chromosomes. "Women's verbal aptitude accounts for the fact that they like to gossip *and* have the last word." Women "like to see pictures of food" and have a "relatively low interest in travel." They are "not inclined to be interested in automobiles and business," and their "interest in sports and mechanical objects is extremely low." All these notions, most of them snide, condescending, and stupid, constituted the commonsense, taken-for-granted assumptions about my mother, and week in, week out, I watched her chafe under them.

My mother despised doing housework, and she was extremely unpleasant to be around when, on her weekends "off," she vacuumed, stripped the beds, cleaned the oven, ironed, and so forth. Yet she was determined to have the house neat and clean at all times, because a clean house was the primary way you were assessed as a wife and mother. June Cleaver made having a spotless house look so effortless; for Mom, it was so hard. I resolved early on to become a slob when I grew up, since housework seemed to produce nothing but misery. (I succeeded spectacularly, by the way.)

By 1963, women like my mother were in an untenable position. They worked all the time, yet their work inside and outside the home was taken for granted and poorly valued. To even approach the level of material comforts that *Leave It to Beaver* and *Father Knows Best* suggested everyone had, millions of families needed Mom in the workforce. And to have their houses approach the standards of tidiness and cleanliness also set by these shows, Mom had to come home from work and mop till she dropped. The ideological yo-yo they had been spun on since 1941—hey, be a feminist, you're equal to men; hey, wait a minute, no you're not; hey, maybe you are—constituted one series of contradictions in our mothers' lives. Being a woman at the height of the feminine mystique meant incorporating a mosaic of traits, most of them negative, and most of them at odds with one another. What persona, which subject position, should our mothers assume, and when? My mother tried out nearly all of them as she navigated her way through her memories, her disappointments, her desire to conform, and her absolute disdain for conformity. I watched her buy into some of the media norms about ideal womanhood, and I watched her defy and lash out at others, for she was pulled in one direction by imagery and in another by economics, and pulled in both by desire and longing. We saw in our mothers acceptance and rebellion, conformity and iconoclasm, especially when it came to work in and outside of the home. By the early 1960s, the tension between my mother's having had her identity—or, more accurately, identities—constituted by the mass media and her increasing resistance to media images that trivialized her worth was becoming unbearable, for her and for me.

But the lessons about women and work that I got from my mother, and from the mass media, were more ambiguous. June Cleaver's life—tossing salad and installing new rolls of paper towels—looked boring, and I knew my mother liked having a job, skills, accomplishments, and friends who were just hers. But my mother, like millions of mothers across the country, made it clear that my work would be different, because, unlike her, I was going to go to college. She wanted me to set my sights higher. And so did I.

There were, however, still cautionary tales about women and work, about setting your sights too high, about actually taking your work seriously. For there was one narrative about women and work that tied my mother and me together in unspoken ways, and ties me to millions of other women—and men—in a twisted, destructive spell we seem unable to exorcise. This is the story of *A Star Is Born,* one of my mother's favorite movies and a real whopper of a melodrama with the telling hit song "The Man That Got Away." This sick story has somehow been so compelling that it's been made into a film three times and spawned lots of imitators, from *Valley of the Dolls* to *Mahogany* to *Funny Girl.* Here's the basic premise. A young, extremely talented but unknown actress meets an older, extremely successful actor-mentor, who helps launch her career, and, in short order, she becomes a star. But there is a finite amount of success allotted to any one male-female couple: the more she gets, the more he loses, as if her success can only be parasitic on his. According to this immutable law of physics, as her star rises, his must fall in direct proportion. Her fame and fortune emasculate him and turn him into a suicidal drunk. The moral is clear: you can work, but if you have a career and are really good at it, if you become "a star," you will diminish your man and suck the very lifeblood out of his manhood and sense of self-worth. It doesn't matter how much you love him, you simply can't defy the following law of nature: become a success, you castrate your man.

Neither my mother nor I could anticipate that thirty years later we would still be trying to exorcise the two central cultural messages of her era, which continue to cling to the deepest recesses of our psyches: first, the suggestion that working mothers are somehow delinquent mothers; and second, the notion that working moms are primarily responsible for cleaning the house, cooking dinner, and playing Uncle Wiggily with the kids. Study after study shows that while working dads have time to read the paper, watch guys with arms the size of Smithfield hams run into each other, go out with the boys for a frosty one, or simply take a nap, working moms barely have the time—or the opportunity—to pee with the bathroom door fully closed.[23] Like a toxic spill from 1950s ideology that we can't seem to clean up or bury, the notions that working mothers are, ipso facto, depriving someone, usually a loved one, of something, that they shouldn't be too ambitious, and that they should be constantly guilty, contaminate our lives. They don't stop women from working any more today than they did in the 1950s, because most of us haven't much choice. But this tension between old images and new realities, the kind of media lag our mothers lived with, still corrodes women's sense of self-worth, of what we're entitled to, and what we can rightly ask of our men. We see that even though we and our mothers resisted media messages about women and work, the insidious cultural norms have been nearly impossible to expunge.

Watching my mother and watching what was said to and about her, there was one big lesson I got. Whatever this category "woman" was, I didn't want a big part of it, since it meant you'd be torn in a million directions and be ridiculed as dumb yet overbearing, incompetent yet scheming, and frivolous yet dangerous. Of course, there were always exceptions to every rule, and that's what I wanted to be, an exception. It turned out that millions of other girls my age wanted the same. But then puberty hit—irreversible, inexorable, and excruciating—forcing us to recognize that, like it or not, womanhood was where we were destined. And it started to seem as if we had only two choices: sink or organize a mutiny.

CHAPTER 3

Sex and the Single Teenager

By the early 1960s, millions of baby boomers were confronting that hideous abyss, puberty. The growth rate of the teenage population took off at four times the average of all other age-groups: a staggering 46 million Americans entered their teens in this decade. One thing you become obsessed with during puberty is, of course, sex. And, not coincidentally, magazines and movies became obsessed with sex as well, for the early 1960s marked the beginning of what came to be called the Sexual Revolution. There had already been a few harbingers, like the introduction of the bikini in 1959 and the appearance on the best-seller list of the unexpurgated version of *Lady Chatterley's Lover*. And then, in 1960, the FDA approved distribution of the birth control pill. According to a nervous *Reader's Digest,* "one vast, all-pervading sexological spree" was about to begin.[1] Teenagers were in the middle of a hyped-up Sexual Revolution we were supposed to ignore or reject at the very moment that massive amounts of sex hormones were being pumped through our bloodstreams. Fat chance.

In the same way that we girls had gotten mixed messages about our role in changing the world, and about women and work, we started to get mixed messages about sex. The legacy of the 1950s was that no "nice" girl ever, *ever,* went all the way before marriage, and no nice woman ever really liked sex. But by the early 1960s, there were indications to the contrary, in best-selling books, in suggestive ads ("Does She—Or Doesn't She?"), in pop music, and in James

Bond movies. And as we grew from preteens to teens, these media became even more daring, pushing the boundaries of what you could show and what you could say. And we became a lot less sure about what was right and wrong when it came to sex.

I was just about to hit puberty myself when this revolution began, and I remember the secrecy, shock, and horror that accompanied its early tremors. Being raised Catholic, as I was, meant going to church and hearing the priest all of a sudden start screaming about birth control, which I quickly learned was a really, really big sin. (We're talking a beeline to hell unless you said 500 rosaries and put a big contribution in next Sunday's collection.) Now, I had no idea what birth control meant, and I quickly discovered that no one, especially my parents, was going to tell me. But then I learned from someplace—I think it was *Life* magazine—that there was this new pill, and if women took it they wouldn't get pregnant. Why was the priest so flipped out over this, I wondered, since I knew even at this tender age that getting pregnant when you didn't want to was the number one terror for females? This pill idea sounded pretty good to me, so I started getting confused some more. Didn't this represent progress, and wasn't progress, especially medical progress, what made America America?

Then (and I'll never forget *this*), Liz Taylor made this scandalously immoral movie, *Cleopatra,* while cheating on the husband she'd "stolen" from Debbie Reynolds by stealing yet another woman's man, and we all had to stand up in church and take an oath together out loud that we would never go see it. If we did, well, now we're talking serious church time, including novenas, and helping add a wing to the rectory. Naturally, I wanted to go see it right away, and when I did, I was extremely disappointed in how tame it was (and how bad it was). Meanwhile, Ann Landers began stepping up her "Just Say No" campaign against girls doing anything except holding hands before marriage, and, well, it started to seem like maybe something was up. As it turned out, something was. That rigid code meant to keep middle-class girls' pants on until after they got married—the double standard—was starting to crumble.

You could see it in magazine articles everywhere, with titles that used to be reserved for the likes of *True Confessions:* "If Only They Had Waited," "My Daughter Is in Trouble," "Today It Could Be *Your* Daughter," or "How to Tell Your Daughter Why She Must Keep Her Self-Respect." Landers, in addition to her endless newspaper columns on the differences between necking and petting, and the perilous dangers of both, wrote pieces like "Straight Talk on Sex and Growing Up" for *Life* magazine and published more advice in her book *Since You Ask Me* in 1961.[3] The message in these articles was always the same. Girls, who didn't have much, if any, sexual desire, had to protect themselves from boys, who were, from the age of fourteen on, completely governed by their crotches. Females never really liked sex—they only did it with their husbands so they could have what they really found satisfying, babies. If a girl did it before she was married, she risked getting pregnant, but, even worse, no boy, not even her steady boyfriend, would ever respect her again, and no decent man would marry her, because she wasn't a virgin.

This was pretty scary stuff, ruining your entire life over something you wouldn't like very much anyway. And if you got pregnant, your whole family would be humiliated and you'd have to either get married immediately or be shipped off to one of those homes where bad girls in angel blouses were hidden until the offending abdominal bulge disappeared. But a few things happened that started making these warnings seem a tad hysterical. First, the Kinsey Reports that came out after World War II suggested that some women actually liked sex and that premarital intercourse wasn't as rare as everyone thought. But not too many kids read this clinical, jargon-filled stuff. No, for the most part we hid in garages or basements, hungrily devouring some purloined copy of *Lady Chatterley's Lover,* or we snuck *Tropic of Cancer* out of our parents' bookshelves and furtively flipped to the "good parts," which, as I recall, weren't too hard to find. Two major surprises awaited girl readers: the women in these books liked sex, sometimes a lot, and the young girls themselves felt a pleasant tingling between their legs as they turned the pages. Holy cow—sex might be fun, exciting, fabulous, exhilarating, and not just for boys.

The real coup de grace came in 1960, with the introduction of the birth control pill. Boy, did *this* create an uproar, and not just in my church. Popular magazines from *Life* to *Reader's Digest* were crammed with articles about the birth control controversy. Americans were beginning to realize that there were other countries on the planet besides the United States and the Soviet Union, and that there was something called a population explosion going on in many of them. They were also learning that there were millions of poor people right here in America who couldn't afford the kids they had and certainly didn't want any more. Plus there were tens of millions of middle-class women, many of whom weren't yet thirty, or even twenty-five, who'd already had all the kids they wanted and didn't want any more either. So you might say there was a big demand for birth control information and devices, and several transcendently obvious, commonsense arguments for making all these available as soon as possible.

But there were also these celibate, overfed, busybody bishops and priests who'd never administered a 2:00 A.M. feeding or cleaned up a projectile vomit puddle of mashed bananas, cottage cheese, and spaghetti who kept issuing bulls and encyclicals insisting that birth control be banned, or at least made very hard to get. Guys like this lobbied to get people fired who tried to make birth control available to poor people.[4] And in some states, like Connecticut, the use of birth control devices, let alone the sale or prescription of them, was forbidden by law. There, in 1961, Estelle Griswold, head of the state's Planned Parenthood League, was arrested for giving out information on things like contraceptive foam. To a lot of people—including many Catholics like me—this all seemed extremely silly, especially since Mrs. Griswold was a woman in her sixties who looked respectable enough to be the head of the DAR. Finally, in 1965, the Supreme Court overturned Griswold's conviction and ruled that the Connecticut ban against contraceptives was unconstitutional. By this time, millions of women were already on the pill, with millions more, like me, age fifteen, waiting in the wings.

By the early and mid-1960s, the Sexual Revolution was one of the biggest stories in the print media. Publishers and editors discovered that sex helped sell magazines—even newsmagazines. They greatly exaggerated the speed and scope of the Sexual Revolution, suggesting that young people, especially young women, all over the country were shedding their virginity en masse. The truth was that while some college women, especially those pinned or engaged, were violating the taboos against premarital sex, most young women in and out of college in the early and mid-1960s still kept their undies on until they were married. While *Time* and other publications panted over the "cult of pop hedonism" and an "orgy of openmindedness," several researchers in the mid-1960s documented that sexual permissiveness had not yet overtaken the youth of America.[5] The magazines sensationalized the Sexual Revolution with their suggestions that sex-crazed coeds were watching *La Dolce Vita* and then sleeping with whomever was available. That behavior didn't really start on a large scale until 1968.

Yet no comment, no prediction, no assessment of the contemporary scene was too hyperbolic to print. Margaret Mead, who was always quoted about pretty much everything, complained that "we have jumped from puritanism to lust," while Pearl Buck, another magazine regular and trusted sage, opined, "The change is so abrupt, so far-reaching, that we are all dazed by it."[6] "The Puritan ethic," announced *Time,* "so long the dominant force in the U.S., is widely considered to be dying, if not dead, and there are few mourners."[7]

Popular magazines expressed a blend of panic and puerile excitement over the prospect of young, white, middle-class women thumbing their noses at the double standard. As one writer put it, it was "not girls from lower income levels [but] girls from our so-called 'best' families" who were shocking adults by their sexual behavior.[8] Previously, in pop culture iconography, the "bad" girl—meaning the one who did have sex before marriage—was easily identified by class and ethnicity. She came from the "wrong side of the tracks," had dark hair and was not fair-skinned, wore spit curls and skirts with slits, and was the kind of girl boys were urged to sow their "wild oats" with before marrying the girl with the pageboy and the circle pin. In other words, her willingness or desire to be sexually active could be dismissed as the allegedly hypersexualized, unrestrained behavior of the lower classes. But when fair-skinned, well-bred, middle-class girls started claiming and expressing their own sexuality, this was news, for it suggested that the cherished class boundaries were being violated, that girls of the "better" classes were being contaminated by whatever corrupted the values and behavior of their inferiors.

Magazines like *Life, Reader's Digest, Esquire,* and the *Ladies' Home Journal* all looked for deeper explanations for the Sexual Revolution. With the availability of contraceptives and penicillin, the three age-old deterrents to premarital sex—conception, infection, and detection—began to lose their power to terrorize middle-class girls. But the magazines saw deeper causes, from the postatomic dread of Armageddon to the spread of existentialism. In one of the most air-headed references to Simone de Beauvoir ever uttered, one boy reportedly told *Newsweek* that "living together makes me feel like an intelligent person—like Sartre and his mistress."[9] But the magazines did get one cause right, and that was the rise of relativism in the 1960s. Imposing one's own sexual standards on others was now as anachronistic as a Jonathan Edwards sermon; sophisticated tolerance was in. As one girl told *Esquire,* "I used to think it was terrible if people had intercourse before marriage. Now I think each person should find his own values."[10] A boy told *Time* that the only test of sexual conduct should be "Do I want to do it? Does it hurt anyone else?"[11]

There were two other explanations for the imagined "sexological spree," and you will not be surprised that one of the people especially deserving of blame was Mom. It was Mom, with her pathetic need to live through us and her ambitious desire to shove us prematurely onto the social stage, who pushed "champagne parties for teen-agers, padded brassieres for twelve-year-olds, and 'going steady' at ever younger ages." *Saturday Review* attacked "the mother who fosters sexual precocity in her daughters and who herself has a very shaky concept of values, responsibility, and true affection." The article had special contempt for "the girls who, sometimes with the connivance of their ambitious mothers, deliberately trap desirable young men by getting pregnant."[12] I, unfortunately, never met any of these pimping moms so popular with male commentators; the moms I knew thought we should all have our legs glued together for about a decade.

The other culprit in promoting the Sexual Revolution was, according to the magazines, the "mass media," which emphasized the "gratification of sexual drives as natural and glamorous."[13] What's so rich about this is that publishers and editors were hardly above using sex whenever possible to sell their magazines, yet they acted as if they were above and apart from the media system they decried. In a cover story called "The Second Sexual Revolution" and clearly designed to lure in extra readers, *Time* cited the "innumerable screens and stages, posters and pages" that flashed "larger-than-life-sized images of sex."[14] *Esquire,* the magazine noted for its portraits of barely clad women, complained about "the stridently phallic movie heroes of today" and the "sleazy paperbacks [that] compete with each other in a gaudy Olympiad of sex and sadism."[15] Articles like "How to Stop the Movies' Sickening Exploitation of Sex," "Speaking Out: Movies Are Too Dirty," and "Must Our Movies Be Obscene?" singled out films as the worst culprits.[16] It was true, books and movies were getting much more explicit than they had been, but so were magazines. And while the magazines gave voice to concerns about the new morality, they also accelerated its acceptance by making it seem reasonable and inevitable. The magazines often structured their articles in the classically "objective" on-the-one-hand, on-the-other-hand format as they sought to lure in some readers without alienating others.

In the midst of this sea change in American morality, a book appeared that must have made the priests of America long for the reintroduction of the chastity belt. *Sex and the Single Girl,* by Helen Gurley Brown, became an instant best-seller in July 1962 and stayed on the list for nearly seven months. The book created a sensation because it put the words *sex* and *single girl* in bed together in the very same phrase, in direct violation of 1950s Legion of Decency morality. I mean, even married people on TV had to have twin beds so there was no suggestion that any body parts below their clavicles ever made contact, and here was this brazen hussy blithely announcing in her book and in countless television interviews that America should get over it, already, about premarital sex for women. Within a few years of the book's publication, the previously unknown Brown became the darling on the TV talk show circuit, was named editor of the languishing *Cosmopolitan* magazine, and received the highest amount ever paid, up to that time, for the movie rights to a nonfiction book.

Now, I don't want to hold Helen Gurley Brown up as some paragon of feminism, since the bottom line of her message has always been the absolute importance of pleasing men. But looking at her book, thirty years later, with all its fatuous advice about buying wigs, bleaching your leg hair, and making "chloroform cocktails" (coffee, ice cream, and a fifth of vodka), we see some startling stirrings of female liberation. And, for her, liberation came through sex, by throwing the double standard out the window.[17]

For many young women, Brown was a welcome iconoclast. She made being single and having a job sound glamorous and exciting, while she equated marriage—especially marriage at too young an age—with drudgery and boredom. "You may marry or you may not. In today's world that is no longer the big question for women. Those who glom on to men so that they can collapse with relief, spend the rest of their days shining up their status symbol and figure they never have to reach, stretch, learn, grow, face dragons or make a living again are the ones to be pitied. They, in my opinion, are the unfulfilled ones." The fulfilled ones were out in the world and had jobs. "A job," gushed Brown, "can be your love, your happy pill, your means of finding out who you are and what you can do . . . and your means of participating, instead of having your nose pressed up to the glass."[18] This did sound better than scrubbing diaper pails.

Most important, the single girl had great sex. "Theoretically a 'nice' single woman has no sex life. What nonsense! She has a better sex life than most of her married friends. She need never be bored with one man per lifetime. Her choice of partners is endless and they seek *her*."[19] Challenging the stuffy women's magazines, Brown insisted that you didn't have to marry early just to have children, since "you can have babies until you're forty or over."[20] Here Brown was clearly ten to twenty years ahead of her time. Despite the fact that Brown's ideal single woman was a frivolous ditz who took voice lessons so she could sound sexier and had "a memorable beach hat or two," she was also an active agent in the world, in control of her sex life and her future. This was a new kind of role model, and while she was highly convenient to men (and to advertisers), she also opened up new possibilities for women. For once women started thinking that they could be equal in the bedroom, after a while they started thinking they should be equal in other venues as well.

With Brown's book perched at the top of the best-seller charts, another soon-to-be-famous woman published "The Moral Disarmament of Betty Coed" in the September 1962 issue of *Esquire*. Gloria Steinem was just beginning her writing career and made a splash with this piece, which announced that on college campuses the double standard was going the way of the poodle skirt. Increasing numbers of college girls didn't think premarital sex was any big deal; they did it when it felt right, and many of them were quite eager to get hold of the pill. These girls thought their sex practices were "none of society's business," and they didn't "feel forced to choose between a career and marriage." We see the prefeminist stirrings in Steinem as she writes, "The development of the 'autonomous' girl is important and, in large numbers, quite new . . . she expects to find her identity neither totally without men nor totally through them." She concluded the article with an especially prescient comment: "The real danger of the contraceptive revolution may be the acceleration of woman's role-change without any corresponding change of man's attitude toward her role."[21] Say amen somebody.

How accurate was this portrait of college girls giving the double standard a giant raspberry? Gael Greene decided to find out. Hoping to capitalize on Brown's success, she titled her 1964 book *Sex and the College Girl*. Greene interviewed hundreds of students, mostly female, from colleges and universities throughout the country, and while she found no statistical evidence she felt she could trust, she affirmed people's suspicions: premarital intercourse in college dorm rooms, dugouts, arboretums, and Chevy station wagons was increasing. Most of the girls she talked to were preoccupied with sex, and they refused to impose their judgments on other people's sexual behavior.

At the same time, Greene found that college girls were deeply conflicted between the old message that "sex is sin" and the new message that "sex [is] the ultimate expression of romantic love." These girls told Greene that they had been terrorized by the double standard warnings, only to get to college and discover it was all a whopping lie. A student from Radcliffe said, "I mean we all get sort of the same 'nice girls don't' routine at home. Well, I for one really believed it. There just wasn't any doubt in my mind that I would be a virgin when I got married. But then I came up here and there they were—all those nice girls, much nicer than I if you talk about family and background—and they were doing it. I felt betrayed. . . . My virginity lasted exactly four months. . . . The truth is, nice girls do." Greene reported a "fury" among college girls "at being so unfairly misled" and a sense that their intelligence had been insulted. Their confusion and ambivalence about what was right led them to ricochet on a daily basis between "two contradictory values" and to cobble together some compromise they could live with.

Greene reported that movies, magazines, and books often played a key role in convincing some college girls to shed their virginity. A graduate of Hunter College cited *Marjorie Morningstar* as one such text. "I suspect Herman Wouk would be somewhat upset if he realized how many nice middle-class Jewish girls lost their virginity because of him. . . . Silly as it sounds, I know for sure at least three girls who gave up the good fight just to prove they weren't Marjories." Other girls singled out *Where the Boys Are,* a successful book and movie, whose heroine Merritt asserted, "It's ridiculous and picky of society to turn it [virginity] into an *institution.*"[22] Greene herself cited the on- and off-screen affairs between glamorous costars like Taylor and Burton or Natalie Wood and Warren Beatty as a double whammy slap in the face to American puritanism.

The puritan ethic was indeed taking a thrashing in the movies, fanning the sexual confusion many young women felt. Despite the unfortunate plethora of Doris Day films (*Pillow Talk, That Touch of Mink*) in which a thirty-five-year-old maidenhead was as sacred and well-guarded as the Pietà, there was a new sexual frankness in films, which had started in the 1950s with movies like *Peyton Place* and *Baby Doll* and was accelerating with the arrival of foreign films. With the great decline in movie attendance in the late 1940s and early 1950s, Hollywood had begun to exploit more sexually risqué themes to lure adults back into the theaters. But the success of *Rebel Without a Cause* (1955), *April Love* (1957), *Love Me Tender* (1956), and *I Was a Teenage Werewolf* (1957)—the last of which cost $150,000 to make and quickly grossed $2.5 million—established the importance of the teenage audience. At the end of the 1950s, three-quarters of the movie audience was teenagers.[23] And what was foremost in these viewers' minds were their ongoing romantic and sexual dilemmas. By 1965, one Hollywood executive complained to *The New York Times,* "Teenage tastes are exerting a tyranny over our industry. It's getting so show business is one big puberty rite."[24]

But because of the importance of this audience, the film industry did play a leading role in breaking down sexual taboos long before television would touch them. In the first James Bond movie, the wildly successful *Dr. No* (1962), Sean Connery and a luscious Ursula Andress made it clear that unmarried men and women did have sex simply because they were attracted to each other, and the rest of the series featured a string of sex objects who, despite their objectification, made sex for single women glamorous and satisfying. And when the virginal Maria in *West Side Story* (1961) admitted Tony into her bed, the audience was urged to be sympathetic, even approving. In 1965, the Motion Picture Association of America, the industry's office of self-censorship that enforced what was known simply as "the code," approved a scene in *The Pawnbroker* that showed a woman naked to the waist, and the T & A floodgates were opened. The following year, *Variety* proclaimed, "The Code Is Dead."[25]

Movies have always been an especially powerful medium, particularly for the young. There you are, in the dark, small, almost faceless, lost and anonymous in the audience, your eyes upturned to the huge, perfect, idealized face of the movie star. Various writers, drawing on psychoanalytic theory, have likened movie viewing to infancy, when the baby, not yet knowing the difference between Mom and herself, idealizes the huge, all-nurturing mom, and identifies with her, thinking she and Mom are the same. The size of the movie screen, the darkened, blurry irrelevance of everything around it, the perfections of its heroes and heroines, re-create this delicious moment in infancy, compelling us to identify with the idealized characters before us in an especially thoroughgoing fashion. It is this intensity of identification that has prompted do-gooders of various stripes since the early 1900s to try to censor movies, especially those that seem to promote sexual license. And it is also this intensity of identification that makes films from this era about young girls and sex so important to remember.[26]

It was during the beginning of the Sexual Revolution that a new kind of film emerged, the pregnancy melodrama. A cross between the women's film and the youth film, the pregnancy melodrama placed premarital sex between young people at the center of its often preposterous narrative. At the heart of these films was the battle between American puritanism—often personified in frigid, shriveled-up moms and brutish, spiritually dead dads—and the new morality, which truly allowed for a more healthy marriage between love and sex. Since films of this era rarely showed people doing it—or even in bed together, for that matter—the pounding of the ocean surf, or of waterfalls, was called upon again and again to serve as the metaphor for you-know-what.

Having said this, it is important to emphasize that I'm not talking about those fake, sanitized beach movies like *Beach Blanket Bingo* or *How to Stuff a Wild Bikini*. Annette and Frankie generated about as much sexual heat as two snails in a cistern, and we were actually supposed to believe that a bunch of guys and gals slept together in the same beach house without any hanky-panky going on. We knew these movies were phony. Pregnancy melodramas, in contrast, acknowledged that young people were fed up with bourgeois hypocrisy about everything from status seeking to sex, and that they were struggling with often irresistible sexual urges. Cast adrift in an amoral world, the protagonists in these films struggled in a sea of relativism as they rejected the unyielding and, to them, heartless dictates of sexually constipated adult America.

Several themes and features were common to pregnancy melodramas. The desirable boys were often feminized in some way, by being overly sensitive and brooding, by rejecting the corporate ethos and monetary standards of male success, and by having wavy hair that dipped suggestively over their foreheads. They also equated sex with love. Father figures (often obvious metaphorical symbols of patriarchy and capitalism) were frequently crippled—lame, drunk, sickly—to make clear how their obsession with material goods had paralyzed them emotionally and spiritually. While attacking the sterility of American materialism and patriarchy, these films offered a prescription: that society had to be rehabilitated through an embrace of more traditionally female traits.

Most important, the young female characters had sexual desires that they acted on without being killed or otherwise banished by the end of the story. Now these were girls we could identify with. In *A Summer Place* (1959), Sandra Dee willingly goes "all the way" with Troy Donahue, and when she gets pregnant, he doesn't jilt her but says instead that the prospect of having a baby makes him feel "warm all over." In *Love with the Proper Stranger* (1963), Natalie Wood gets knocked up by Steve McQueen during a one-night stand he barely remembers, but by the end of the film he is head over heels in love and proposes.

The young women in these films acknowledged the contradictions pulling them in different directions. Pregnancy melodramas provided female viewers with multiple personas to try on: there were stark differences between the female characters in each film, but there were also contradictions within the same character. It was this latter type of character, deeply conflicted and unsure whether to act on her sexual impulses or obey the double standard, a girl inclined to rebel yet still every bit a "good girl," who was held up as the new role model. The various female characters in pregnancy melodramas offered points on the continuum of female sexuality, from prudish to promiscuous. The big-breasted, out-of-control sluts on one end of the continuum and the tight-lipped ice maidens on the other served as monoliths to be rejected, while the ones in the middle, caught in the crosscurrents of discourses about "good" and "bad" girls, were the ones meant to be recognized as authentic by teenage girls. In other words, young girls were socialized as viewers to identify with ambivalence itself.[27]

One of my favorites of this genre is *Susan Slade* (1961), which I wasn't allowed to see when it came out because it was too risqué. Connie Stevens is Susan, a naive, sheltered virgin who has a shipboard romance with a dashing mountain climber, Con White (?!), who wastes little time mounting her as well. From the soft-focus close-ups of Susan with her eyes barely opened and lips slightly parted, the audience sees that this girl knows sexual desire and likes it. By the time they dock, the young lovers are secretly engaged, but they won't make it official until after Con completes his next climb in Alaska. While Susan waits in vain to hear from him, she discovers, you guessed it, that she's pregnant. Then she learns the worst—Con has been killed in a climbing accident. Now what? She has to tell her parents, and to save face, her father takes a job in Guatemala, where they move for two years. When they return to California, Susan's mother, played by Dorothy McGuire, pretends the baby is hers. Meanwhile, Susan is being courted by two boys, Hoyt Brecker (Troy Donahue), the sensitive, brooding local stable hand and poor, aspiring novelist, and Wells Corbett (Bert Convy), the rich, cocky son of her parents' wealthy friends.

Then comes the best scene in the film. One night while Susan is home watching her "baby brother," the kid gets hold of a cigarette lighter while Susan is chatting with Hoyt, and before you know it, there's a rubber toddler mannequin on screen engulfed in a small bonfire. Susan and Hoyt rush the baby to the hospital (the kid survives), and it is there that Susan realizes she can't live this lie anymore. Surrounded by Wells and his parents, Hoyt, and her own mother, Susan confesses that the baby is hers and that she doesn't care who knows it. Wells, the status-obsessed hypocrite, withdraws his previous commitments of love and marriage, while Hoyt skulks off. But he has simply gone back to Susan's to wait for her and, when she arrives, declares his undying love for her, no matter what she did before.

Now, despite the double helix contortions of the plot, several themes emerge that dominated in other pregnancy melodramas. Most important, of course, is that the girl is not punished for her premarital exploits but emerges as a morally principled girl who also gets Troy Donahue, who, even though he couldn't act, was extremely cute. Upper-class values and pretensions, like Wells Corbett's, are seen as buttressing a thoroughly retrograde and hypocritical form of sexual sterility and deceit. And the truly attractive, decent, and lovable boy is the one who sees a girl for what she is and doesn't judge her by some outmoded, barbaric double standard.

Time and again, the double standard was attacked as a source of unnecessary misery, and as an unnatural code left over from some less enlightened era. By the end of these films, viewers wanted to cudgel it back to the Stone Age. In *A Summer Place,* American puritanism was given its most perverse and demonic personification in the form of a frigid and tyrannical mother, Helen Jorgensen (grimly played by Constance Ford). She and her husband, Ken (Richard Egan), are trapped in a loveless marriage marked by separate bedrooms and Helen's abhorrence of sex. We know Helen's an evil bitch from the get-go because she's frequently shot in harsh light and from an unflattering low angle, she rarely smiles, and we always see her spying on other people, especially her daughter, Molly (Sandra Dee), and Molly's boyfriend, Johnny (Troy Donahue). Everyone knows that women in films are to be looked *at;* if they do much looking themselves—for information, for sex, for clues—they usually pay the consequences and are hated by all the other film characters and the entire audience.[28] By contrast, we learn right away that Johnny's mom, Sylvia (Dorothy McGuire), is the good mom, because she's always lovingly framed in warm, rosy, soft-focus shots. Molly, too, is caressed by the camera, so girls knew they could—and should—identify with her, even though she loses her virginity.

In a fight with Helen, Ken castigates her for the monstrous, twisted levels of her prudery, and we, the audience, are right there with him. "Are you antipeople and antilife? Must you suffocate every natural instinct in our daughter too? Must you label young lovemaking as cheap and wanton and indecent? Must you persist in making sex itself a filthy word?" After this heated exchange, Molly goes to her father's room to say good night. As she snuggles against him in his bed, Molly complains of her mother, "She's antisex. She says all a boy wants out of a girl is that, and when a girl marries it's something she has to endure. I don't want to think like that. Poppa, she makes me feel ashamed of even having a body." But apparently not for long.

Later in the film, whatever fleeting shame Molly may have felt has clearly given way to lust for Johnny, and the two of them go off to a deserted building along the beach that Molly, not Johnny, has found for the specific purpose of doing the wild thing. Molly is anything but passive here—she struggles with whether or not to go all the way with Johnny, and when he ventures that maybe they should try to be good, she runs her finger suggestively over his lips and whispers, "You don't really want that." Fade to black; next stop, the gynecologist's office for the bad news.

While Ken and Sylvia wait up nervously for the kids to return from the beach, Ken delivers yet another indictment of 1950s morality: "Just what honest advice can I give her? To be a half-virgin? To allow herself to be fondled, to go halfway in the backseats of parked cars but always draw back in time? . . . I can't tell her to be half-good—I feel like a hypocrite. . . . Is the only answer that youth must be a time of suspended animation?" Throughout the picture it is Ken, the new, humanized kind of dad, who attacks sexual repression as deadening. He represents a recuperated patriarchy, in which the fathers gain even greater authority by taking on the female traits of empathy, nurturance, and compassion. And it is in Johnny, the tender, loyal boy with his blond hair waving softly, even girlishly, over his forehead, that the young girl sees her fantasy of a more humane and feminized patriarchy realized.[29]

In the end, when Molly and Johnny (whom we are to believe are somewhere around seventeen and eighteen) marry, the moral of the story isn't that premarital sex is bad or that getting married that young is really dumb. The moral is that denying your sexual instincts is stultifying, and acting on them liberating. Molly gets sexual fulfillment, respectability, and her man. The movie ends happily, well before the baby arrives, which is good, because after that sex for Johnny and Molly will be only a fond memory.

For many baby boomers, *Splendor in the Grass* (1961) was the most powerful of the pregnancy melodramas, in part because it was a "serious" film—William Inge won an Oscar for the screenplay—and because Natalie Wood and Warren Beatty were so convincing as young lovers trapped between their sexual desires and their repressive parents. One minute Deanie (Wood) has to listen to her frigid, moneygrubbing mother hiss, "Boys don't respect a girl they can go all the way with. Boys want a nice girl for a wife," and the next she has to decide whether to go all the way with Bud (Beatty), who is irresistible and truly in love with her. As we watch Bud and Deanie struggling with their desires, usually against the backdrop of a pounding waterfall, we see that this isn't the usual Ann Landers portrait of the predatory, only-one-thing-on-his-mind guy trying to seduce some unwilling, sexually disinterested girl. Deanie is often as overcome by her passion as Bud, and for them both, love and passion are inseparable. In this film, *not* going all the way completely ruins the young couple's lives. Deanie goes crazy as a result of her abstinence and has to be institutionalized, and Bud, after collapsing on a basketball court from sexual frustration, ends up pathetic and defeated, a barefoot dirt farmer in overalls with snot-nosed kids and an ever-pregnant, slatternly wife.

Like most of the girls in the audience in 1961, Deanie has no place to stand. Torn between her overwhelming physical desires and a moral code that pretends they don't—and shouldn't—exist, Deanie is divided against herself, her mind and body pitted against each other, wanting to succumb to her passion and not daring to do so. Because she feels the costs of restraint and the costs of passion in the same moment, Deanie provides a powerful point of identification for the girl in the audience reacting against the moral strictures of the 1950s.

In contrast, *Where the Boys Are* (1960) sought to resolve the prevailing questions about premarital sex through a melodramatic ending that showed the horrible costs for girls of going all the way. Four girls go to Florida for spring break; three remain virgins and end up with steady boyfriends. The fourth (Yvette Mimieux), mistaking sex for love, goes all the way with the first guy she meets, then takes up with his best friend, whom she shamelessly chases, and by the end of the film is a victim of date rape who wanders aimlessly through traffic until she is hit by a car. (She lives.) But throughout this film, which is also supposed to be a comedy and a musical, there are so many contradictions about girls and sex that the final message is "Every girl must decide for herself." Even the opening sequence, seemingly sexist and stupid at first, actually reveals that for girls, attitudes and behaviors are changing.

Opening with an aerial shot of Ft. Lauderdale, a slightly sarcastic male voice intones that during spring break droves of students 20,000 strong swarm to these shores. "The boys come to soak up the sun and a few carloads of beer. The girls come, very simply, because this is where the boys are." Already the major tension of the film is established. According to this narration, it is boys who venture forth into the world, autonomous, self-motivated, and considerably more indifferent to girls than they are to malted beverages. Here girls are cast as the sexual aggressors, the ones who take the initiative in courtship rituals and pursue the boys. Throughout the film, however, we see that this initiative is restricted to positioning themselves in the right place at the right time so as to be spotted by the right boy. Was this passivity or was this taking action? Just how much a girl should do, how assertive she should be, how far she should go, drove the narrative of the entire movie.

A film like *Where the Boys Are* offered viewers the opportunity to try on a range of attitudes toward premarital sex by presenting a variety of stock female archetypes, from the confirmed virgin to the fallen angel to the tomboy type who didn't have such worries because no man found her sexually attractive (the role Connie Francis got stuck with). Tuggle (Paula Prentiss), the virgin, gets to utter lines like "I promised myself I'd try for a man the chaste way, and so help me I'll keep it if I have to drop into the local blacksmith and buy a belt." She adds, "Girls like me weren't meant to be educated. We were made to have children. That's my ambition—to be a walking,

talking baby factory, legal of course." The character no one was supposed to want to emulate was Lola, the balloon-breasted, squeaky-
voiced, low-class, dumb-blond party girl who earned a living by
swimming in a giant fish tank under the billing "Sea Nymph of the
Tropical Isles."

Meanwhile, the main heroine, Merritt (Dolores Hart), the one
we're really supposed to identify with, is a bundle of contradictions.
In the opening of the film, we see her challenging the postmenopausal female professor who is trying to teach them about
"Courtship and Marriage." "Why don't we get down to the giant
jackpot issue," Merritt demands, "like should a girl or should she not,
under any circumstances, play house before marriage?" She then
asserts, "My opinion is yes," which gets her thrown out of class and
into the dean's office. Later in the film, however, when she's in
Florida being wooed by Ivy Leaguer Rider Smith (George Hamil-
ton—and where did they get these names, anyhow?), she talks like an
experienced woman but rebuffs all his advances. When the moment
of truth comes and she can't resist Rider anymore (the waves are just
too powerful *and* he wears an ascot), she admits she's a virgin and that
she's confused about what to do. Just as she's about to give in, she
hears that her friend Melanie (Mimieux) is in trouble and dashes off
to tend to her. Everyone is horrified by the date rape, and Melanie,
of course, wants to kill herself. The subtext is that Melanie brought
this on herself because she slept with a boy before being sure he really
loved her.

At the end of the film, with spring break over, Merritt and Rider
meet on the beach. Merritt says no girl is strong "when it comes to
love—what she thinks is love. How do you know the difference?"
Rider invites her to come up to Brown to visit him, and she accepts.
When she does go, will Merritt sleep with Rider? We aren't sure. If
she does, will it be wrong, or destroy her, or cost her his love? We
doubt it. So despite what happened to Melanie, it's simply not clear
that premarital sex in all cases is bad, especially if you're smart and
sensible, like Merritt.

In the early 1960s, the voices of the schoolmarm, the priest, the advice columnist, and Mom insisted, "Nice girls don't." But another voice began to whisper, "Oh yes they do—and they like it, too." Audiences saw the desirable boys in these movies look at the girls who said yes not with contempt but with love. We saw these girls lovingly lit and shot from camera angles that made them look like morally decent beauty queens, not like tramps. In the temporary fantasy world of the darkened movie theater, we could try on different roles, from starlets who said yes to starlets who said no to those who said, "Maybe, but I'm just not sure yet." And as we saw on the big screen that it was sometimes possible *not* to get punished for having sex with your boyfriend, some of us began to wonder.

Even so, the double standard exerted a powerful hold over most teens in the early and mid-1960s. For one thing, the majority of us were still too young to say yes anyway, and it was no small feat to shake the warnings from one's parents or Ann Landers—especially for girls who lived in small towns, where gossip traveled quickly and imposed rigid codes of behavior.[30] Nonetheless, the seeds of doubt and eventual rebellion were planted, and they grew rather quickly. Like the other mixed messages we were getting, the ones about sex were at war with each other, some telling us we should never, ever behave like boys, the others telling us we had every right to as much sexual freedom and license as they did, especially now that we could avoid getting pregnant.

But we didn't get these contradictory messages just in the movies or in magazines. We got them every time we turned on the radio, or our record players, or threw a quarter in the jukebox. We sang these mixed messages to ourselves day in and day out for years, branding ambivalence, defiance, and fear onto the innermost reaches of our psyches.

CHAPTER 4

Why the Shirelles Mattered

OK—here's a test. Get a bunch of women in their thirties and forties and put them in a room with a stereo. Turn up the volume to the "incurs temporary deafness" level and play "Will You Love Me Tomorrow" and see how many know the words—all the words—by heart. If the answer is 100 percent, these are bona fide American baby boomers. Any less, and the group has been infiltrated by impostors, pod people, Venusians. But even more interesting is the fact that non–baby boomers, women both older and younger than my generation, adore this music too, and cling to the lyrics like a life raft.

Why is it that, over thirty years after this song was number one in the country, it still evokes in us such passion, such longing, such euphoria, and such an irresistible desire to sing very loudly off key and not care who hears us? And it's not just this song, it's girl group music in general, from "He's So Fine" to "Nowhere to Run" to "Sweet Talkin' Guy." Today, the "oldies" station is one of the most successful FM formats going, in no small part because when these songs come on the radio, baby boomers get that faraway, knowing, contented look on their faces that prompts them to scream along with the lyrics while running red lights on the way home from work. None of this is silly—there's a good reason why, even on our deathbeds, we'll still know the words to "Leader of the Pack."

First of all, girl group music was really about us—girls. When rock 'n' roll swiveled onto the national scene in the mid-1950s and

united a generation in opposition to their parents, it was music performed by rebellious and sexually provocative young men. Elvis Presley was, of course, rock 'n' roll's most famous and insistently
masculine star—in 1956, five of the nine top singles of the year were
by Elvis. At the same time, there would be weeks, even months,
when no woman or female group had a hit among the top fifteen
records.[1] When women in the fifties did have hits, they were about
the moon, weddings, some harmless dreamboat, like Annette's "Tall
Paul," or maybe about kissing. But they were never, ever about doing
the wild thing.

Then, in December 1960, the Shirelles hit number one with
"Will You Love Me Tomorrow"; it was the first time a girl group,
and one composed of four black teenagers, had cracked the number
one slot.[2] And these girls were not singing about doggies in windows
or old Cape Cod. No, the subject matter here was a little different.
They were singing about whether or not to go all the way and wondering whether the boyfriend, so seemingly full of heartfelt, earnest
love in the night, would prove to be an opportunistic, manipulative,
lying cad after he got his way, or whether he would, indeed, still be
filled with love in the morning. Should the girl believe everything
she'd heard about going all the way and boys losing respect for girls
who did? Or should she believe the boy in her arms who was hugging and kissing her (and doing who knows what else) and generally
making her feel real good?

Even though this song was about sex, it didn't rely on the musical instrument so frequently used to connote sex in male rockers'
songs, the saxophone. Saxes were banished, as were electric guitars;
instead, an entire string section of an orchestra provided the counter-
point to Shirley Owens's haunting, earthy, and provocative lead
vocals. The producer, Luther Dixon, who had previously worked
with Perry Como and Pat Boone, even overlaid the drumbeats with
violins, so it sounded as if the strings gave the song its insistent, puls-
ing rhythm. While Owens's alto voice vibrated with teen girl angst
and desire, grounding the song in fleshly reality, violin arpeggios flut-

tered through like birds, and it was on their wings that our erotic desires took flight and gained a more acceptable spiritual dimension. It was this brilliant juxtaposition of the sentimentality of the violins and the sensuality of the voice that made the song so perfect, because it was simultaneously lush and spare, conformist and daring, euphemistic yet dead-on honest. The tens of millions of girls singing along could be starry-eyed and innocent, but they could also be sophisticated and knowing. They could be safe and sing about love, or dangerous and sing about sex. "Will You Love Me Tomorrow" was about a traditional female topic, love, but it was also about female longing and desire, including sexual desire. And, most important, it was about having a choice. For these girls, the decision to have sex was now a choice, and *this* was new. This was, in fact, revolutionary. Girl group music gave expression to our struggles with the possibilities and dangers of the Sexual Revolution.

What were you to do if you were a teenage girl in the early and mid-1960s, your hormones catapulting you between desire and paranoia, elation and despair, horniness and terror? You didn't know which instincts to act on and which ones to suppress. You also weren't sure whom to listen to since, by the age of fourteen, you'd decided that neither your mother nor your father knew anything except how to say no and perhaps the lyrics to a few Andy Williams songs. For answers—real answers—many of us turned to the record players, radios, and jukeboxes of America. And what we heard were the voices of teenage girls singing about—and dignifying—our most basic concern: how to act around boys when so much seemed up for grabs. What were you to do to survive all those raging hormones? Why, dance, of course.

There's been a lot of talk, academic analysis, and the like about how Elvis Presley and rock 'n' roll made rebelliousness acceptable for boys. But what about the girls? Did girl group music help *us* become rebels? Before you say "no way" and cite "I Will Follow Him," "Chapel of Love," and "I Wanna Be Bobby's Girl" to substantiate your point, hear me out. Girl group music has been denied its rightful place in history by a host of male music critics who've either ignored it or trashed it. Typical is this pronouncement, by one of the contributors to *The Rolling Stone History of Rock & Roll:* "The female group of the early 1960s served to drive the concept of art completely away from rock 'n' roll. . . . I feel this genre represents the low point in the history of rock 'n' roll."[3] Nothing could be more wrong-headed, or more ignorant of the role this music played in girls' lives. It would be ideal if this section of the book were accompanied by a customized CD replaying all these fabulous songs for you. Since that's not possible, I do urge you to listen to this music again, and to hear all the warring impulses, desires, and voices it contained.[4]

By the late 1950s, Tin Pan Alley realized that Perry Como, Doris Day, and Mantovani and his orchestra weren't cutting it with the fastest-growing market segment in America, teenagers. Even Pat Boone was hopelessly square, having foisted on us the insufferable "April Love" and his goody-two-shoes advice book to teens, *'Twixt Twelve and Twenty,* which said kissing "for fun" was dangerous. Music publishers and producers grasped two key trends: rock 'n' roll was here to stay, and there was this flourishing market out there, not just boys, but girls, millions of them, ready and eager to buy. And they were not buying the Lennon Sisters or Patti Page. At the same time, the proliferation of transistor radios meant that this music could be taken and heard almost everywhere, becoming the background music for our desires, hopes, and fears, the background music to our individual and collective autobiographies.

Teenage songwriters like Carole King and Ellie Greenwich got jobs in the Brill Building in New York, the center of pop music production in America, and in the aftermath of the Shirelles hit, all kinds of girl groups and girl singers appeared, from the pouf-skirted Angels ("My Boyfriend's Back") to the cute and innocent Dixie Cups to the eat-my-dirt, in-your-face, badass Shangri-Las. There was an explosion in what has come to be called "girl talk" music, the lyrics and beat of which still occupy an inordinately large portion of the right— or is it the left?—side of my brain.

The most important thing about this music, the reason it spoke to us so powerfully, was that it gave voice to all the warring selves inside us struggling, blindly and with a crushing sense of insecurity, to forge something resembling a coherent identity. Even though the girl groups were produced and managed by men, it was in their music that the contradictory messages about female sexuality and rebelliousness were most poignantly and authentically expressed. In the early 1960s, pop music became the one area of popular culture in which adolescent female voices could be clearly heard. They sang about the pull between the need to conform and the often overwhelming desire to rebel, about the tension between restraint and freedom, and about the rewards—and costs—of prevailing gender roles. They sang, in other words, about getting mixed messages and about being ambivalent in the face of the upheaval in sex roles. That loss of self, the fusing of yourself with another, larger-than-life persona that girls felt as they sang along was at least as powerful as what they felt in a darkened movie theater. And singing along with one another, we shared common emotions and physical reactions to the music.

This music was, simultaneously, deeply personal and highly public, fusing our neurotic, quivering inner selves with the neurotic, quivering inner selves of others in an effort to find strength and confidence in numbers. We listened to this music in the darkness of our bedrooms, driving around in our parents' cars, on the beach, making out with some boy, and we danced to it—usually with other girls—in the soda shops, basements, and gymnasiums of America. This music burrowed into the everyday psychodramas of our adolescence, forever intertwined with our most private, exhilarating, and embarrassing memories. This music exerted such a powerful influence on us, one that we may barely have recognized, because of this process of identification. By superimposing our own dramas, from our own lives, onto each song, each of us could assume an active role in shaping the song's meaning. Songs that were hits around the country had very particular associations and meanings for each listener, and although they were mass-produced they were individually inter-preted. The songs were ours—but they were also everyone else's. We were all alone, but we weren't really alone at all. In this music, we found solidarity as girls.[5]

Some girl group songs, like "I Will Follow Him," allowed us to assume the familiar persona *Cinderella* had trained us for, the selfless masochist whose identity came only from being some appendage to a man. As we sang along with Dionne Warwick's "Walk On By," we were indeed abject martyrs to love, luxuriating in our own self-pity. But other songs addressed our more feisty and impatient side, the side unwilling to sit around and wait for the boy to make the first move. In "tell him" songs like "Easier Said Than Done," "Wishin' and Hopin'," and, of course, "Tell Him," girls were advised to abandon the time-wasting and possibly boy-losing stance of passively waiting for *him* to make the first move. We were warned that passivity might cost us our man, and we were urged to act immediately and unequiv-ocally, before some more daring girl got there first. Girls were urged to take up a previously male prerogative—to be active agents of their own love lives and to go out and court the boy. Regardless of how girls actually behaved—and I know from personal experience that what was derisively called "boy chasing" was on the rise—now there were lyrics in girls' heads that said, "Don't be passive, it will cost you."

Was being cautious too safe? Was being daring too risky? Girl group music acknowledged—even celebrated—our confusion and ambivalence. Some of us wanted to be good girls, and some of us wanted to be bad. But most of us wanted to get away with being both, and girl group music let us try on and act out a host of identi-ties, from traditional, obedient girlfriend to brassy, independent rebel, and lots in between. We could even do this in the same song, for often the lead singer represented one point of view and the backup singers another, so the very wars raging in our own heads about how to behave, what pose to strike, were enacted in one two-minute hit single.

Few songs capture this more perfectly than one of the true girl group greats, "Sweet Talkin' Guy" by the Chiffons. Here we have a tune about a deceitful and heartless charmer who acts like he loves you one day and moves on to another girl the next. Nonetheless, since he's "sweeter than sugar" (ooh-ooh) with "kisses like wine (oh he's so fine)," this heel is irresistible. The lead singer warns other girls to stay away from such a boy, since he'll only break their hearts, but she also confesses he is "my kinda guy." The female chorus backs her up, acknowledging that it is indeed understandable to be swept up by such a cad.

On the face of it, we have lyrics about the unrequited love of a young woman with, no doubt, a few masochistic tendencies. But the song achieves much more. With the layering of voices over and against one another, some of them alto and some of them soprano, we have a war between resisting such boys and succumbing to them. The music, with its driving beat and a tambourine serving as metronome, is dance music. At the end of the song the layered vocal harmonies run ecstatically up the octaves, like girls running jubilantly across a field, ending with a euphoric chord that suggests, simultaneously, that young female love will win in the end and that it will transcend male brutishness. Singing along to a song like this, girls could change voice, becoming singing ventriloquists for different stances toward the same boy, the same situation. As altos, sopranos, or both, back and forth, we could love and denounce such boys, we could warn against our own victimization, yet fall prey to its sick comforts. We could feel how desire—irresistible, irrational, timeless—was shaping our destinies. The euphoric musical arrangement made us feel even more strongly that the power to love and to dream would enable us somehow to burst through the traps of history. In "Sweet Talkin' Guy," being divided against yourself is normal, natural, true: the song celebrates the fact not just that girls *do* have conflicting subjective stances but that, to get by, they *must*. Yes, we can't help loving them, even when they're bastards, but we have to be able to name how they hurt us, and we must share those warnings with other girls. And if we're dancing while we do it, moving our bodies autonomously, or in unison with others girls, well, maybe we'll escape after all.

Girl group songs were, by turns, boastful, rebellious, and self-abnegating, and through them girls could assume different personas, some of them strong and empowering and others masochistic and defeating. As girls listened to their radios and record players, they could be martyrs to love ("Please Mr. Postman"), sexual aggressors ("Beechwood 4-5789"), fearsome Amazons protecting their men ("Don't Mess with Bill" and "Don't Say Nothin' Bad About My Baby"), devoted, selfless girlfriends ("My Guy," "I Will Follow Him"), taunting, competitive brats ("Judy's Turn to Cry," "My Boyfriend's Back"), sexual sophisticates ("It's in His Kiss"), and, occasionally, prefeminists ("Don't Make Me Over" and "You Don't Own Me"). The Shirelles themselves, in hit after hit, assumed different stances, from the faithful romantic ("Soldier Boy," "Dedicated to the One I Love") to knowing adviser ("Mama Said," "Foolish Little Girl") to sexual slave ("Baby, It's You"). The songs were about escaping from yet acquiescing to the demands of a male-dominated society, in which men called the shots but girls could still try to give them a run for their money. Girls in these songs enjoyed being looked at with desire, but they also enjoyed looking with desire themselves. The singers were totally confident; they were abjectly insecure. Some songs said do and others said don't. Sometimes the voice was of an assertive, no-nonsense girl out to get the guy or showing off her boyfriend to her friends. At other times, the voice was that of the passive object, yearning patiently to be discovered and loved. Often the girl tried to get into the boy's head and imagined the boy regarding her as the object of his desire. Our pathetic struggles and anxieties about popularity were glamorized and dignified in these songs.

In girl group music, girls talked to each other confidentially, primarily about boys and sex. The songs took our angst-filled conversations, put them to music, and gave them a good beat. Some songs, like "He's So Fine" (doo lang, doo lang, doo lang), picked out a cute boy from the crowd and plotted how he would be hooked. In this song the choice was clearly hers, not his. Songs also re-created images of a clot of girls standing around in their mohair sweaters assessing the male talent and, well, looking over boys the way boys had always looked over girls. Other songs, like "Playboy" or "Too Many Fish in the Sea," warned girls about two-timing Romeo types who didn't deserve the time of day, and the sassy, defiant singers advised girls to tell boys who didn't treat them right to take a hike. Opening with a direct address to their sisters—"Look here, girls, take this advice"— the Marvelettes passed on what sounded like age-old female wisdom: "My mother once told me something/And every word is true/Don't waste your time on a fella/Who doesn't love you." Urging the listener to "stand tall," the lead singer asserted, "I don't want nobody that don't want me/Ain't gonna love nobody that don't love me."

The absolute necessity of female collusion in the face of thoughtless or mystifying behavior by boys bound these songs together, and bound the listeners to the singers in a knowing sorority. They knew things about boys and love that they shared with each other, and this shared knowledge—smarter, more deeply intuitive, more worldly wise than any male locker room talk—provided a powerful bonding between girls, a kind of bonding boys didn't have. And while boys were often identified as the love object, they were also identified as the enemy. So while some of the identities we assumed as we sang along were those of the traditional, passive, obedient, lovesick girl, each of us could also be a sassy, assertive, defiant girl who intended to have more control over her life—or at least her love life. In numerous advice songs, from "Mama Said" to "You Can't Hurry Love," the message that girls knew a thing or two, and that they would share that knowledge with one another to beat the odds in a man's world, circulated confidently.

Other songs fantasized about beating a different set of odds—the seeming inevitability, for white, middle-class girls, of being married off to some boring, respectable guy with no sense of danger or adventure, someone like David Nelson or one of Fred MacMurray's three sons. Here we come to the rebel category—"Leader of the Pack," "Uptown," "He's a Rebel," "Give Him a Great Big Kiss," and "He's Sure the Boy I Love." Academic zeros, on unemployment, clad in leather jackets, sporting dirty fingernails, and blasting around on motorcycles, the boy heroes in these songs were every suburban parent's nightmare, the boys they loved to hate. By allying herself romantically and morally with the rebel hero, the girl singer and listener proclaimed her independence from society's predictable expectations about her inevitable domestication. There is a role reversal here, too—the girls are gathered in a group, sharing information about their boyfriends, virtually eyeing them up and down, while the rebel heroes simply remain the passive objects of their gaze and their talk. And the girls who sang these songs, like the Shangri-Las, dressed the part of the defiant bad girl who stuck her tongue out at parental and middle-class authority. The Ronettes, whose beehives scraped the ceiling and whose eyeliner was thicker than King Tut's, wore spiked heels and skintight dresses with slits up the side as they begged some boy to "Be My Baby." They combined fashion rebellion with in-your-face sexual insurrection.

In "Will You Love Me Tomorrow," Shirley Owens asked herself, Should she or shouldn't she? Of course, the question quickly became Should I or shouldn't I? The answer wasn't clear, and we heard plenty of songs in which girls found themselves smack in the grip of sexual desire. Sexuality emerged as an eternal ache, a kind of irresistible, unquenchable tension. But in the early 1960s, sex and sexual desire were still scary for many girls. The way many of these songs were produced—orchestrated with violins instead of with electric guitars or saxophones—muted the sexual explicitness and made it more romantic, more spiritual, more safe. "And Then He Kissed Me" alluded to some kind of new kiss tried on the singer by her boyfriend, one she really liked and wanted to have a lot more of. In "Heat Wave," Martha Reeves sang at the top of her lungs about being swept up in a sexual fever that just wouldn't break, and the whispering, bedroom-voiced lead in "I'm Ready" confessed that she didn't really know quite what she was supposed to do but that she was sure ready to learn—right now. Claudine Clark desperately begged her mother to let her go off to the source of the "Party Lights," where one helluva party was happening, and she sounded like someone who had been in Alcatraz for twenty years and would simply explode if she didn't get out.

The contradictions of being a teenage girl in the early and mid-1960s also percolated from the conflict between the lyrics of the song and the beat of the music. Girl group music had emerged at the same time as all these new dance crazes that redefined how boys and girls did—or, more accurately, did not—dance with each other. Chubby Checker's 1960 hit "The Twist" revolutionized teenage dancing, because it meant that boys and girls didn't have to hold hands anymore, boys didn't have to lead and girls didn't have to follow, so girls had a lot more autonomy and control as they danced. Plus, dancing was one of the things girls usually did much better than boys. As the twist gave way to the locomotion, the Bristol stomp, the mashed potatoes, the pony, the monkey, the slop, the jerk, and the frug, the dances urged us to loosen up our chests and our butts, and learn how to shimmy, grind, and thrust. This was something my friends and I did with gleeful abandon.

Many of us felt most free and exhilarated while we were dancing, so bouncing around to a song like "Chains" or "Nowhere to Run" put us smack-dab between feelings of liberation and enslavement, between a faith in free will and a surrender to destiny. Both songs describe prisoners of love, and if you simply saw the lyrics without hearing the music, you'd think they were a psychotherapist's notes from a session with a deeply paranoid young woman trapped in a sadomasochistic relationship. Yet with "Chains," sung by the Cookies, girls were primed for dancing from the very beginning by the hand clapping, snare drums, and saxophones, so that the music worked in stark contrast to the lyrics, which claimed that the girl couldn't break free from her chains of love. Then, in a break from the chorus, the lead singer acknowledged, "I wanna tell you pretty baby/Your lips look sweet/I'd like to kiss them/But I can't break away from all of these chains." At least two personas emerge here, coexisting in the same teenager. One is the girl who loves the bitter-sweet condition of being hopelessly consumed by love. The other is the girl who, despite her chains, has a roving and appreciative eye for other boys. The conflict between the sense of entrapment in the lyrics and the utter liberation of the beat is inescapable. The tension is too delicious for words.

It was the same for one of the greatest songs ever recorded, "Nowhere to Run." The opening layers of drums, horns, and tambourines propelled us out onto the dance floor—I mean, you couldn't not dance to this song. While we were gyrating and bouncing around to a single about a no-good boy who promised nothing but heartache yet had us in his sadistic grip, we were as happy as we could be. The best part was the double entendre lyrics in the middle, which we belted out with almost primal intensity. "How can I fight a love that shouldn't be?/When it's so deep—so deep—it's deep inside of me/My love reaches so high I can't get over it/So wide, I can't get around it, no." In the face of our entrapment, Martha Reeves made us sweat, and celebrated the capacity of girls to love like women. She also articulated a sophisticated knowingness about how sexual desire overtakes common sense every time, even in girls. In a very different kind of song, the effervescent "I Can't Stay Mad at You," Skeeter Davis told her boyfriend that he could treat her like dirt, make her cry, virtually grind her heart under the heel of his boot, and she'd still love him anyway, and all this between a string of foot-tapping, butt-bouncing shoobie doobie do bops. So even in songs seemingly about female victimization and helplessness, the beat and euphoria of the music put the lie to the lyrics by getting the girl out on the dance floor, moving on her own, doing what she liked, displaying herself sexually, and generally getting ready for bigger and better things. Dancing to this music together created a powerful sense of unity, of commonality of spirit, since we were all feeling, with our minds and our bodies, the same enhanced emotions at the same moment.

While a few girl groups and individual singers were white—the Angels, the Shangri-Las, Dusty Springfield—most successful girl groups were black. Unlike the voices of Patti Page or Doris Day, which seemed as innocent of sexual or emotional angst as a Chatty Cathy doll, the vibrating voices of black teenagers, often trained in the gospel traditions of their churches, suggested a perfect fusion of naivete and knowingness. And with the rise of the civil rights movement, which by 1962 and 1963 dominated the national news, black voices conveyed both a moral authority and a spirited hope for the future. These were the voices of exclusion, of hope for something better, of longing. They were not, like Annette or the Lennon Sisters, the voices of sexual repression, of social complacency, or of homogenized commercialism.

From the Jazz Age to rap music, African American culture has always kicked white culture upside the head for being so pathologically repressed; one consequence, for black women, is that too often they have been stereotyped as more sexually active and responsive than their white-bread sisters. Because of these stereotypes, it was easier, more acceptable, to the music industry and no doubt to white culture at large that black girls, instead of white ones, be the first teens to give voice to girls' changing attitudes toward sex. But since the sexuality of black people has always been deeply threatening to white folks, black characters in popular culture also have been desexualized, the earth-mother mammy being a classic example. The black teens in girl groups, then, while they sounded orgiastic at times, had to look feminine, innocent, and as white as possible. Berry Gordy, the head of Motown, knew this instinctively, and made his girl groups take charm school lessons and learn how to get into and out of cars, carry their handbags, and match their shoes to their dresses.[6] They were trapped, and in the glare of the spotlight, no less, between the old and new definitions of femininity. But under their crinolined skirts and satin cocktail dresses, they were also smuggling into middle-class America a taste of sexual liberation. So white girls like me owe a cultural debt to these black girls for straddling these contradictions, and for helping create a teen girl culture that said, "Let loose, break free, don't take no shit."

The Shirelles paved the way for the decade's most successful girl group, the Supremes, who had sixteen records in the national top ten between 1964 and 1969. But of utmost importance was the role Diana Ross played in making African American beauty enviable to white girls. As slim as a rail with those cavernous armpits, gorgeous smile, and enormous, perfectly made-up eyes, Diana Ross is the first black woman I remember desperately wanting to look like, even if some of her gowns were a bit too Vegas. I couldn't identify with her completely, not because she was black, but because when I was fourteen, she seemed so glamorous and sophisticated. Ross has taken a lot of heat in recent years as the selfish bitch who wanted all the fame and glory for herself, so it's easy to forget her importance as a cultural icon in the 1960s. But the Supremes—who seemed to be both girls and women, sexy yet respectable, and a blend of black and white culture—made it perfectly normal for white girls to idolize and want to emulate their black sisters.

Another striking trend that grew out of the girl group revolution was the proliferation of the male falsetto. From Maurice Williams in "Stay" to Lou Christie in "Two Faces Have I" to Roy Orbison in "Crying" and Randy and the Rainbows in "Denise" (ooo-be-ooo), and most notably with The Four Seasons and The Beach Boys, boys sang in high-pitched soprano ranges more suited for female than for male sing-along. What this meant was that girls belting out lyrics in the kitchen, in the car, or while watching *American Bandstand* had the opportunity to assume *male* roles, male subjective stances as they sang, even though they were singing in a female register.

This was nothing less than musical cross-dressing. While the male falsettos sang of their earnest love for their girls, about how those girls got them through the trials and tribulations of parental disputes, loneliness, drag-car racing ("Don't Worry Baby"), or being from the wrong side of the tracks, girls could fantasize about boys being humanized, made more nurturing, compassionate, and sensitive through their relationships with girls. This is an enduring fantasy, and one responsible for the staggeringly high sales of romance novels in America. It was a narcissistic fantasy that the girl was at the center of someone's universe, that she did make a difference in that universe, and that that difference was positive. This practice of assuming male voices later enabled girls to slip in and out of male points of view, sometimes giving girls a temporary taste of power. Several years later, in a song much maligned by feminists, "Under My Thumb," girls could and did sing not as the one under the thumb but as the one holding the thumb down.

While girl group music celebrated love, marriage, female masochism, and passivity, it also urged girls to make the first move, to rebel against their parents and middle-class conventions, and to dump boys who didn't treat them right. Most of all, girl group music—precisely because these were groups, not just individual singers—insisted that it was critically important for girls to band together, talking about men, singing about men, trying to figure them out.

What we have here is a pop culture harbinger in which girl groups, however innocent and commercial, anticipate women's groups, and girl talk anticipates a future kind of women's talk.[7] The consciousness-raising groups of the late sixties and early seventies came naturally to many young women because we'd had a lot of practice. We'd been talking about boys, about loving them and hating them, about how good they often made us feel and how bad they often treated us, for ten years. The Shirelles mattered because they captured so well our confusion in the face of changing sexual mores. And as the confusion of real life intersected with the contradictions in popular culture, girls were prepared to start wondering, sooner or later, why sexual freedoms didn't lead to other freedoms as well.

Girl group music gave us an unprecedented opportunity to try on different, often conflicting, personas. For it wasn't just that we could be, as we sang along first with the Dixie Cups and then the Shangri-Las, traditional passive girls one minute and more active, rebellious, even somewhat prefeminist girls the next. Contradiction was embedded in almost all the stances a girl tried on, and some version, no matter how thwarted, of prefeminism, constituted many of them. We couldn't sustain this tension forever, especially when one voice said, "Hey, hon, you're equal" and the other voice said, "Oh no, you're not."

The Shirelles and the other girl groups mattered because they helped cultivate inside us a desire to rebel. The main purpose of pop music is to make us feel a kind of euphoria that convinces us that we can transcend the shackles of conventional life and rise above the hordes of others who do get trapped. It is the euphoria of commercialism, designed to get us to buy. But this music did more than that; it generated another kind of euphoria as well. For when tens of millions of young girls started feeling, at the same time, that they, as a generation, would not be trapped, there was planted the tiniest seed of a social movement.

Few symbols more dramatically capture the way young women in the early 1960s were pinioned between entrapment and freedom than one of the most bizarre icons of the period, the go-go girl dancing in a cage. While African American performers like the Dixie Cups or Mary Wells sang on *Shindig* or *Hullabaloo,* white girls in white go-go boots pranced and shimmied in their cages in the background. Autonomous yet objectified, free to dance by herself on her own terms yet highly choreographed in her little prison, seemingly indifferent to others yet trapped in a voyeuristic gaze, the go-go girl seems, in retrospect, one of the sicker, yet more apt, metaphors for the teen female condition during this era. It's not surprising that when four irreverent, androgynous, and irresistible young men came over from England and incited a collective jailbreak, millions of these teens took them up on it. For we had begun to see some new kinds of girls in the mass media—some perky, some bohemian, some androgynous—who convinced us that a little anarchy was exactly what we, and American gender roles, needed.

CHAPTER 5

She's Got the Devil in Her Heart

"Four Party-Givers: Which Type Are You?" demanded the cover of *Glamour* magazine. You could only fall into one of four categories: planner, traditionalist, romantic, and extemporizer. "How Good Is Your Swim Suit Figure? Special Pinch Test," offered another issue. Don't miss the "Know Yourself Quiz: What Does Your Color Choice Tell About You?" Month after month, we sharpened our pencils and took yet another quiz, and we could also pinch, measure, and poke ourselves as per the carefully illustrated instructions in the magazine. We were desperate to know which type we were, to know ourselves, and we looked to the mass media for answers. No doubt the magazines kept offering quizzes, often as many as four or five in one issue, because they were quite popular with us, their abject, quivering, insecure readers.

As we struggled through our teens, we were bombarded with questions such as these, which were stand-ins for the big ones. Who were we? Who should we be? How could you fit in with everybody else yet still be a distinctive individual with traits all your own? Now there's little doubt that a pathological level of self-consciousness is what being an adolescent is all about, at least in America. But for girls, self-scrutiny—of our thighs, our pores, our eyebrows, our breasts, our hair follicles, our cuticles, and our "true" inner selves—was drummed in by magazines like *Seventeen, Glamour, 'Teen,* and *Mademoiselle,* with their increasingly skinny models, their advice columns, and those endless, moronic quizzes. Boys simply didn't have such magazines—*Boys' Life* was about fishing and tying knots and they were too young for *Esquire*—but there were plenty geared for us, especially if you also count *True Confessions* and *Photoplay.*

There is no doubt that as these magazines demanded increased self-scrutiny—so important to selling cosmetics, clothes, and Relaxa-cizors—they also exaggerated our psychic schizophrenia, our sense of being a mosaic of traits that didn't quite fit together. The magazines were themselves schizophrenic about whether to approach us as if we were coherent, unified individuals or a bundle of contradictory, inchoate multiple personalities. The major literary devices here were the ceaseless, countless, repetitious, judgmental, and certainly asinine quizzes we were invited to take each month. These quizzes were especially insidious. They always addressed us directly and intimately as "you," as if they were personally designed for each and every one of us. They asked us a lot of personal questions and invited us to confess—in private, of course, and to an understanding listener who would never tell anyone. And they promised enhanced self-knowledge if you'd only pick up a pencil and check off a few answers. Through their multiple choice or true and false formats, these quizzes reaffirmed that we were indeed different people at different times, and *should be* different people at different times.

What fragrance type are you, floral or spicy? Take a quiz and find out; your perfume will tell you who you *really* are. Are you attractive to boys? How feminine are you? Are you shy or stuck up, too loud or too quiet? Are you too easy or too hard to get? Take another quiz. Is your skin oily or dry, your face heart-shaped or square? Don't forget to check your "Happiness Index." The monthly "It's All Jake" col-umn—in which a chatty, omniscient, sophisticated guy, we were supposed to believe, writing under the ever-so-cool pseudonym Jake—gave girls the real lowdown about men and themselves. Jake plotted, one month, "to find the real you" by giving a word associa-tion quiz. As Jake acknowledged, "Any paperback treatise in psy-chology will tell you that the real you is very hard to locate."[1] The most maddening quizzes and advice columns told us, over and over, that, in order to be popular, we simply had to be ourselves. But how could you be yourself if you didn't know what "yourself" was? And what if the "yourself" you thought you might be didn't correspond to any of the categories at the end of the quiz?

The insistence that you absolutely *had* to be able to pigeonhole yourself quickly was an obsession in these magazines, but the pigeon-holing was tied to particular situations. One quiz told you that you were a romantic; another, that you were decisive; yet another, that you were afraid of commitment and that each trait, under different circumstances, could be good or bad. So these quizzes reinforced the notion that you had to assume different roles for different occasions—that there was not a "real" you, just an actress performing a variety of parts. Certain roles, traits, and impulses were, of course, completely unacceptable, and they were either condemned in these quizzes or simply never mentioned, as if their existence was unimaginable. I remember all too well looking at the possible answers and thinking that either all of them or none of them captured my response. But there were your possible choices, A, B, or C, and you had to pick one and only one.

As we surveyed our compartmentalized selves, we sought role models to emulate, women who seemed to embody a way to feel more whole and less fragmented. And, by the mid-1960s, there was no shortage of pop culture teen girls to latch on to. I may not have been sure who I was, but one thing was clear to me early on—I did not want to end up like my mother, pissed off, overworked, under-paid, and trapped in New Jersey. In fact, my main mission in life was to be as different from her as possible. My mother, I thought simply back then, had been stupid and hadn't planned things very well. She had allowed herself to be trapped. She had willingly fallen into that despised category Woman and now acted like one and was paying for it. Not me: I was determined to be different and to escape the prison of traditional womanhood. Plus, I wanted to have fun when I grew up. No, I definitely did not want to be like my mother, and I didn't want to be like June Cleaver or Margaret Anderson either. No thank you. I wanted to be Holly Golightly and stay up all night. I wanted to be Cricket Blake from *Hawaiian Eye* and ride around in a convertible with Edd "Kookie" Byrnes. I wanted to be Gidget, the perky tomboy type who still had plenty of dates and got to spend most of her time on the beach. And I especially wanted to go on tour with the Beatles. By 1964, they had recorded a song that tapped into these feelings: "Devil in Her Heart." Even though it was a call and response song about whether the girl in question would be faithful or fickle, I saw a higher meaning: just how long were we going to behave ourselves, anyway, especially when behaving yourself as a girl meant not having any fun? Wasn't it about time we had the devil in our hearts?

There were so many boundaries I wanted to cross, especially those marked "teenage girls don't belong here." And during this critical transition period in the mid-1960s, as the forces of various revolutions were coalescing, I had a host of young role models—some of them serious and some of them frivolous—to try on for size. But no matter how dumb some of them seem now, together they pushed me closer to a wholesale break with Mom's lot in life. All of them were about masquerade, about looking the part of the teenage girl while, underneath, sneaking in less "feminine" behaviors and traits. There were all sorts of disguised, furtive insurgencies going on that emboldened me and girls like me in surprising ways, and legitimized our pushing against the already crumbling boundaries of 1950s-style femininity.

At the same time that rebellion was erupting in tens of millions of teenagers, the advertisers, moviemakers, and TV producers of America realized that we weren't just a big market: we were humongous. In a 1963 article titled "Teens Grow as Top Target for Many Products," *Printer's Ink* estimated that already "some 20-million teenagers personally spend an average of $550-million plus annually" and that "smart marketing men" would be well-advised to concentrate on the kids.[2] We were a tricky market to pitch things to, however, because we wanted to rebel against grown-ups and the establishment while feeling grown-up ourselves. We also wanted desperately to conform with one another, or at least with those of us who were cool. A successful ad campaign or TV show or musical group spoke simultaneously to these conflicting desires and made us feel like distinctive individuals with traits all our own who defied mindless, knee-jerk conformism yet still fit in. What this led to by the mid-1960s was a plethora of images of teenage girls and young women, some of them cynically manufactured, some of them much more genuine, who personified the blending, or management, of both defiance and conformity.

As something resembling my teen identity began to coagulate, there was a cavalcade of female archetypes to consider, and each, in her own way, embodied a reaction against the identity with which our mothers had been saddled. They also represented a compromise between obeying gender norms and subverting them. Even so, the absolute importance of having flawless skin, thick, shiny hair, a slender figure, and great clothes remained indisputable. This hadn't changed, and maybe even had intensified as more products, from Stri-Dex to Summer Blonde to poor boy sweaters and miniskirts, were marketed exclusively to us. We were still terrified of being ugly, unpopular, smelly, fat, and dorky, and as lemminglike in our desire to imitate what we saw in *Seventeen* and *Glamour.* (Models like Twiggy would shortly raise the stakes considerably on how much weight we all had to lose and how much eyeliner we had to apply to be truly fashionable.) Yet these new female icons, as strikingly different as they all were—the bohemian, the career girl, the folk singer, the Beatles fan, the perky TV teen—were about repudiating certain prescribed female traits, like being docile, obedient, apolitical, and sexually passive. Even *Glamour,* by the early 1960s, assumed its readers would either work or go to college after high school, and there were many more articles like "From Campus to Career" and quizzes asking, "Are You in the Right Job?" than there were pieces about marriage, let alone babies, which were rarely mentioned. The 1963 "Happiness Index" asserted that "happiness is . . . an eight dollar raise; the boss's compliment; not having to shave your legs." Yes, this was chatty and cute; it was also prefeminist.

Through these new archetypes we could imagine and emulate a new kind of agency for ourselves and for our generation of girls. And the celebrity girls and boys we identified with were blurring one of the most important boundaries of all, the one demarcating what it meant to be a boy and what it meant to be a girl. As longer hair and dandified clothes for boys became cool, many of us began doing what boys did, acting like them, and even looking like them. Mia Farrow and Twiggy had shorter hair than John Lennon. We wore pants, instead of skirts, whenever we could, man-sized watchbands, and, if we were preppy, the same Bass Weejuns the boys wore. We stopped wearing Heaven Sent and bought Canoe from the men's counter. Sure, these were just cosmetic gestures of style, but they mattered. No one called it gender bending at the time, but that's what was happening. And it gave us just that little bit of latitude we craved as we collectively cast ourselves against Mom. Referring to the unisex fad, *Glamour* cautioned, "Try On His Shoe in '66, *But Don't Try to Fill It.*"[3] But once you tried it on and felt how comfortable it was, well, as men found out, they didn't always get those shoes back.

The first irresistible, androgynous, and nonconformist female character many of us remember is Holly Golightly from *Breakfast at Tiffany's* (1961). She partied all night and slept all day, usually in the nude, watered the plants with scotch, kept her slippers in the refrigerator and her phone in a suitcase, refused to decorate her apartment, used a two-foot-long cigarette holder, and earned her living as a quasi–call girl, quasi-escort. She lived a glamorous life in New York City, hosting wild cocktail parties, dining at the "21" Club, and getting drunk whenever she felt like it. She could whistle for a cab as loudly and effectively as any burly doorman. She was definitely not a virgin, and she was completely charming. She was totally cynical about marriage, setting her sights only on millionaires. She shoplifted for fun, played the guitar on her fire escape, and called everyone darling.

Here was a young woman on her own, flouting all sorts of old-biddy conventions about how single women should conduct themselves, having a ball. But it was the fact that Audrey Hepburn played this character that made so many of us fantasize about becoming Hollys ourselves when we grew up. It wasn't just that Audrey Hepburn was stunningly gorgeous, or that she was slimmer than most models, or that whatever she wore automatically looked so incredibly stylish. Wide-eyed and small-breasted, Hepburn was still girlish, and while it was quite clear that Holly Golightly was sexually active, Hepburn seemed, well, not quite presexual or asexual but like a fairy or a storybook princess, above it all. She made sexual maturity for girls less scary, as if on the other side of puberty you could be child-like and androgynous and still be attractive to men. Beautiful women with boyish bodies and upper-crust accents, women like Hepburn and Jackie Kennedy, were critical icons during this period, for they made being boyish "classy" and very "in." After the mammary mania of the 1950s, flat-chestedness was fashionable and soon came to signify intelligence and breeding, as if flat-chested women were ipso facto the special exceptions to all those negative stereotypes about female irrationality, incompetence, and stupidity. Audrey Hepburn made me feel a lot better about not looking remotely like the "after" picture in ads for Mark Eden Bust Developers, and this explains, in part, why she was one of the most popular actresses in America among young women.

The narrative of *Breakfast at Tiffany's* was so compelling because it is about a young woman's struggle with her own identity and her passage to womanhood, a passage she and many of us in the audience regarded with dread. After meeting this sophisticated New York City glamour girl, we learn that in a previous life she was Lulamae Barnes, a tomboy, child-bride hillbilly from the sticks, Holly's complete opposite. When her former husband comes looking for her, she refuses to go back with him, explaining simply, "I'm not Lulamae anymore." Later in the film, when Paul Varjack (George Peppard) pressures her for a commitment, she announces that she is neither Lulamae nor Holly, she isn't sure who she is.

This never-ending invention of selves, of masks, of poses was all too familiar to us, and when Paul asks her to give up certain aspects of being Holly to be his wife instead, we were as torn as Holly. Paul insists, "I love you—you belong to me," but Holly snaps back, "No—people don't *belong* to people. I'm not going to let anyone put me in a cage." Loving someone, she asserts, is tantamount to imprisoning him or her. (Even as a preteen viewer, I saw the way marriage had entrapped a lot of adults I knew, so I tended to agree with Holly.) Holly validated my own emerging antagonism to the institution of marriage. Nevertheless, there was George Peppard, handsome, caring, and smart, who loved her despite all her previous dalliances and who seemed to be offering something different. I wanted Holly to be able to stay Holly *and* keep Peppard. The final scene, in which Holly finds her cat (named Cat, of course) and kisses Paul in a teeming downpour, is ambiguous. Do I cry every time because she's found Cat and Paul, or because she's lost Holly? And it's not clear how important the film's resolution was anyway, since what we all remembered and found thrilling wasn't that Holly got George Peppard in the end but that she got away with all sorts of nonconformity without paying any price—on the contrary, she got one reward after the next. She made female eccentricity, and deliberately not fitting in, glamorous.

It's not embarrassing, after all these years, to admit that Holly Golightly/Audrey Hepburn had a strong impact on you when you were young, making you long for bigger and better things. Cricket Blake, however, is another matter. It takes a certain amount of guts to admit that you bonded on some primal, coursing level with Cricket Blake. Played by Connie Stevens, whom I idolized in the early 1960s, Cricket was the sidekick of Tom Lopaka (Bob Conrad) and Tracy Steele (Anthony Eisley), the two chisel-faced, freewheeling bachelor detectives with a posh poolside office in the ABC show *Hawaiian*

Eye, which ran from 1959 to 1963. But I shouldn't be that embarrassed—Cricket, like Holly, offered an inviting alternative to Mom in New Jersey. She also showed me a way out of the identity problem by being perky: energetic, an individualist, if only in speech, manner, and style, puckish and attractive in a childlike way. A single career girl with a long, blond, bouncy ponytail, Cricket worked as a photographer by day and a nightclub singer by night. She referred to Tom as "lover," flirted with whomever she felt like, and sometimes helped solve cases. She was very much an individual, often cast as eccentric and—that most favorite of TV qualities—"zany." Living in a glamorous place, surrounded by these hunky guys, and never, ever seen vacuuming or cleaning up baby sputum, Cricket had it made, as far as I was concerned. This was the life—single in Hawaii with lots of adventure and no responsibilities, behaving exactly as you wanted and being your own person.

The show was produced by Warner Bros., which specialized in detective shows such as *Bourbon Street Beat, Surfside Six,* and, its most famous, *77 Sunset Strip.* They all featured two or three debonair, handsome private eyes, with dark, steel oblongs of their own, and one beautiful young woman, who was their secretary, switchboard operator, or simple sidekick. Two young guys with their hair waved suggestively over their foreheads, Edd Byrnes of *77 Sunset Strip* and the ubiquitous—and robotic—Troy Donahue of *Surfside Six,* were used by ABC to capture the teen and preteen audience, and the ploy worked. I know I was there every week. Both were teen idols for a few years, and Byrnes had a gold record hit with his novelty song "Kookie, Kookie, Lend Me Your Comb," a duet with my girl, Connie Stevens.

Now, looking back on these shows, it's obvious that starlets like Stevens, Diane McBain (Daphne on *Surfside Six*), Jacqueline Beer (Suzanne on *Sunset Strip*), and Dorothy Provine (Pinky Pinkham [!] on *The Roaring Twenties*) served primarily as decorative sex objects and as occasional helpmates to those involved in the real action, the men. But they also offered young girls a fantasy about life outside domesticity, away from some respectable, dull thud of a crew-cut husband and whiny, needy children. They offered a fantasy of an escape from masochism, of a life freer, more fun, and much less angry than Mom's. They suggested, if only in a whisper, liberation.

Eight days after *Hawaiian Eye* went off the air, on September 18, 1963, *The Patty Duke Show* premiered. The teenage girl was now so important to advertisers and producers that entire shows were built around her and her zany antics. The network with the lowest ratings, ABC, was trying to improve its pathetic showings in the Nielsens, and clearly targeted the teen audience, and girls in particular, as the path to success. Hence Patty Duke, *Shindig, The Farmer's Daughter,* and the show that really hit pay dirt, *Bewitched.* By 1965, *The Patty Duke Show* and *Gidget* aired back to back on Wednesday nights. Here we had teenage girls possessed by an almost virulent strain of perkiness. And while perkiness seems so nauseating now, it was then an absolutely critical mask for girls who wanted to take an active role in the world yet still be thought of as appealing.

In both shows, a perky, cute, and slightly tomboyish teenage girl was the central character and, thus, the center of attention. Her parents doted on her, she was popular, she had a steady boyfriend, but she also got to date other boys. The struggle for a comfortable, "natural," yet socially successful female identity was what animated these shows, so they resonated well with all those quizzes in *Glamour, Mademoiselle,* and *Seventeen.* Patty and Gidget liked to take charge, set up new situations, and control events, but they also wanted to be appealing to boys, who were sometimes put off by girls who were too spunky and aggressive.

It was usually "perkiness"—assertiveness masquerading as cuteness—that provided the middle ground they needed to get their way and get male approval, two goals that were often mutually exclusive. By donning this disguise, Gidget and Patty got to be thought of as girls while assuming some of the prerogatives of boys. They disdained the passivity and helplessness of overly feminized girls. Lady was a category they actively rebelled against, reinforcing a negative definition of womanhood while angling to be the delightful exception. The appeal here was watching these girls move between more "masculine" and "feminine" positions and having fun doing so. For many teenage girls struggling with all their warring selves, perkiness was a satisfying compromise, a veneer over the fragmented mosaic. For if you were perky·you were, by definition, unpredictable and highly individualistic, and could get away with behaviors no one quite expected. Perkiness repressed and channeled teen girl sexuality into antics and plots, while giving girls some sense of control. Perkiness was fabulous camouflage.

The Patty Duke Show sought to capitalize on Patty Duke's considerable success portraying the young Helen Keller in *The Miracle Worker*. Rarely has such a talented young actress been more poorly served (except when Sally Field got stuck with *The Flying Nun*). The show featured identical cousins (have you *ever* heard of identical cousins?), Patty and Cathy Lane (both played by Patty Duke), the former an all-American, outspoken, slang-speaking, rock 'n' roll–loving girl with the dorkiest boyfriend in TV history, and the latter a more ladylike, refined, soft-spoken young woman from England with high-culture tastes. Both characters were pretty insufferable because they were so patently unrealistic, and you could never imagine anyone having the hots for the dork-boyfriend, Richard. This show actually pretended that normal boys and girls would rather sip a milk shake at the local soda shop than French kiss at the local drive-in. Although Patty was clearly the more "normal" and hip of the two, there were times when Cathy's polish and quiet demeanor were shown as attractive and desirable.

Having two Pattys was quintessentially mid-1960s, when TV shows, with the help of special effects, sought to hail as many types of teenagers as possible. The purpose of the show seemed to be to provide girl viewers with two points of identification, Patty and Cathy, both of them deliberately asexual and providing two outlying points on the spectrum of teen girl femininity. Oscillating between these two personas, the narrative rewarded perkiness sometimes and reticence at others. *The Patty Duke Show* reinforced the notion that a girl was a grab bag of traits and masks, some more feminine and some more masculine, that could be deployed in different situations. Patty and Cathy often traded places, providing a fantasy of being able to change one's identity while showing all the pitfalls that accompany such impersonations.

Gidget was more appealing. Not only were Sally Field's hairdos and clothes cuter, but also the show featured the great Electra fantasy: Mom gone and a kind, handsome, well-to-do, and indulgent Dad all to yourself. The show also sought to appear more authentic to girl viewers by opening and closing each segment with voice-over narration by Gidget herself, allowing us to be privy to her innermost thoughts. In an episode demonstrating how the show navigated the shoals of femininity, Gidget and her college professor father host a Swedish exchange student, Inge, until the college dorms open. Raised by a very strict, old-fashioned father and engaged to an overly serious and overbearing boor named Gunnar, Inge is a drudge who carries her own luggage, constantly volunteers to cook and clean, and spends the rest of her time studying. Quoting her father, she says, "To be a woman is to be useful." Anticipating the Cyndi Lauper hit of twenty years later, Gidget asks incredulously, "Don't you want to have fun?" When Inge tells her that her life and behavior have already been decided for her, Gidget urges, "Well, fight back." Gidget repeatedly describes Inge as a slave to her father and boyfriend, as a second-class citizen deprived of the special privileges of being a girl, and tells her that in America she can behave differently because here everybody's equal. From Gidget's point of view, and thus the audience's, Inge needs to be liberated. Let's see just what liberation means here.

Gidget takes it upon herself to socialize Inge in the ways of femininity so that Inge can begin to enjoy her rights. She teaches Inge how to act helpless and seductive to get boys to carry her books, buy her food, and take her out on dates. The problem is, Inge is too good a student and becomes a Swedish femme fatale in no time flat. (Given the stereotypes about Swedish girls, we saw this one coming like a Mack truck.) Soon all the boys in Gidget's crowd, including Gidget's current boyfriend, Mark, are calling on Inge, and in one scene Inge uses a combination of flattery and sexual display to try to seduce Gidget's father. Clearly Inge has gone too far on the femininity spectrum, not knowing how to modulate, inflect, and strategically deploy these traits the way Gidget does. She hasn't gotten it that an out-and-out display of sexuality, inadequately disguised by perkiness or anything else, is too dangerous and too threatening for a girl of her age. By the time Gunnar returns, Inge is a petulant, self-indulgent, narcissistic brat who sashays around the house expecting to be catered to hand and foot. Gidget has created a monster.

Gidget decides to show Gunnar and Mark how far Inge has fallen by hosting a quiet dinner at home for the four of them, during which the usually effervescent, assertive Gidget displays all the self-effacing, domestic, ladylike traits she knows Gunnar admires. While Gidget cooks, serves dinner, and asks Gunnar solicitously about his work, Inge insists that she's not having fun, demands to be taken out, and refuses to help Gidget with the dishes. While Gidget and Mark retreat to the kitchen, Gunnar tells Inge he is ashamed of her. She tells him he is just like Pappa, "Study, verk, learn. Well, I vanna haf a little fun." "Of course," answers Gunnar. "But is that all? I vant a voman for a vife, not a child who only vants to haf fun. Look at Gidget. She's quiet, pleasant, thoughtful." As the argument escalates, he accuses Inge of being "a spoiled child," takes her over his knee, and spanks her. This restores Inge to her formerly docile self, although we sense that Gunnar may compromise too. Please note that the spanking falls happily into the "Thanks, I needed that" category of abuse: upon overhearing it, even Gidget smiles with approval that this is the best way to restore Inge to the proper mode of female behavior. Gidget, meanwhile, is the model of teen femininity, not so much because she is a lady but because she knows how to impersonate one at the right time. There is a recognition here that femininity is a masquerade, and one that is essential for female survival.

The next day at the beach, Mark says to Gidget, "The other night I sorta saw you differently. You were quieter, you know, more feminine, and I liked that. I mean, you used to come on full of plans, a take-charge girl, but no more. I mean, a guy likes to feel like he's out with a girl, not a platoon sergeant." As Gidget responds, "Whatever you say, Mark," we see her loading him up with all the beach supplies from the back of the car, her actions contradicting her words and the laugh track underscoring the futility of his words. "A man has to be boss," asserts Mark. "You're right, you're the boss," says Gidget as she smiles knowingly to herself. Then her voice-over cuts in. "And that's when I realized I'd set back women's rights a hundred years—exactly where they belong," at which point Mark collapses under the load Gidget has piled on him.

What constitutes "equality" for girls remains confused throughout the episode, and indeed throughout the series itself. The show insists that girls not be slavish doormats for fathers or boyfriends. But, to get their way, girls need to flatter boys into thinking they're superior so boys will, instead, wait on girls. Without such manipulations, girls would have no privileges, so "women's rights" jeopardizes these prerogatives. Yet to be too feminine, meaning too self-centered, helpless, and sexualized, can also isolate a girl. The message here was about balance, and about a position of equality that required subordination, and a position of subordination that required equality. Perkiness allowed for such machinations, deceptions, and contortions.

During these years, we also acted out the flip side of perkiness: hysteria. The most prominent image of the teenage girl in the mid-1960s was the victim of Beatlemania. Everything that perkiness disguised and repressed—sexual energy, impudence, rebellion against adult authority, a defiance of traditional gender codes, and a howling sense of outrage—all these hysteria unleashed. And it was our overpowering identification not with celebrity girls but with four young men from Britain that showed what could happen when containment and repression fail.

Only two months after *The Patty Duke Show* premiered, John F. Kennedy was killed. The sense of possibility, of optimism, of inevitable progress had been so buoying in the first three years of the 1960s that the youth of America took Kennedy's death especially hard. I was too young to know about all the hidden corruptions and hypocrisies of the Kennedy administration. I didn't know then that behind the images of John-John and Caroline frolicking in the Oval Office, behind the nationally televised speeches asserting that segregation was immoral and would not be tolerated, behind the glittering White House parties for artists and intellectuals, it was old-style politics as usual. So when I saw that vulgar turkey neck, Lyndon Johnson, being sworn into office, I felt that youth had been robbed and betrayed. I felt that the forces of reaction and cynicism had triumphed over idealism. I was disillusioned and very, very sad. It was as if optimism itself had been gunned down in Dealey Plaza.

It was to fill this emotional and spiritual void, this deep grieving over a beloved, charismatic, and witty young man, that we would react to a group of four different young men, also attractive, witty, and a clear departure from the past. Just as Frank Sinatra served as a pop culture surrogate for young women when millions of young men went off to war in the 1940s, the Beatles became a mass phenomenon at a time of profound loss. And the resonance between Kennedy and the Beatles—young, spirited, funny, energetic— allowed for a powerful and collective transference of hope.

The Beatles had cut their first record, "Love Me Do," in 1962 and, by 1963, had become a huge success in England. Capitol Records, however, did little at first to promote them in the United States. Then, in December 1963, no doubt sick of listening to "Dominique" by the Singing Nun for the 800th time, several DJs began playing imported copies of "I Want to Hold Your Hand." It went to the top of the charts in January 1964, sales having soared to 1.5 million. Quickly other songs were released, and by April the Beatles held the top five slots on *Billboard*'s charts, the only time in history this occurred. (The songs were "Can't Buy Me Love," "Twist and Shout," "She Loves You," "I Want to Hold Your Hand," and "Please Please Me.") ⌈Beatlemania had arrived, mutating the previously "normal" American girl into the hair-tugging, screaming, tranced-out Beatles fan.⌋

It was their February 9 appearance on *The Ed Sullivan Show*—the highest-rated show in TV history up to that time[4]—that signaled to the adult world that a new hysteria was gripping the teenagers, and especially the girls, of America. Just as I will never forget where I was when I heard that Kennedy had been shot, I will always remember the Beatles on Ed Sullivan like it was yesterday. I sat six inches away from the TV, hugging an orange Naugahyde hassock to keep me grounded. While I didn't scream (because I was recording them on my dad's reel-to-reel tape recorder), I sure felt like it. I was elated—actually filled with joy. I couldn't stop smiling while they performed. They made me so happy, the kind of happy that overflows all the breakers in your neural system and makes you feel free. This was a happiness I could barely contain, the kind that made me want to shake my best friend and jump for joy. I adored them. I understood completely why 73 million Americans watched them on Ed Sullivan, and why 10,000 screaming fans had greeted them when they had landed at Kennedy Airport two days earlier. Throughout their brief visit to New York City and Washington, DC, the Beatles were chased, run after, and swarmed over by teenage girls who kept breaching the barriers set up between them and their heroes.

I remember when they were scheduled to perform at Shea Stadium in August 1965. One of the New York radio stations had a contest to win tickets to the concert. Fans were to draw pictures of the Beatles and send them in to be judged. The category my best friend and I entered was "biggest" picture of the Beatles. My father was an artist and had rolls and rolls of drawing paper, which we painstakingly taped together and spread out over my backyard. In our white eyeshadow and black eyeliner, we painted the faces of all four Beatles on what we thought was a huge expanse of paper—probably about thirty feet by three feet. It cost a fortune to mail in—evidence enough to us that we had a great chance of winning. But we had been thinking too small—the winner in this category was, I recall, as big as an acre or two.

Adults didn't know what to make of this behavior, and soon there were two major cottage industries in America. The first produced Beatles wigs, bubble-gum cards, magazines (with pictures of each Beatle's lips blown up to life size so you could kiss each one), and so forth. The second produced scores of articles by educators, sociologists, and Dr. Joyce Brothers with titles like "Why the Girls Scream, Weep, Flip," "What the Beatles Prove About Teenagers," and "Brace Yourself, They're Back." It's hard to believe some of the assessments that so-called grown-ups came up with, like "Musically they are a near-disaster [and] their lyrics (punctuated by nutty shouts of 'yeah, yeah, yeah!') are a catastrophe,"[5] and "Beatle music is high-pitched, loud beyond reason, and stupefyingly repetitive."[6]

Much of this drivel was sarcastic and condescending, suggesting that we were "possessed" and that, if parents were patient, it would all pass. The visual images of girls fainting, screaming, biting their knuckles, and pulling their hair out simply reinforced this notion of possession. David Dempsey, writing for the Sunday *New York Times Magazine,* observed, "The Beatles, who provoke the most violent response among teenagers, resemble in manner the witch doctors who put their spell on hundreds of shuffling and stamping natives." He described Beatlemania as a "seizure" that put teens in a "Zen-like trance." "The female members of this cult," he added, "go berserk." But Dempsey also got the point: "Whether dancing, or merely listening and jumping, those taking part are working off the inner tensions that bedevil a mixed up psyche."[7]

Were we just mindless twits, empty-headed bimbos swept up in some inexplicable mass hysteria, witches in a twentieth-century electronic Salem? What was it about the Beatles that spoke to girls so powerfully, that made thousands of otherwise obedient, law-abiding teens willing to cross police barricades, to risk seizure and even arrest, to get near their idols? Beatlemania, always made to look foolish then and now, in fact marked a critical point in the evolution of girl culture that wasn't foolish at all, and was particularly dangerous to the status quo.[8]

First of all, the Beatles were good—really good—and they took their female audience seriously. It wasn't just that they wrote their own music and lyrics, which was itself a major departure from most other performers and a sign to us of a new authenticity in rock. For girls, it was that they so perfectly fused the "masculine" and "feminine" strains of rock 'n' roll in their music, their appearance, and their style of performing. It wasn't just their long hair, or Paul's eyelashes, the heels on their boots, or the puckish way they clowned for the camera. Without ever saying so explicitly, the Beatles acknowledged that there was masculinity and femininity in all of us, and that blurring the artificial boundaries between the two might be a big relief.[9]

A common sign displayed by Beatles fans was "Elvis Is Dead. We Love the Beatles." It wasn't that the Beatles weren't sexy—they were. But they weren't as threateningly masculine as Elvis. They didn't sneer, they didn't direct attention to the pelvic area, they eschewed anything resembling Brylcreem, and, as David Reisman put it, they didn't remind one of "a hoodlum."[10] Elvis shoved the wrong side of the tracks into middle-class America's faces: he looked like a working-class tough, and he sounded like a black man. The Beatles, in contrast, even though they had come from Liverpool, one of the most benighted and roughest working-class enclaves in England, had traded in their T-shirts and leather jackets for pseudo-Edwardian suits and ties. Yet unlike all those fake, obviously packaged, and eminently safe boy idols—Tommy Sands, Frankie Avalon, Paul Anka—the Beatles exuded a kind of sexual energy that was perceived as completely genuine yet nonaggressive. They personified sexual sublimation, in which primal instincts and threats to the existing order weren't denied—they were just dressed up in Nehru suits and, as a result, better disguised. Even though their hair was shockingly long by 1964 standards—"great pudding bowls of hair" as *Newsweek* put it[11]—they still seemed convincingly clean cut. Without being able to put it into words, but quite able to put it into screams, girls instinctively recognized the Beatles as a Trojan horse, smuggling androgyny, a contempt for middle-class conventionalism, and sexual release into their protected, middle-class worlds. The Beatles insisted that all kinds of barriers could be finessed.

Their music bridged safety and danger as well. Drawing from the "hard" rock 'n' roll of Chuck Berry and Little Richard, as well as from the "soft" call-and-response layered harmony styles of the girl groups, the Beatles pushed the conventional musical codes of masculinity and femininity up against each other in a way that evoked making love with your clothes on. In England they often toured with the Ronettes or Mary Wells, whose music they admired and borrowed from. Electric guitar riffs, driving bass and drums, and John's gravelly voice led into falsetto cries of "ooh" and "yeah," suggesting that male sexuality wasn't so threatening, female sexuality was perfectly normal, and the two could exist together harmoniously. After all, they only wanted to hold our hands, or dance with us, and love us, and all this said with a winning and suggestive wink. When they recorded their own versions of girl group songs like "Please Mr. Postman" and "Chains," they showed that boys could find themselves in exactly the same spot as girls and feel just as trapped and helpless.

Onstage, they were irresistible. The most striking thing about them was their sheer joy of performing. No languid, sleepy-eyed Ricky Nelson here, or some overly solemn Andy Williams or mooning Johnny Mathis. They had the spirit, the openness, and the freshness of cheerleaders; they didn't stand still, and their moves weren't choreographed. And these were white boys who definitely did not have poles up their sphincters. They channeled sexual energy away from where Elvis had located it, in the male crotch, and moved it through safer, nonsexual parts of the body—their feet, their legs, their heads, their hair. Like electricity, it arced to the audience, where it surged safely through female limbs and faces. Sexual energy was simultaneously activated and repressed. These boys were having fun, stomping their feet and smiling broadly while they sang, smiling, in part, at themselves and at the performance they were giving. Their self-mockery was like a magnet, and their enthusiasm infectious. The way Ringo bounced his hair while drumming embodied carefreeness, and suggested that no one should take him or herself too seriously, especially if young. Their own barely controlled ecstasy and abandon while performing captured the state teenage girls found themselves in, racked by overpowering feelings but constantly warned to contain themselves. The Beatles showed how you could mock conventions while obeying them, how you could have fun within the confines of established expectations, how you could push the boundaries of public performance and get away with it. The Beatles affirmed that youthful optimism was a force to be reckoned with yet again, and that, for all its naivete, it was hip. For this, girls screamed in gratitude.

The Beatles made it clear that they were quick-witted and smart and that they would tweak pretension every chance they got. Their particular form of rebellion, masquerading at first as clowning for reporters, was palatably packaged in witty remarks, mugging, and pranks. Social conventions about money, about taking fame seriously, about deferring to authority figures, and about how to behave in public were all treated with irreverence. Already John Lennon's remark before the British royals—"People in the cheaper seats, please clap. The rest of you just rattle your jewelry"—was infamous. When they arrived in New York, they were asked when they were going to get haircuts. George quipped, "I had one yesterday." When asked which Beatle he was, John replied, "Eric." They made fun of themselves and of the supposed seriousness of the entire press conference ritual. No one had had this much fun with the press since, well, JFK.

Since I am not a shrink (although I play one in my job), I can't provide the definitive, clinically validated reasons why millions of girls, in 1964, were cast under the spell of Beatlemania. But I don't think Beatlemania was at all silly. In fact, in Beatlemania the seeds of female yearning and female revolt germinated with the speed of those exploding flowers in time-lapse photography. Given the timing of their arrival in America, a mere eleven weeks after Kennedy's assassination, the collective catharsis they evoked is hardly surprising. Lyndon Johnson—old, singularly unattractive, shifty-eyed, and with all the charisma of raw poultry—personified, for me, the deliberate thwarting of youthful exuberance. His installation as president seemed a direct repudiation of Kennedy's call for a "new generation," including a new generation of young women, to try to change the world. And then the Beatles arrived, making fun of the establishment and getting away with it, and reaffirming that the spirit and vitality of this new generation was indeed alive and well and would not be daunted, stunted, or denied. Through the Beatles, some of us began to believe again that things were going to be all right.

Because they sang so directly to and about young women, and did so without pandering to them, this reaffirmation was especially compelling for girls. Folded in with this was the Beatles' challenge to "the Marlboro Man" version of masculinity. So when we watched these joyful, androgynous young men, we saw not just a newly feminized, distinctly friendlier form of manhood. We also saw our *own* reflection. In these boys were glimpses not only of a new masculinity but also of the best part of 1960s adolescent femininity—an eagerness to reach out to others, a faith in love, a belief in progress, and a determination to leave behind hoary conventions about staying in one's place. Most girls had a favorite Beatle, the one they claimed as "theirs," the one they loved above the others. If you think about it, girls often chose the Beatle that they themselves most resembled, either physically or as a personality type, or the one they most wanted to be like. (OK, with this mouth, how could I have been anything but a John girl?) This imaginary bonding brought a brief but satisfying feeling of completion. For it wasn't just that by loving one or all of the Beatles you could indulge in a safe, pretend relationship with some idealized love object. Through this powerful identification with John, Paul, George, or Ringo, you could, on some semiconscious level, become a Beatle yourself, part male, part female, out in the world having fun. As one girl recalled, "I didn't want to grow up and be a wife and it seemed to me that the Beatles had the kind of freedom I wanted. . . . I wanted to be like them, something larger than life."[12]

With the arrival of the Beatles, girls congregated in public in packs, in swarms, waiting for tickets, waiting for concerts, waiting for the Beatles themselves, united in a determined, shared cause. Girls wantonly jettisoned social conventions about female decorum by screaming, jumping up and down, even fainting in public. They yelled "I love you" at the top of their lungs. They actively chased these boys out in the streets, for all to see. The established authority of the state was totally irrelevant to dedicated Beatles fans: they crawled under, climbed over, and simply burst through police barricades, demonstrating that arbitrary boundaries, and the laws of old men, meant nothing to them. Perplexed and horrified adults trying to make sense of this seeming anarchy knew on some level what they were witnessing: a very public unleashing of sublimated female sexual energy. But they were also seeing something more: what Barbara Ehrenreich and her coauthors have identified as "the first mass outburst of the sixties to feature women—in this case, girls."[13] This was terrifying—and it was a premonition.

Girls looking and acting more like boys, boys looking and acting more like girls, all of them trying to figure out what constituted individualism and what constituted conformity—this was the turbulence of the mid-1960s, and it was embodied in a variety of teen girl archetypes. Beatlemania was a manifestation of our sense, our fear even, that we knew nothing more about ourselves than that each of us was a mass of unchanneled longing and desire who didn't want to end up like Mom. But much of the pop culture of this period—layouts on unisex fashions, Gidget's and Patty's constant orchestration of events, the whopping success of the Beatles—showed that girls wanted some gender boundaries blurred. When taking all those quizzes and wondering whether we, like Holly Golightly, could ever be individuals who stand out from the herd, we began to think of individualism itself as a pose, a collection of jaunty, saucy, irreverent gestures that might hide the contradictory mess inside. The mass media reinforced the importance of both individualism and conformity, of being more like boys yet still very much a girl, and offered perkiness as a temporary compromise. But cracks were beginning to appear in the walls restraining female energy and sexuality. These compromises weren't calming us down; they were making us worse.

CHAPTER 6

Genies and Witches

While my friends and I were upstairs blasting Beatles records and planning how many times we would go see *A Hard Day's Night,* our mothers were downstairs in the kitchen or the laundry room fuming, and fantasizing about a jailbreak of their own. They soon discovered they weren't alone. Political rumblings about women's second-class status, and their desire for more opportunities and choices, now registered on America's media seismographs. Some of our mothers, it turned out, wanted to break down some barricades themselves. The prevailing line in the print media of the early 1960s was that American women, as the *Ladies' Home Journal* put it, "never had it so good": they controlled the family's purse strings and the nation's wealth, had an array of household technologies that made housework effortless, had plenty of free time to play bridge or do volunteer work, and enjoyed unprecedented equality. The *Journal* continued, "They have rights and opportunities today the likes of which the Western world has never seen. . . . Indeed, women today are in many respects much better off than men." In its special supplement of October 1962 entitled "The American Female," *Harper's* maintained that American women were "repelled by the slogans of old-fashioned feminism."[1]

But *Harper's* also thought it saw a trend in 1962 and named it "crypto-feminism." Women were reexamining their roles as "wives, mothers, and members of the human race" because motherhood was short-lived as a full-time job, more women wanted or needed to work outside the home, yet many women found that "the institutions that are supposed to serve women are not very helpful." Women, in fact, faced a "void." Articles kept appearing in the early and mid-1960s with titles like "Our Greatest Waste of Talent Is Women," "Women—Neglected Assets," and "Women—Emancipation Is Still to Come," articles at odds with the "women have it made" line. Clearly, a new turbulence was emerging.

Professional women, in particular, were fed up with their second-class salaries and their image as freaks of nature, and they lobbied the Kennedy administration to do something. In one of the more famous scenes from John Kennedy's press conferences, the indefatigable journalist May Craig stood up and asked the president what he was doing for women. Kennedy quipped that he was sure that, whatever it was, it wasn't enough, implying that women were *never* satisfied, and shared a big laugh with the predominantly male press corps. Nonetheless, in 1961, Kennedy established a Presidential Commission on the Status of Women, with Eleanor Roosevelt as its head, to ascertain how to eradicate the "prejudices and outmoded customs [that] act as barriers to the full realization of women's basic rights." The Kennedy administration also outlawed discrimination in the federal civil service and in 1963 pushed through Congress the Equal Pay Act, which prohibited paying men and women different salaries for the same jobs. The Kennedy Commission's report, *American Women,* published just six weeks before the president's death, recommended the establishment of child-care services, advocated equal opportunities for women in employment and education, urged women to seek public office, and argued that the government's mission should be to secure "equality of rights for women." The front-page story in *The New York Times* headlined the report with "U.S. Panel Urges Women to Sue for Equal Rights."[2]

The real tip-off that many of our mothers hated their assigned positions, weren't sure whether to hate themselves or the men around them, and were tired of straddling the untenable contradictions in their lives was the eagerness with which thousands of them ran out to buy Betty Friedan's *The Feminine Mystique,* which they put on the best-seller list from April through July 1963. In 1964, while teenagers were discovering the Beatles, older women made *The Feminine Mystique* the number one best-selling paperback in the country.[3] Trashing "biology as destiny," Freud, and penis envy, castigating the phony happy housewife heroine of the women's magazines, and enumerating the emptiness, resentments, and self-doubt of many housewives' lives, Friedan reminded women of the unfinished work of the women's movement and urged her sisters to stop being doormats and to fight for equality.

Portions of Friedan's book were condensed in women's magazines, and the book inspired other investigations into the status of women. In "Whatever Happened to Women's Rights?" published in the *Atlantic Monthly* in March 1964, Paul Foley stacked up a tower of statistics to emphasize women's second-class status. Only two U.S. senators and 11 of the 435 members of the House of Representatives were women. Only 3 of the 422 federal judges were female. Women were confined to low-paying, dead-end jobs, they married too young, and they were not encouraged to pursue advanced degrees. Foley's article was condensed and reprinted in *Reader's Digest.*[4] *U.S. News and World Report* in 1966 also itemized the various ways in which women were discriminated against and underrepresented in American business and political institutions, and it noted that sociologists "warn that the U.S. may be building up a new generation of 'unhappy women.' " The article also focused on a significant trend: women were "going to work in droves," often combining a job, marriage, and motherhood. But the article concluded that " 'full equality' for women appears far off."[5] Foley, however, claimed that "for public scrutiny on the American woman, 1963 was a banner year," and he was right: this was to be a turning point.

It was within this context of prefeminist agitation, combined with the unsettling phenomenon of wild packs of girls chasing the four mop-tops across America, that there appeared on TV, and with a vengeance, a new female mutant, a hybrid of old and new, of negative and positive stereotypes. We saw the ghoulish Morticia in *The Addams Family* as a femme fatale; a genie who was not a rotund, balding man but a shapely and beautiful young woman; a witch who was not a murderous old hag but an attractive young housewife; a cute, perky nun who could fly.

All of a sudden, female characters in TV sitcoms were capable of magic. They had fantastic supernatural powers. Yet this was more than just the ultimate in kitsch or the triumph of special effects. If we put these TV shows and the impulses behind them on the shrink's couch for a minute, we see that a significant proportion of the pop culture moguls were trying to acknowledge the impending release of female sexual and political energy, while keeping it all safely in a straitjacket. Sure, it would be great if women, especially young women, were more sexually liberated. But prefeminist rumblings about economic and political liberation were another matter. You could almost see these guys holding their nuts for dear life. Sensing they were playing with fire, they tried to contain it technologically, through images of levitation, twitching noses, and poofs of fake smoke.

In these shows, the potentially monstrous and grotesque was beautified and tamed; what we saw, in other words, was the containment of the threat posed by unleashed female sexuality, especially in the wake of Beatlemania and Helen Gurley Brown. Since viewers had been socialized to regard female sexuality as monstrous, TV producers addressed the anxieties about letting it loose by domesticating the monster, by making her pretty and sometimes slavish, by shrinking her and keeping her locked up in a bottle, and by playing the situation for laughs.[6]

In shows like *Bewitched, I Dream of Jeannie,* and *The Flying Nun,* a new version of Pandora's box was acted out. Seemingly normal-looking female characters possessed magical powers, which men begged them not to use; if women did use them, their powers had to be confined to the private sphere. Whenever women used these powers outside the home, in the public sphere, the male world was turned completely upside down. Business simply could not be conducted as usual, and logic and rationality were often overthrown and rendered useless. Men were made impotent by these powers, and the husbands (or husband figures) of such women were stripped of their male authority and made to look foolish and incompetent in front of their male superiors. After all, how can you explain men turned into dogs, or co-workers sent to Antarctica? Although the men insisted (usually unsuccessfully) that their women not use these powers, there were three exceptions that the shows' narrative systems permitted: to complete domestic chores, to compete over men, and to help the men out of embarrassing situations, which usually had been created by the woman's unauthorized use of her magic powers in the first place.

The two most successful examples of this genre were *Bewitched* and *I Dream of Jeannie*. *Bewitched* was extremely popular; it was the biggest hit series produced by ABC up to that time, running from 1964 to 1972. For its first five seasons it was among the top twenty highest rated shows; the year of its debut, it soared to number two, topped only by *Bonanza*.[7] It is easy to dismiss *Bewitched* as one of the dumbest and kitschiest shows ever produced, but it would be a mistake to do so. *Bewitched* was such a success in part because of its novelty and its skillful use of special effects, which played to some fairly basic fantasies about magic and control. But it was also successful because it was one of the few shows with an appealing female lead character who offered female viewers a respite from, as well as a critique of, male domination. In *Bewitched* we have a woman's dream and a man's nightmare. Darrin was surrounded by an endearing yet constantly troublesome matriarchy, a domestic situation in which his wife, mother-in-law, daughter, and other relatives were all witches, endowed with magical powers, which constantly threatened his professional status and his authority as head of the household.

A show like *Bewitched* was an updated, blander, yet trickier version of *I Love Lucy*. Lucy didn't have magical powers, and she certainly didn't need them to get into trouble. Always struggling to break out of the confines of the domestic sphere and enter Ricky's glamorous world in the public limelight, Lucy was set up by the physical slapstick of the show as a clown, as a woman constantly using her face and body to fight the strictures of femininity. Samantha, however, was not a clown: she always remained a lady. This was one of the show's many concessions to traditional femininity and conventional gender roles. Elizabeth Montgomery didn't have to use her face or body the way Lucy did: she had technically mastered special effects to be disruptive for her. Aside from twitching her nose, nodding her head, or raising her hands, she did not become physically grotesque when disrupting Darrin's world. Young, slim, blond, and beautiful, with practical, intelligent ideas about what needed to be done in her community, yet a witch, Samantha stood at the intersection between middle-class definitions of the ideal young wife and rebelliousness against those definitions.

Samantha embodied important contradictions, for she was a happy, respectable suburban housewife who exerted power beyond the kitchen or the living room. She was at once traditional and modern. The show often suggested that women, especially younger women, were smarter, more creative, and more versatile than men. Samantha had magical powers, but she also excelled at the more mundane female duties of ensuring that social interactions ran smoothly. Often it was up to her to come up with an explanation to Darrin's boss or other outsiders for the bizarre goings-on. Invariably, her explanation placated the irate or confused father figure, and often she succeeded in using the explanation to make Darrin or some other hapless man look good in the eyes of the older male authority figure. Samantha engineered the outcome so that Darrin got the credit for coming up with a great idea or doing a great job, but the audience knew who was the real power behind the throne. And it was key to the show that Darrin have all the sex appeal of egg albumen. Had he really been handsome, sexy, or magnetic, her magic and power would have been too threatening, both to the man and to the viewer.

The question of whether Samantha could use her powers, and under what circumstances, defined the entire series. In the first show, on their wedding night, just before they are supposed to go to bed,

Samantha reveals to Darrin that she is a witch. Dressed in her peignoir, Samantha shows a skeptical Darrin just what she can do by making a broken cigarette lighter he's trying to use suddenly ejaculate a flame and by moving an ashtray around the coffee table so he can't successfully flick his ash. (And you thought all that subliminal stuff only went on in liquor ads.) When he nearly faints realizing she really is a witch, Samantha kisses him seductively and he says they'll discuss the problem tomorrow. We know what happens next. The mere suggestion that these two are going to have sex was revolutionary for television at that time. The next day, Darrin makes Samantha promise never to use her powers again. Samantha assures him, "Darling, I'll be the best wife a man ever had." He gets specific. "You're going to have to learn how to be a suburban housewife. . . . And you'll have to learn to cook and clean and keep house and go to my mother's house every Friday night." Samantha says it sounds wonderful. We don't believe her for a minute. There wasn't a woman in the audience who would have given up that kind of power.

We know she won't be able to keep her promise, and her restraint is tested right away. A former girlfriend of Darrin's, dark-haired, rich, seductive, and patronizingly sophisticated—in other words, a bitch—invites Darrin and Samantha over for dinner. During the course of the evening, she openly flirts with Darrin while making insufferably catty remarks to Samantha about her hair and clothes; she's clearly the real demon here. Under an assault like this, when another woman is challenging her for her man, Samantha can't possibly keep her promise to Darrin. Using her magical powers, she makes the rival's hair fall into her eyes, places a large hunk of spinach on one of her front teeth, has her dinner slide into her lap, her dress nearly fall off, and her wig blow off her head. The rival is humiliated and Samantha's use of witchcraft completely justified. At the end of the show, in what became a classic scene in *Bewitched,* Darrin is urging Samantha to come up to bed, and we know exactly what he's got on his mind. But the kitchen is a mess. Samantha says she'll be right up, then raises her arms and zaps the kitchen clean. She says with a self-satisfied smile, "Maybe I'll taper off," a joke rife with ambiguity. Taper off, my ass.

It is also important to note that Samantha's mother—indeed, all her relatives—is strongly opposed to Samantha not using her powers just because of Darrin. Endora constantly casts him as a mere mortal to whom Samantha is superior, and as someone who is constraining Samantha, trying to make her life too confined, boring, and predictable. For Endora, Samantha has another, more exciting destiny, a destiny that spans history and geography. And while Samantha insists that marriage to Darrin is what she wants, she gets to have it both ways, to have the reassurances of being a suburban wife and the adventures of being a more unconventional woman.

What is especially interesting about the show, premiering as it did in 1964, not long after Betty Friedan's *The Feminine Mystique* was a best-seller, is the way it offered, yet sought to diminish, a criticism of female confinement in the home. It is hard to imagine a woman watching who did not identify with the fantasy of cleaning the kitchen or preparing dinner just by twitching her nose. But there were other telling fantasies, repeated week in and week out, about having some real influence in the outside world, and how the world might be better if men just listened to women once in a while. In an episode from the first season, Samantha and Endora eat at Mario's Pizza and decide the food is so good that Mario deserves some publicity. Samantha, by twitching her nose, stops the presses at the local paper and inserts a full-page ad that reads "Eat at Mario's." When the ad comes out, Mario's competitor, the head of Perfect Pizza, is outraged and drops Darrin's ad agency for letting Mario's get the upper hand. When Samantha learns that her husband's account is in jeopardy, she works to repair the damage. She and Endora, using their magic, fill the town's billboards with ads, cover the sky with skywriting, and place "Eat Perfect Pizza" placards on all the pedestrians in town. The delight they take in orchestrating this ad campaign is clear as each tackles a new medium, giggling and saying, "It's your turn," and "Now yours." At the end of the show, with the account saved,

Darrin complains, "I'd appreciate your letting me handle my accounts by myself," to which Endora responds sarcastically, "Do you think you can?" Samantha insists with a smile, "Of course he can— except under special circumstances."

In other episodes, Samantha uses her magic to get the mayor to fix the town's traffic lights, to persuade a French fashion designer to design clothes that look good on "the average American woman" and not just on fashion models, and to expose political corruption and help get a reform candidate elected to the city council. In this last episode, Darrin wrongly accuses a corrupt councilman of fraudulent dealings in a city construction contract. Samantha and Endora transport themselves to the councilman's office and use their witchcraft to open his locked file cabinet and study his records. It takes Samantha just a few seconds to confirm that all his dealings, with the sole exception of the one that pea-brained Darrin had tried to expose, had been crooked, another Darrin blunder that causes Endora great mirth. Yet Endora casts various spells to vindicate Darrin and indict the councilman. At the end of the show, we see Darrin, completely befuddled, mumbling to himself as he walks upstairs, while Samantha and Endora stand shoulder to shoulder, leaning slightly into each other with their arms crossed over their chests, smiling knowingly and patronizingly at poor, dumbo Darrin.

The repeated combination of magic, diplomacy (her forte), and good common sense made Samantha's solutions to problems the ones that were clearly the most viable and sensible. Here was a housewife with logical and creative ideas about how to make the world better, and with an ability to act on those ideas and get them a fair hearing, even if she had to do so through her bumbling surrogate, Darrin. (The character was such a zero that Dick York, Darrin number one, was easily replaced in 1969 by another Dick, last name Sargent, as Darrin number two.) Samantha's interventions in advertising, politics, and marketing were a mixed blessing, but often they expedited the solution to a particular problem. And despite his anger and frustration over the personal humiliations, Darrin always loved and admired Samantha. This was one of the first post-1950s sitcoms to show a husband and wife sharing a double bed, and we often saw Darrin looking at Sam with desire.

Samantha stood in contrast to the older women in the show, who were grotesque by comparison and conformed more closely to the age-old archetype of the witch as a wrinkled and disorderly crone.[8] Grotesque women—the battle-axes, villainesses, shrews, and over-the-hill whores of popular culture—with their aging faces and sagging, protruding bodies, were ostracized, pitied, and often destroyed in movies and TV shows because they had moved outside the norms of femininity. But such women also rebelled against and often disrupted the rigid gender codes of society, and the female grotesque par excellence of *Bewitched*—Endora—was no exception. With her overly bouffant, bright red hairdos, two-inch-long false eyelashes, and thick eyeliner that shot up at a forty-five-degree angle to her eyes, Endora made gestures to femininity that were exaggerated, like a Mardi Gras mask. But it was this defiance that gave her power, and made her such a liberatory character. Darrin hated her interventions, and often Samantha did too. She was blunt, honest, catty, and self-indulgent, and she did not waste her time trying to soothe others' feelings or placate men the way Samantha did. She was a caricature of the meddling, hard-edged mother-in-law girls were supposed to cast themselves against. But as played by Agnes Moorehead, Endora also had an arch sophistication and a biting tongue that enabled her to get away with—and enjoy—her assaults on arbitrary male authority, especially when it was imposed on her daughter. Female viewers agreed with her dismissive assessment of Darrin as an impotent doofus and took great delight in her outrageous transgressions, and in her unmovable loyalty to Samantha. Endora got to say what many women wished they could say, and her complete indifference to the approval of men was a joy and relief to watch, even as we knew we did not want to be like her.

The other grotesque female, the baggy-faced, chinless, relentlessly nosy neighbor Mrs. Kravitz, was given none of Endora's protective coloration. There was no masquerade of femininity here. Mrs. Kravitz was a warning, the darker side of female aging. She kept spying on the Stevens house, looking where she wasn't supposed to. Thus, even though she saw "the truth," her reports made her appear crazy. Ugly, unadorned, shrill, she never succeeded in getting anyone else to see what she saw. She was the parody of the old housewife with too much time on her hands and nothing to do except live through others. Old women who become voyeurs, who neglect their appearance and their husbands, are pathetic. This, girls, is who you could become if you pay too much attention to the outside world and not enough to your face, body, and home. Mrs. Kravitz embodied the costs of not adhering to traditional femininity: her husband held her in contempt, and everyone else laughed at and pitied her. Unlike Samantha, who knew how to juggle her domestic duties and her forays into the outside world, Mrs. Kravitz had lost her balance. She spent too much time looking out her window and not enough looking in her mirror, too much surveillance in the wrong direction.

The character we identified with, Samantha—most frequently referred to by her masculine nickname, Sam—was passive and active, flouted her husband's authority yet complied with the role of suburban housewife, was both conforming and rebellious: she gave expression to traditional norms and prefeminist aspirations. The show hailed young female viewers by providing, and seeking to reconcile, images of female equality—and, often, even images of female superiority—with images of female subordination. Samantha's talent and success as a wife lay in knowing when to intervene and when to hold back. She often made mistakes, but because she had the traditional female traits of empathy, tact, flattery, and the ability to craft a compromise, all coupled with her magic, she was able repeatedly to rescue her husband, herself, and her marriage.

The show acknowledged that young women wanted more than confinement in the home, that housework was drudgery, and that husbands were often inept clods. Samantha skillfully managed the contradictions of being a superior being (a witch with power) and a subordinate being (a wife with a husband). She made these contradictions work for her, and she also smoothed them over, demonstrating the juggling act young girls were meant to do when they got married. While the show reaffirmed the primacy of traditional female roles and behaviors, it also provided powerful visual representations of what many young women would like to do if they just had a little power: zap that housework and a few men as well.

I Dream of Jeannie ran from 1965 to 1970 and also featured a woman with magical powers, but this show was predicated on a more flagrant sexual display of Jeannie's body and her desires, even if the network censors made sure Barbara Eden's belly button was discreetly hidden. The premise rested on a male fantasy of a regular guy discovering a beautiful, naive, unworldly woman who will do anything for him and calls him "master," or, more formally, by his military title. (That the "regular guy" was an astronaut played into another male fantasy for good measure.) But the implied power and availability of Jeannie's sexuality were always a threat to her master, Captain (later, Major) Tony Nelson, and sometimes he was most relieved and happiest when she was "in her bottle." Jeannie was always more amorous and sexualized than her master, and this, of course, is what got them into so much trouble. Captain Nelson tried in vain to contain Jeannie both physically and sexually, and in those episodes where Jeannie's bottle was lost, there was considerable tension until it was found and Jeannie could get back inside it again.

I Dream of Jeannie differed from *Bewitched* in crucial ways that already suggested a backlash against the earlier show's discourse of empowerment. Jeannie did not intervene in community affairs the way Samantha did; in fact, she cared little for the public sphere. She was not the ideal 1960s wife who happened to have magical powers. In her pink chiffon harem pants, red bra, pom-pom-trimmed bolero jacket, and chiffon-draped headpiece, Jeannie was from another place and time, an anachronism in 1960s suburban America. She was the dumb, shapely, ditzy blonde with too much power, which she often used impetuously. Hyperfeminized, Jeannie was unreasonably jealous and possessive, giggled a lot, and was overly enthusiastic about whatever her master did: in fact, she often behaved and was treated like a child. Although she got her master into embarrassing situations, unlike Samantha she left him to explain his own way out. She was not seen as shrewder or more creative than Captain Nelson; after all, he was an astronaut, embedded in a world of science, technology, and the military-industrial complex women allegedly *couldn't* master. Jeannie's main goal was to serve Captain Nelson obsequiously, get him to pay more attention to her, and, she hoped, get him to marry her. Although Captain Nelson kept insisting he was the master of the house, Jeannie's magic constantly undermined that assertion. Yet the balance of power always tilted toward him, because Jeannie was more devoted to him and more emotionally dependent on him than he was on her.

The fact that Jeannie didn't know how to behave like a "normal" woman was the basis for a number of the plots in the show. In one telling episode, we see how this show, despite its reliance on many of the same visual gags and tricks as *Bewitched,* differed ideologically from its predecessor. In a 1965 episode, "The Americanization of Jeannie," Jeannie comes to feel that Captain Nelson devotes too much time and attention to his work and not enough to her. She reads a women's magazine and finds an article titled "The Emancipation of Modern Women." She asks, "What does emancipation mean?" and he answers, "You don't have to worry about anything like that." "Oh, yes I do," she insists. "I want to understand your way of life so I can please you." She continues reading the article. "Are you a loser in the battle between the sexes? Is the man in your life aloof, indifferent, difficult to please? Does he fail to appreciate what you have to offer as a female? Answer: Challenge his masculine arrogance. Be independent, self-reliant, unpredictable. You must learn to cope with him on his own grounds. In short, you must become a modern, American woman."

The next day, Nelson comes home to find the house a mess and no dinner on the table. Jeannie walks into the living room in a bathrobe and curlers and says, "Hiya, old boy," instead of her usual, more fawning greeting. Nelson accuses her of not doing any housework, but Jeannie responds by citing part of her magazine article, "How Not to Be a Drudge." " 'Share the work with him,' " reads Jeannie as she reaches for a box of chocolates. "I'm an astronaut, not a housekeeper," explodes Nelson. "You must broaden your horizons," retorts Jeannie as she hands him a broom.

Needless to say, Nelson tells Jeannie that a real woman doesn't behave this way, and his reactions, as well as the narrative, repudiate the role reversal she proposes. At the end of the episode, their original relationship is restored, and Nelson advises her, "You need an outlet for your affection. You need a pet." Advice from a magazine about female emancipation turns out to be very bad advice because it undermines the woman's femininity, makes her appear ridiculous, and alienates the man's affections. The advice, of course, is a parody of feminism, for it urges women to be deliberately unattractive and completely self-indulgent, and to make men do the housework while the women do nothing at all.

Bewitched never took such a head-on approach to role reversal, thus it didn't draw such stark boundaries between male and female spheres. *Bewitched* blurred gender roles; *I Dream of Jeannie* accentuated them. Yet both shows anticipated feminism and hailed the prefeminist viewer. Samantha was clearly a role model, while Jeannie was an extreme version of femininity that girls ought not to model themselves after. When women like that got power, look out. Thus, *I Dream of Jeannie* was more of a warning. In *Bewitched,* Darrin's work in an advertising agency was repeatedly compromised by the inappropriate exercise of female power. In *I Dream of Jeannie,* the ante was upped: now, magic inspired by female desire, jealousy, and possessiveness threatened to disrupt one of the crowning achievements of 1960s male technocracy, the U.S. space program. Even NASA was no match for female power and sexuality run amok. In *Bewitched,* female power could be accommodated; in *Jeannie,* it could not. Because of these differences, the central mixed message remains: female power, when let loose in the public sphere, is often disruptive to male authority, but sometimes it also bolsters that authority. These colliding messages made *Bewitched* and *I Dream of Jeannie* simultaneously cautionary and liberatory. The schizophrenic female persona such shows helped constitute saw female obsequiousness amply rewarded. But she also had empowering images of physically zapping things—and men—into their proper place.

In 1964 and 1965, images of female possession were everywhere. In two sitcoms, *The Munsters* and *The Addams Family,* the mothers were black-clad female vampires with often macabre idiosyncrasies. The antithesis of Donna Reed, these moms did not bake chocolate chip cookies or take the PTA seriously. They were more likely making frog-eyeball stew or teaching the kids how to tie hangman's knots and build toy guillotines. Again, it was only through such quasi-monsters—totally unrealistic yet unthreatening women from the realms of the supernatural—that females' rebellion against their traditional roles got expressed on TV. And as with *Bewitched* and *I Dream of Jeannie,* the sexual tension between regular guys and newly empowered women was a prominent subtext. A running joke on *The Addams Family* had Gomez unable to restrain himself from planting passionate kisses all along Morticia's irresistible arm. Here we saw the clearest connection between female sexuality and ghoulishness: her monstrous power turned him into a helpless, slavering fool.

Then, in the 1967–68 season, we had a fusion of *Bewitched* and *Gidget,* in the form of the poor, benighted Sally Field as Sister Bertrille. In *The Flying Nun,* perkiness took to the air. It took Sally Field ten years and the ability to portray dozens of personalities in *Sybil* to live down this role. Now we had a female character who could fly, but lest anyone do a Freudian reading, she was, by vocational choice, chaste and asexual. Her flying wasn't always in her control, but when you walk around with headgear shaped like a paper airplane on steroids, the updrafts sometimes just take you away. She often ended up in places where females, especially those from nunneries, weren't supposed to be; she was once nearly shot down as an enemy plane and, on another occasion, pursued by a lovestruck pelican.[9] Here we see the progression from Samantha to Sister Bertrille, from the woman having control of her magical powers and using them, at times, in ways that embarrassed men to the woman's magical powers having control of and embarrassing her. This was, of course, wishful thinking on the part of TV producers, for out in the viewing audience young women were feeling more, not less, empowered.

It is no surprise that, at the moment girls took to the streets in an outpouring of female resistance against the status quo, and in pursuit of new, supposedly false gods, while their mothers flocked to buy a book demanding equal rights for women, the witch and other women with supernatural powers would reappear on the cultural landscape of America. Television shows tried to suggest that if girls and women were feeling a bit restless, a tad mischievous, a mite defiant, these unruly impulses could be managed. But in an effort to co-opt this rebellion, and to translate it into Nielsen ratings, this media strategy backfired. For as we watched Darrin Stevens turned into a Yorkshire terrier, or Major Tony Nelson transported to seventh-century Persia, we saw that male authority wasn't so impregnable or impressive at all.

In real life, teenage girls blithely ignored or pushed through police barricades, with few negative consequences. What many of us experienced and saw, although we barely knew it at the time, was the beginning of a war. It was a battle between sexual rebellion and sexual containment, between the old masculinity and the new androgyny, a fight over how much more masquerading had to go on between men and women. After trying on the personas of the rebel, the sexual sophisticate, the knowing girl who was bonded to other girls in a group, the pursuer, and the witch, some girls decided they didn't want to imagine, fantasize, or pretend anymore. Girls were stepping over old boundaries, and there was no going back. We were on the verge of revolt.

CHAPTER 7

Throwing Out Our Bras

On September 7, 1968, Robin Morgan, who had played Dagmar on the TV show *Mama,* organized several busloads of women to attend the annual Miss America pageant in Atlantic City. What these women did there was, by the standards of the day, completely shocking. They were not there to attend the pageant and choose who was prettier or had a better butt; they were there to put down the pageant, and put it down they did. They swung brassieres in the air like lassos. They crowned a live sheep "Miss America" to dramatize that the contestants, and all women, are "oppressed and judged like animals at a county fair."[1] They carried signs that read, "Welcome to the Miss America Cattle Auction" and "Miss America Sells It," and held up a poster of a naked woman with her body parts labeled "rump" and "loin," as if she were nothing more than a side of beef. They chanted, "Atlantic City is a town with class. They raise your morals and they judge your ass." And they set up a "Freedom Trash Can," into which they tossed stenographer's pads, hair rollers, high heels, copies of *Playboy,* and, the most titillating symbol of female containment, all those brassieres. These women weren't perky, they were pissed; yet, at the same time, they seemed to take a cheerful delight in trashing one of the country's most sacred and closely followed rituals, the only TV show, claimed Richard Nixon, that he let Tricia and Julie stay up late to watch. No one had ever seen anything quite like it. This was a completely outrageous event and marked a watershed in American history, a watershed virtually ignored in retrospectives on the 1960s in general and 1968 in particular.

The Miss America demonstration defined my earliest days in college. One of the first photographs taken of me and my roommate freshman year featured us braless, wearing men's undershirts instead, holding a sign that read, simply, "Ban the Bra." We also saw fit to paint the following epigram in huge letters on our window facing out to the street: "The more I see of men, the more I like dogs." As I recall, the letters were in fluorescent paint, which was set off nicely by the black light we lit each night. This created such a stir it was photographed and featured in the local paper amid much head shaking. The seniors down the hall in their Villager dresses, fraternity pins jutting out from their chests like the Croix de Guerre, thought we were barbarians who were wrecking the college; we informed them that they were, in the parlance of the times, douche bags.

I wasn't a feminist yet, not by a long shot; I was not in the mood, politically or hormonally, to see American society as a patriarchy. At first, many of us regarded the Miss America demonstration as nothing more than the latest in guerrilla theater, not the opening salvo in a revolutionary social movement that would change our lives forever. But as a result of the Sexual Revolution, which by 1968 was quite real, and all the other cultural trends that had shaped me throughout the 1960s, my chutzpah level was at record heights and in 1968 would soar to new levels, precisely because of what I saw on television, heard on my stereo and the radio, and read in newsmagazines. For me, Robin Morgan and her compatriots linked the cultural with the political, compelling me to take another fateful step away from the girl I used to be. They emboldened me and got me thinking, revealing the chasm not just between me and those older girls in their Peter Pan collars but also between me and men. They suggested that the sense of cultural and social collectivity many young women felt when they sang along together with the Shirelles or the Beatles was about to be extended into a political movement that would change

America. They put us on notice that the politically innocent word *girl* was about to give way to the politically conscious word *woman*.

That same year, Valerie Solanas circulated the SCUM Manifesto, which she sold at first on the streets of Greenwich Village.[2] The acronym SCUM stood for Society for Cutting Up Men, and I still can't read the manifesto without laughing out loud at its over-the-top, in-your-face bravura. As you would imagine, the SCUM Manifesto was a far cry from "I Will Follow Him." "Life in this society being, at best, an utter bore and no aspect of society being at all relevant to women," began Solanas, "there remains to civic-minded, responsible, thrill-seeking females only to overthrow the government, eliminate the money system, institute complete automation, and destroy the male sex." Asserting that "the male is a biological accident" because the Y chromosome is really an incomplete X chromosome, Solanas continued that the male "has made of the world a shitpile" and therefore should be killed—unless he joins the Male Auxiliary of SCUM. In her final coda, Solanas really let it rip: "The sick, irrational men, those who attempt to defend themselves against their disgustingness, when they see SCUM barreling down on them, will cling in terror to Big Mama with her Big Bouncy Boobies, but Boobies won't protect them against SCUM; Big Mama will be clinging to Big Daddy, who will be in the corner shitting in his forceful, dynamic pants."[3] In June of '68, Solanas acted on her words and shot—and nearly killed—Andy Warhol. In a few short years, we had gone from Gidget to this, in part because of what we saw and heard in the mass media.

There was, in fact, a level of rebellion in the 1960s that the media could neither manage nor contain, despite *Bewitched* and *I Dream of Jeannie*. Two media in particular—television news and rock and folk music, and the interaction between them—stoked the flames of this rebellion. While the most prominent female icons early in the decade were Jackie Kennedy, hysterical Beatles fans, perky TV teens, and go-go dancers in cages, behind the scenes, out of the spotlight, there were real girls getting real political. And what led them to this awakening was that they now had the opportunity to go to college. Magazines like *Glamour* added regular columns and articles about getting into and attending college, and while their back-to-school issue each August featured the ten "best dressed" college girls (as opposed to the smartest, most accomplished, or most likely to succeed), the magazines nonetheless imparted a taken-for-granted quality to college attendance for girls. In 1965, the number of degrees awarded to women was double what it had been in 1955; by 1969 the number had tripled, and it kept zooming up.[4] At the vanguard of this social change were our older sisters, women born in the early 1940s, many of whom thought of themselves as baby boomers even though the boom didn't "officially" start until 1946.

Many of these girls, in addition to discovering sex, drugs, and rock 'n' roll, also discovered they had real problems with the status quo, so they discovered politics. Some joined the Peace Corps. Others were more radical and joined Students for a Democratic Society (SDS), which in the early 1960s was committed to community organizing and working for a more egalitarian society grounded in participatory democracy. Still others joined the Student Non-Violent Coordinating Committee (SNCC) and spent their summers in the South working in the civil rights movement. There was, on many campuses, a new ethos of achievement for girls, an understanding that they would use their education for more than deciphering the rules of "Careers" and reading *The Joy of Cooking*. And it was these girls, who were in college in the early and mid-1960s, who became the early leaders of the women's liberation movement. Before the Miss America demonstration, few outside the New Left knew of such women. As a result, they seemed to come from nowhere—or, as the press seemed to suggest, from outer space or under a rock.

There are many possible explanations for young, middle-class women to have been challenging the status quo in these years. Maybe it was because, at the same time that we listened to the Shirelles and the Beatles, or watched Samantha turn Darrin's boss into a poodle, we also read books like *The Catcher in the Rye, On the Road, Silent Spring, Growing Up Absurd,* and *Black Like Me.* Maybe it was hearing Bob Dylan, Joan Baez, and Peter, Paul, and Mary sing social protest songs. Certainly it was seeing the nightly news start showing us a very different picture of the world than the one we saw on *The Patty Duke Show.* In fact, after we'd watched the perfect, secure, harmonious families on *The Donna Reed Show* or *My Three Sons,* we watched our parents fight with each other, yell at us and hit us, and plot their divorces. We also saw, on the same TV that brought us fictional, conflict-free towns like Mayfield and Springfield, all-too-real places like Selma and Birmingham, where real Americans couldn't vote or send their kids to college, where real parents lost their children to bombs planted in churches, and where real teenagers were clubbed mercilessly by police for sitting at a Woolworth's counter.

We were starting to gag, in fact, on the widening disjunctures between our lives, what we saw on the news, and the increasingly infantile and surreal offerings of network television: *Mr. Ed, My Favorite Martian, Gilligan's Island, F Troop,* and, worst of all, *Hogan's Heroes,* which transformed the grotesque horrors of a Nazi POW camp into a half hour sitcom with a laugh track. This gap between our experiences of current events and a realm populated by Munsters, talking cars, flying nuns, and the overly fertile and supposedly musical King family defined our adolescence. For girls in particular, old assumptions were silted over by a whole host of new questions, new rebellions, new ways of looking at the world and our place in it. The change in outlook was gradual, a progression that took longer for some than for others and was less overtly political for some than for others. The first step was girls thinking they had a duty to champion the rights of others. The next step was realizing they had a duty to champion rights for themselves.

As the 1960s progressed, television became increasingly divided against itself, a schizophrenic medium that during certain portions of the broadcast day pretended there were no such things as social problems but at others shoved these problems right in our faces through news reports and exposés like *Harvest of Shame*. We knew that we were choking on artifice and lies, and we wanted the cloying taste out of our mouths. In time, our desires would crystallize as the great quest for the authentic, the genuine, the spontaneous, and the true, fueled by raging teenage hormones itching to rebel against grown-up society.

Nothing drove home the gap between TV land and reality more than the civil rights movement, which by 1963 dominated the national news. The movement provided network news executives with what they wanted most: powerful, dramatic, and spontaneous images. From the early days of television, news shows like John Cameron Swayze's *Camel News Caravan* on NBC were only fifteen minutes long and consisted primarily of stories read by the anchorman or newsreel footage of staged events like ribbon cuttings, press conferences, dam dedications, and beauty contests. The sponsor, Camel cigarettes, made sure that Swayze puffed away while presenting the news and forbade NBC from showing anyone, no matter how newsworthy, smoking a cigar, making only one exception, for Winston Churchill. Any news footage containing a "no smoking" sign could not be aired.[5]

The civil rights movement blew apart this artifice and in the process transformed the political outlook and political participation of hundreds of thousands of young people. And the civil rights movement and then the antiwar movement, the first major social movements to be brought to people by television, transformed television news and baby boomers' relationship to the news and TV in general. Many complacent Americans were shocked by the murder of Medgar Evers in June 1963, and the slayings of Andrew Goodman, Michael Schwerner, and James Chaney a year later. When viewers turned on the nightly news in May 1963 and saw the snout-nosed, porcine Birmingham police attack slender, helpless schoolchildren with fire hoses and German shepherds, many were ashamed, horrified, and disgusted. To those of us who loved the Shirelles, the Marvelettes, and Sam Cooke, and who were just becoming familiar with

Martin Luther King's eloquence, all of this seemed outrageous, and George Wallace's 1963 inaugural chant, "Segregation now! Segregation tomorrow! Segregation forever!" which we also saw on the news, confirmed that there were some authority figures who needed serious defying.

It is hard to believe that with all this going on, the nightly news was only fifteen minutes long. But it was precisely such dramatic, visually arresting stories that prompted CBS, in September 1963, to extend its nightly newscast, anchored by Walter Cronkite, to a half hour. A week later, NBC did the same, with *The Huntley-Brinkley Report*. Both networks increased the number of their news bureaus so they could have film footage of events instead of relying primarily on still photos or the anchor's storytelling abilities. Adolescents whose newspaper reading consisted only of "Mary Worth" and Ann Landers now could see current events in their homes every day without having to read at all.

One of the things they saw were more women and more young people engaged in dangerous and disruptive oppositional politics. Young black women were as much a presence as black men, in the vanguard of the struggle for integration, and the dignity and resolve they conveyed on the nightly news as they tried to enroll in college or participated in sit-ins showed how powerful young women could be. Behind the media spotlight, young women, black and white, learned invaluable lessons about political organizing. In front of the camera, women from Rosa Parks to Coretta Scott King made political protest by women seem not just natural but necessary. The Vietnam War also brought increasing numbers of women to the streets, to participate in highly publicized moratoriums and demonstrations. The notion that politics and social protest were things women should ignore and avoid was, quite simply, eroding.

That young women could be political, even radical—and be admired for it—was becoming accepted on the fringes of American popular culture and powerfully reinforced through the huge folk music revival of the 1960s. The revival was started by the older brothers and sisters of kids like me, but through radio, record albums, and TV, it quickly trickled down to us. These older kids had outgrown the fare of AM radio—"Johnny Angel," "Papa-Oom-Mow-Mow," and "Ahab the Arab"—but were hardly about to switch over to what passed for adult fare, Dean Martin, Steve and Eydie, and the sound-track to *The Sound of Music*. What these kids wanted in their music, as elsewhere, was authenticity, relevance, and, last but hardly least, iconoclasm. And they got it in songs about persecuted labor organiz-ers, the ordeal of African Americans, and the utter folly of war.

Listening to and playing folk music was one way that kids who didn't ride down south on freedom buses or go to sit-ins could par-ticipate, if only vicariously, in the civil rights movement. Folk music legitimized the sense of urgency many young people felt about extending social justice throughout America. There was a critically important resonance between this music and what we saw in the news from Selma and Birmingham. And this music also reinforced, quite powerfully, the notion that not just young men, but young women too, needed to speak out and to take to the streets if they had to.

Certainly the pioneer here was Joan Baez. Her debut at the New-port Folk Festival in 1959 signaled a new kind of female performer, one who eschewed makeup, satin dresses, and sexual come-ons, and instead played her own guitar, dressed simply, sang social protest songs, and talked oppositional politics between numbers. By the summer of 1962, Baez had sold more records than any female folk singer in history, and two of her albums had gone gold, without the usual promotional hype on AM radio.[6] Baez became so big that she made it onto the cover of *Time* in November 1962. In a little hatchet-job piece called "Sibyl with Guitar," *Time* described Baez as an "otherworldly beatnik" with a "remote manner, long hair, bare feet and burlap wardrobe" who was often contemptuous of her audience and had only one friend, an "aimless . . . sulky, moody, pouting fel-low whose hair hangs down in golden ringlets."[7]

What *Time* couldn't get over the most was the fact that Baez, who was young and beautiful, absolutely refused to buy into existing gender norms about proper female behavior and appearance, and was hugely successful anyway. The magazine kept marveling that she and her contemporaries, like Judy Collins, didn't wear makeup—not even lipstick—and that their hair hadn't seen a curler in years. The burlap clothes really made them nuts. Baez seemed to defy feminine conventions at every turn—her house was "squalid," and while *Time* insisted on pointing out that she was "palpably nubile," they were surprised to note that there was "little sex" in her singing. Worst of all, she was "earnestly political," taking part in "peace marches and ban-the-bomb campaigns" and also championing civil rights for black people. But the magazine had to acknowledge, even while being stupefied by it, that Baez "speaks to her generation" and was enormously popular with young people, especially college students.

The folk music revival became so popular that ABC tried to cash in on it in 1963 and 1964 with the TV show *Hootenanny,* which featured live performances taped at college campuses around the country. And here we saw another female folk singer, more of a crossover artist than Baez, more of a compromise. Her hair was like a sheet of platinum, straight, blunt cut, unteased. She dressed simply, the way I imagined the really cool girls in Greenwich Village did, in solid color sweaters and skirts: no spike heels, no sequins, no crinolines, no aquamarine eyeshadow. We began to hear her voice, perfectly blended with her partners', singing about war, peace, and social justice. Her name was Mary Travers, and the group she was part of, Peter, Paul, and Mary, helped popularize the folk music revival of the 1960s well beyond the ivied walls of colleges and universities. They became the most popular pop acoustic group of the 1960s. The "new" form of music they sang, the protest song, was, of course, not new at all, but after "Duke of Earl" or Paul Petersen's "She Can't Find Her Keys," it seemed revolutionary. The music that had been suppressed all too hysterically by blacklisting in the 1950s was now a commercial gusher. Within a year of their debut, Peter, Paul, and Mary had had three major hits, all of them politically oppositional: "Lemon Tree," "If I Had a Hammer" (which hit number two on the singles charts), and "Blowin' in the Wind." Their debut album—one of the top ten sellers in 1962—went platinum, having sold over a million copies. Also in the top ten was the Kingston Trio's *College Concert,* which featured their antiwar hit "Where Have All the Flowers Gone."

Mary, with her striking good looks and strong, arresting voice, had more to say to us girls than some allegorical stuff about magic dragons. She told us that we had a right—even a duty—to express and act on our sense of political outrage. Most important for the times, she sang harmoniously with men, and did not threaten existing conventions about the importance of female gentleness when engaging in political commentary. Nonetheless, she sang with obvious commitment, force, and carefully modulated indignation. She was a highly energetic and passionate performer, who broke the rules for girl singers by stomping her foot and whipping her platinum hair from side to side as she sang.[8] Mary, more than the more outspoken and defiant Baez, embodied the contradictory position of the young woman committed to fight for social justice. She could be a pacifist, an advocate for desegregation, an opponent of government militarism and mindless materialism; these aspects of American society she could publicly reject, as long as she looked the part.

What she could not reject completely, if she wanted acceptance for herself and her message, were equally well-established norms about female behavior and appearance. But she could undermine them, making them seem frivolous and unnecessary, and that's exactly what young female folk singers with their plain clothes, strong voices, and indifference to lipstick did. They made it clear that you could ignore the fashion industry, regard cosmetics as ridiculous, and still be cool. They showed that being female and being political were not mutually exclusive; in fact, they were complementary. And they made this critically important, if subtle, link: that challenging norms about femininity itself was, in fact, political.

Mary Travers stood out in the early 1960s; she was one of the few women in a field dominated by men. After all, unlike girl group music, the folk revival movement wore its seriousness and self-importance like a black armband. You didn't dance to this music; you read Bertrand Russell to it, or discussed the existence of God, or tried to implement the principles of the Port Huron statement—in other words, did men's work. Joan Baez (who often toured with Bob Dylan), Mary Travers, and their colleagues put another female icon on the pop culture landscape—the politically conscious young woman unwavering in her determination to rectify social ills. So at the same time that young women could try on sexual rebellion as they sang along with the girl groups, they could try on political rebellion as they sang along with these women, and men, of the folk revival.

Singing along with the Beatles also made us, their devoted female followers, more comfortable with challenging authority in a more politically informed fashion than breaching police barricades to try to touch Ringo's hair. In 1967, we listened in amazement to *Sgt. Pepper's Lonely Hearts Club Band,* bursting with references to marijuana, LSD, and sexual ecstasy, and filled with critiques of the spiritual emptiness and stupidity of adult, middle-class society. By 1968, we weren't chasing after the Beatles in the streets, regarding them as love objects; we were taking their politics to heart, regarding them as political role models and cultural gurus as we sang along with "Revolution." Inside our heads now, embedded in lyrics envisioning the overthrow of the existing society and the birth of a new one, was a new persona, a politically defiant girl.

Although 1968, I hesitate to remind you, saw the rise of one of the most loathsome genres of pop music ever, bubble gum ("Yummy, Yummy, Yummy, I've Got Love in My Tummy"), for the most part rock and pop music was more political than ever, attacking militarism, materialism, and sexual repression. It made girls like me receptive to the kind of rebellion we would see in Atlantic City in 1968. Yet even as rock was radicalizing its female listeners, the music itself was becoming remasculinized. Girl groups, except for the Supremes (who had gone Vegas anyhow), were a thing of the past.

The emphasis on the electric guitar and drums, and male virtuosity in playing them, which included smashing them and playing them with your teeth, excluded women, and elevated Jimi Hendrix, the Doors, Cream, and the Who to stardom. A few women broke through, most notably Janis Joplin, who, when I saw her, drank about three quarts of bourbon onstage, cursed at the security guards, and sang her guts out. From "Eve of Destruction" to "White Rabbit" to "For What It's Worth" to "Handsome Johnny" to "Alice's Restaurant," rock music, dominated as it was by young men who seemed to have Bigfoot's sweat socks stuffed in their crotches, nonetheless reinforced young women's anger at the way the world was being run.

Music was so central to our lives because it seemed to tell "the truth." We hungered for "the truth" not only because of the sludge that dominated the prime-time television schedule—*Gentle Ben, The Lawrence Welk Show, Gomer Pyle,* and *The Newlywed Game.* We hungered for the truth because the other person we saw all too much of on TV, our weasel-faced president, was turning out to be a colossal, intransigent liar, and what he was lying to us about was Vietnam. This didn't just matter to young men; it mattered to all of us with brothers, boyfriends, and friends. In July 1965, Johnson doubled the monthly draft calls, so now my friends' older brothers were getting sent over there. When one came back in a casket, his face swollen from malaria, I knew that I didn't know enough about the war yet, except that I hated it. And as I watched the news, which I did now with increased attention, I saw that thousands of young people around the country, including young women, hated the war too, and were taking to the streets to try to stop it. The reverberations between the news and our music accelerated, so that the real commentary to the images we saw wasn't what the newsman said, it was the lyrics to "For What It's Worth."

What I didn't know then, from either the news or rock music—in fact, what most people didn't know until the Miss America demonstration—was that there were young women in the country furious not just about the war and racism but also about the way they, as women, were treated. And behind the scenes, out of the camera's eye, they began organizing.[9] These were young women who had busted their asses—indeed, risked their lives—for organizations like SNCC, only to be told by Stokely Carmichael that "the only position for women in SNCC is prone." Similar directives were given to young women active in SDS and the antiwar movement who wanted to do more than run mimeograph machines and make coffee. Their enlightened, New Left male comrades told these young women that what they needed was a good screw. These were sentiments right out of a crotch novel or Rolling Stones song. The fault line between coming of age during an era of rising expectations—for young people, for blacks, for the society as a whole—and being told that *your* expectations couldn't rise simply because you didn't have a penis, this fault line burst apart for these women.

Being treated like a cross between Pussy Galore and Hazel made these young, radical women snap: media stereotypes were strangling their goals and ambitions. So they singled out the dominant media imagery of women for attack. Through the underground newspapers and newsletters, as well as the conferences of the New Left, these women developed their own communications networks that conveyed information about the status of women deeply antagonistic to what *Cosmopolitan, Vogue,* and the Miss America pageant presented.[10] These networks were crucial to feminist organizing, and to spreading the word that there were women around the country sick of being told they should be a combination of Brigitte Bardot, Donna Reed, and Eleanor Roosevelt. Taking the offensive against the virgin/whore and good mom/evil mom oppositions that women were supposed to navigate, these radical young women started to think that they might not have to gloss over these contradictions (as they had been socialized to do) but that they could, instead, ride full tilt against them.

While feminist activism was going on out of the camera's eye, the media spotlight, especially that of the news media and the rock music scene, offered daily evidence that young women were getting as physically unruly, as politically rebellious, as sexually unconstrained, and as high as young men. The discrepancies between the images of young women we saw in magazines and ads and the images we saw of them on the nightly news had never been more stark. Advertisers defined the emancipated woman as one who wore miniskirts, paper dresses, and Rudi Gernreich bathing suits, a sort of James Bond girl who was sexually liberated, meaning she was willing and available, if not downright promiscuous. Even worse was their version of the "natural look." Joan Baez's version was simple: you stopped wearing makeup and trying to make your hair defy the laws of physics. But you can't keep a cosmetics and hair-care industry going this way. Madison Avenue's "natural look," promoted through pouty, air-brushed models, urged women to look like little girls in short skirts, Mary Jane shoes, white tights, long, straight (often ironed) hair, and big, wide eyes. Products such as Love's Baby Soft, with its model sucking provocatively on something cylindrical, explicitly promoted the pliant, innocent baby-doll image designed, it seems, on the presumption that men are really pedophiles at heart. This imagery infantilized women and exhorted us to embrace, more than ever, the desire to be attractive and gazed upon favorably by men. Implied in this definition was that women in the streets, whether protesting or just walking, were to be seen but not heard; our purpose was to provide erotic stimuli for "girl watchers" and to quietly, privately, consume products such as feminine hygiene sprays and champagne-flavored douches that would prepare us for intercourse with men. As an ad for one such product put it, "Woman's new freedom—Pristeen is part of it."

Colliding with this Lolita image, of woman as an innocent preschooler who loved sex, were the all too real and wrenching events of 1968 that made innocence a thing of the past, and that featured thousands of rebellious, defiant, politically infuriated young women who talked back, got arrested, and went to jail. No year, in my lifetime, was more tumultuous. Exhilarating, infuriating, full of hope, full of despair, 1968 had me on a constant psychic yo-yo.

When the string was up, it left me feeling that my generation could change the world permanently for the better, ending the regimentation, hypocrisy, and alienation that seemed to trap all too many people. I know this sounds naive now, but we really believed this back then, and I'm glad we did. Then the string would snap down, and I was convinced that our destiny was utterly out of our control and in the hands of Satan himself, working through LBJ, the Chicago police, and General Westmoreland. I felt this range of intense feelings not out in the streets but in my living room, watching history transmitted to me over the television. I was not yet in college in the spring and summer of 1968; I wasn't a member of any of the various oppositional political groups that organized against and did battle with government authorities. I was, like the vast majority of young people, still only a spectator. Yet spectatorship in 1968—even in the confines of your own home—was a politicizing activity.

Just think about what we saw in this one year. In January, Dr. Spock, who had helped our mothers raise us, was indicted for "aiding and abetting" draft evasion. In February, we watched the Tet Offensive on TV, which suggested that maybe Vietnam wasn't going to be the Sunday football game rout the president and the Pentagon had assured us it would. On March 12, Eugene McCarthy won the New Hampshire primary, and four days later, Bobby Kennedy declared his candidacy for president. Just two weeks after this, in what I thought would be yet another lie-filled address to the nation, Lyndon Johnson stunned us all by announcing that he was stepping down from the presidency when his term expired. The elation I felt over this blockbuster development lasted exactly four days until, at 6:00 P.M. on April 4—just in time for the nightly news—Martin Luther King was assassinated.

Less than three weeks after this disaster, on April 23, somewhere between 800 and 1,000 students at Columbia barricaded themselves inside campus buildings to protest the university's ties to the Pentagon and its ongoing appropriation of poor, residential neighborhoods in upper Manhattan. The takeover ended the next week when

1,000 cops stormed the buildings, arresting 700 college kids and injuring at least 150 of them. And it was only five weeks later that we watched those sickening images of Bobby Kennedy lying on the floor of the Ambassador Hotel in Los Angeles, his wife cradling his bloody head in her lap.

What did we get instead of Martin Luther King, Gene McCarthy, and Bobby Kennedy? Well, we got a full-blown, televised police riot at the Democratic convention in Chicago, where we watched cops bashing in the heads of college kids, journalists, and bystanders. I remember so vividly hearing the demonstrators chanting to the cops, "The whole world is watching, the whole world is watching!" and thinking surely this will make a difference, to have such state-sanctioned violence exposed. It made no difference at all, of course, except to make people like me more cynical and resigned than we already were, and certainly less willing to trust or obey white male authority figures. The year that had started with such hope ended with Tricky Dick, his sad, robotic wife, and prissy, insufferable daughters, as well as the most repulsive man ever to achieve high office, Spiro Agnew, all in the White House. As a result of viewing all this, I adopted two basic precepts. The first was that America was not a democracy at all, and that some people and interests were much more equal than others. The other was that the status quo was inhumane and monstrous. As I say, I wasn't a feminist yet, but, in retrospect, it is clear where I and millions of others were heading.

The public activism of young people was one of the biggest ongoing stories of 1968. After all, between January and June of that year alone, there were 221 major demonstrations at 101 colleges and universities involving some 39,000 students.[11] Public demonstrations were automatically newsworthy because they provided news organizations with provocative pictures, they represented conflict, and they sometimes produced arrests and violence, two of the news media's yardsticks for determining whether an event merited coverage. But precisely because of such criteria, and the news media's ingrained preference for covering events rather than explaining underlying causes or processes, their desire to identify leaders and spokesmen even in groups that refuse to have them, and their insistence that there are two sides—no more, no less—to every news story, such coverage was a mixed blessing for the young people of the New Left. It would prove to be a mixed blessing for feminists as well.

When feminists staged their own demonstrations, they encountered not just deeply entrenched journalistic conventions but also the more recently established routines and biases shaping the coverage of social movements and demonstrations. By the time of the Miss America demonstration, certain precedents in the press coverage of dissent were well-established. The news media cast the protests of young people as simultaneously dangerous and ineffectual, deeply subversive yet of little consequence. Solemn references to "Communist elements" and constant reliance on two incendiary images— burning draft cards and Vietcong flags—were intermixed with dismissive comments like this wrap-up from CBS's Bruce Morton: "Most people have doubts that U.S. foreign policy can be changed on the streets."[12] *The New York Times* and CBS, by turns, emphasized the extremism of antiwar demonstrators yet ridiculed their beards and blue jeans as signs that they were nothing more than naive, style-over-substance poseurs. The "other side" the media gave time to were often ultraright-wing types, as if there was some equivalence between their politics and those of kids trying to stop the war.[13]

News organizations habitually minimized the movement's numbers, its effectiveness, and its motivations, and acted as if it was as far from mainstream America as Joseph Stalin. Reporters were used to dealing with leaders and spokesmen—that's what the government trotted out—and when deeply nonhierarchical organizations like SDS refused to name someone as "head," the media anointed leaders on their own, which was deeply divisive to the internal operations of SDS. The important precedent was that the news media routinely divided the antiwar movement into what Todd Gitlin termed "legitimate main acts and illegitimate sideshows," meaning the moderate, conciliatory positions worth listening to and all the rest that the news media indicated were not.[14] Yet despite all this, or maybe even because of it—I know for a fact that some young people watching this coverage were throwing tie-dyed T-shirts at their TV sets—thousands of new converts joined SDS and other groups, or organized demonstrations of their own.

The treatment of the Miss America protest made it clear that the media coverage of the women's movement would be strikingly similar to that of the antiwar movement. But where women were involved, there were some extra, important touches. How feminists used, or failed to use, their faces and their bodies, and the extent to which their faces and bodies conformed to those in a Max Factor ad, were central features of the coverage. If these girls were out on the streets and swinging bras around, why, they must be closet exhibitionists, narcissists, or simply hysterical, and language that suggested witchcraft or secret cults resonated darkly with the magical powers of sitcom characters. The media also paid inordinate attention to the way feminists violated physical and social boundaries, and suggested that, by doing so, they were making spectacles of themselves, just as Beatles fans had done a few years earlier. Feminists were cast as unfeminine, unappealing women who were denouncing the importance of the male gaze, yet who secretly coveted that gaze for themselves by protesting in public. These poor girls, it was suggested, sought to get through political flamboyance what they were unable to get through physical attractiveness.

It was not just what was said to or about women in the media that was important; news stories and TV shows were structured so that feminism was positioned as deviant. The standards by which something was judged newsworthy were, in fact, deeply masculine. The emphases on conflict in the public sphere, on crime, on dramatic public events rather than behind-the-scenes processes, on the individual rather than the group, and on competition rather than cooperation all biased the news toward masculine public enterprise. The public sphere was defined, visually and rhetorically, as the place where men make history. The news also exploited the highly emotional as spectacle while denigrating overly emotional commentary about events as not objective and therefore invalid. Because of these journalistic conventions, the only places any female had in the news were as victim, hysteric, sex object, or wife of a prominent man. In other words, the desire to make news, and the act of doing so, two impulses considered perfectly natural in men, rendered feminists as deviant, no longer feminine but not quite masculine either. The overwhelmingly dismissive coverage of the women's movement that followed was in many ways inevitable.

These biases, of course, were reinforced by the structures of the news organizations themselves, which were rigidly hierarchical and male-dominated. In the late 1960s, women journalists were confined to writing about spring hats and thirty-one new ways to cook squash, or they were researchers for male reporters, and they were rarely seen on television except as weather girls. Women trying to break out of these confines faced enormous pressures to conform to how the boys did things, and they also faced editors and publishers deeply hostile to the women's movement.

Perhaps one reason that the Miss America demonstration is not remembered as frequently as it should be is that it happened amidst the swirl of so many shocking events in 1968. Yet retrospectives today on the late 1960s seem all too eager to show young girls smoking pot and dancing partially clad at love-ins while they completely ignore Atlantic City in September. But anyone who cares about the sick proliferation of the anorexic body as the ideal for all women, or who is tired of the constant equation between crow's-feet and female worthlessness, should keep the memory of this protest alive and well, for us and for future generations. Robin Morgan and her organization, the New York Radical Women, took direct aim at what they called "the degrading mindless-boob-girlie symbol" so prevalent in the media and decried the "ludicrous 'beauty' standards we ourselves are conditioned to take seriously." They also attacked "the unbeatable madonna-whore combination" and the mixed messages women had been socialized to internalize. "To win approval, we must be both sexy and wholesome, delicate but able to cope, demure yet titillatingly bitchy. . . . Miss America and *Playboy*'s centerfolds are sisters over the skin."[15]

Yet the New York Radical Women were in a tricky position—as feminists have been ever since—because they needed the same media outlets that they were attacking. If the movement was to grow, its existence and goals would have to be publicized through the news. Radical feminists were extremely wary about the kind of coverage they would get; one fear was that it would drive women away. Robin Morgan successfully used the extensive media contacts she still had from her child-actress days to give the press advance notice of the protest, but once reporters got to Atlantic City, the version of feminism viewers and readers got would be theirs, not hers.

The New York Times's coverage of the protest in Atlantic City indicated how the women's movement would be framed by the news media over the next five years, and some female journalists were just as dismissive as their male counterparts. *Times* reporter Charlotte Curtis, emphasizing what she saw as these women's desperate need for attention, observed, "Television and news photographers were allowed and even encouraged to photograph the pickets, and the women . . . escalated their activities when the cameramen arrived." The women refused to talk to men, including male reporters. "Miss Kathy Amatnick [*sic*], one of the younger women, caught her 65-year-old grandmother, Mrs. Martha Berlin, talking with a male observer and shouted at her to stop. 'You mustn't do that,' Miss Amatnick cried."[16] (She may have been on to something; her last name, Amatniek, was misspelled by the newspaper of record.) What Curtis failed to report was that one of the main political goals of the action was to force the media to hire more women to cover hard news stories, and to get men to see what it felt like to be second-class citizens. Curtis did make a point of describing the protesters' clothes and emphasized that the demonstration was observed by "about 650 generally unsympathetic spectators." She also devoted a paragraph to a counterdemonstration staged by only three women. Curtis also felt obliged to point out that the sixty-five pickets who came from New York arrived in buses driven "by male drivers." This fact, completely irrelevant to the story, implied that the women were more than happy to be dependent on men when it was convenient, and that their convictions were not particularly deep or strong.

Throughout the article, the demonstrators were made to appear ridiculous, frivolous, and hypocritical. All the women's charges about sexism in the United States were placed in quotation marks, suggesting that these were merely the deluded hallucinations of a few ugly, angry women rather than a fact of life. The demonstrators' rhetoric was cast as highly inflated and thus absurd, and their complaints about female oppression seen as representing a wacky, self-seeking, publicity-hungry fringe of distinctly unrepresentative women. So the women who were protesting the public exhibition of women's bodies were themselves cast as nothing more than needy exhibitionists. The contrast was stark: Miss America contestants, beautiful, docile, and compliant, who eagerly sought out and competed for the male gaze, deserved their day in the public spotlight; the demonstrators, unruly, rebellious, excessive, who attacked the institutionalization of male voyeurism, did not.

In this way the protesters played into—as some of them feared they would—the media's love of conflict, especially among women, and the image of feminists as hostile to other women began to crystallize. Yet even as these early feminist activists despaired over their new image as storm troopers jealous of pretty women, they quickly saw another immediate result of this dismissive coverage: it promoted female solidarity. In the aftermath of the Atlantic City protest, New York Radical Women was flooded with new members, and other feminist organizations were founded around the country.[17]

One year later, *Newsweek* would describe the Miss America demonstration as one in which 150 women "gathered in front of Convention Hall and burned their brassieres," even though no bra burning had occurred in Atlantic City.[18] But bra burning had become the news peg for media coverage of the women's movement, a metaphor that trivialized feminists and titillated the audience at the same time. For the press, burning bras was a natural segue from burning draft cards. It fit into the dominant media frame about women's liberation and equated the women's movement with exhibitionism and narcissism, as if women who unstrapped their breasts were unleashing their sexuality in a way that was unseemly, laughable, and politically inconsequential, yet dangerous. Women who threw their bras away may have said they were challenging sexism, but the media, with a wink, hinted that these women's motives were not at all political but rather personal: to be trendy, and to attract men.

Even for those of us who didn't recognize it at the time, 1968 was a turning point. All the prefeminist glimmerings in girl group music, Beatlemania, perky teens, and women with magical powers, the exhortations to make something of ourselves and change the world, and the image of the political woman we first saw in Joan Baez and Mary Travers—these shards started coming together and magnified one another during 1968. The acceptance by millions of us of some version of feminist ideology was a fitful process during which we began questioning, rethinking, and revising our sense of what it meant—or ought to mean—to be an American woman. Baby boomers' sense of being part of something bigger would begin to shape not just a social identity but a political identity, and one with political consequences. The process began accelerating in 1968 as many of us developed a deep antipathy and contempt for the status quo and an inflated sense of our mission to reject it. And then, for a brief moment on the TV screen, there were these women, charging that what completely undergirded that hideous status quo was the subordination and objectification of women.

The standard histories of the women's movement cite the experiences of women in the civil rights movement and the New Left, as well as the women of the National Organization for Women, as the essential—and often the only—histories of feminism that matter. No one disputes that the pathbreaking work of these women was critical to launching a women's liberation movement in the United States. But those of us in the audience mattered too, even as we rebounded between Mary Travers and Lyndon Johnson, Robin Morgan and Miss America, John Lennon and Tricia Nixon. Without us, there would have been no movement. And our struggling prefeminist persona, the one who wanted to "Tell Him," the one who coveted Samantha's power, and the one who belted out "If I Had a Hammer," was gaining strength and chutzpah. With those two voices in our heads, and in the mass media, getting louder and more insistent— "You're equal," "No, you're subordinate"—we were finding the tension unbearable. But in 1968, the voice for equality was starting to get the upper hand.

CHAPTER 8

I Am Woman, Hear Me Roar

On August 26, 1970, Howard K. Smith, the anchorman at ABC News, smirked slightly and read the following lead-in to one of the day's major stories: "Quote. Three things have been difficult to tame. The ocean, fools, and women. We may soon be able to tame the ocean, but fools and women will take a little longer. Unquote." In case viewers missed the gist of the quip, the text of the quotation was projected to the right of Smith on the screen. He continued. "The man who made that statement is Spiro Agnew. He is now touring Asia, wisely, because today all over this nation, the women's liberation movement is marking the fiftieth anniversary of women gaining the vote by demonstrations and strikes." This was the lead-in to ABC's coverage of the Women's Strike for Equality, the largest demonstration in American history up to that time for women's rights. Opening with such a dismissive little epigram from the official verbal hit man and all-around sleazeball—oh, pardon me, vice president—of the Nixon administration, Smith was able to frame ABC's coverage of the strike with considerable condescension while absolving himself and the network of responsibility for such an obviously neanderthal remark. After airing the reports of several correspondents from around the country, Smith ended the segment by quoting West Virginia Senator Jennings Randolph, who characterized the women's movement as "a small band of bra-less bubbleheads." The last thing the viewer saw was the phrase "bra-less bubbleheads" projected on the right portion of the screen. Kinda made you wanna join right up.

Over on CBS, also spurred by the strike, Eric Sevareid, the TV commentator I screamed at most in the early 1970s, dedicated his evening's commentary to the women's movement. He opened by noting that "no husband ever won an argument with a wife, and the secret of a happy marriage is for the man to repeat those three little words, 'I was wrong.' " Dismissing the movement as led by "aroused minorities . . . who are already well off by any comparative measurement," Sevareid asserted that "the plain truth is, most American men are startled by the idea that American women generally are oppressed, and they read with relief the Gallup poll that two-thirds of women don't think they're oppressed either." Reflecting again on the evolution of social movements, he observed, "Many movements grow by simple contagion, thousands discovering they are in pain, though they hadn't noticed it until they were told." After some further commentary about how difficult it was to think of women simply as people, he concluded by lecturing, "As for the organized movement itself, it remains to be seen whether it will unify and remain effective, or will fragment into quarreling, doctrinal groups like the far left student movement and the black movement. It now has the unavoidable opportunity to prove that the masculine notion that women can't get along with other women is another item from the ancient shelf of male mythology." The camera then switched to Walter Cronkite, who added with his usual finality, "And that's the way it is."

These are just two excerpts from the extensive coverage the women's liberation movement received in 1970, but they are typical of how the news media framed what was and continues to be, by almost any measure, one of the most consequential social movements of the twentieth century. Aside from the big yucks the gents shared over "bra-less bubbleheads" and the Agnew quotation, words such as *contagion* likened feminism to a social disease, and there was incessant emphasis on the divisions, real or imagined, within the movement.

The news media's stereotypes about feminism—which flattened this complex, rich, multipronged, and often contradictory movement into a cardboard caricature—were of urgent concern to feminist organizers, since most women first learned about the movement through the media.[1] "Rage would not be too strong a word to describe the emotion felt by large numbers of feminists about the media's coverage of the women's movement," noted the first chroniclers of the movement, Judith Hole and Ellen Levine, in 1971.[2] And though rage was exactly the correct response, it should not have been the only response. For what is provocative here is that despite this coverage—perhaps even because of it—increasing numbers of women, and men, came to support varying versions of feminist ideology, and to change their aspirations and their lives accordingly. Membership in NOW, to pick only one example and the most mainstream of the feminist organizations, skyrocketed from 1,200 in 1967 to 48,000 in 1974, with 700 chapters in the United States and nine other countries. By 1972, the movement had an anthem—Helen Reddy's "I Am Woman"—which went gold, hit number one on the charts, and won Reddy a Grammy.

There is no doubt that the news media of the early 1970s played an absolutely central role in turning feminism into a dirty word, and stereotyping the feminist as a hairy-legged, karate-chopping commando with a chip on her shoulder the size of China, really bad clothes, and a complete inability to smile—let alone laugh. But at the same time, by treating the women's liberation movement as a big story, the news media also brought millions of converts to feminism, even if the version many women came to embrace was a shriveled compromise of what others had hoped was possible. And while some stories were shockingly derisive, others were sympathetic. Many reports were ambivalent and confused, taking feminism seriously one minute, mocking it the next. In this way, the news media exacerbated quite keenly the profound cultural schizophrenia about women's place in society that had been building since the 1940s and 1950s.

In 1970, the women's liberation movement burst onto the national agenda. It would not be an exaggeration to say, even with everything else going on then, that this was the story of the year. And in the capable hands of our nation's highly objective journalists, the women's liberation movement seemed to come out of nowhere—or, more frequently, from Pluto. The movement fit the criteria of newsworthiness perfectly. People were demonstrating in the streets, they were charging that America was *not* the democratic, egalitarian oasis its mythology said it was, they were saying and doing outrageous things, *and* they were women. The protesters clashed starkly with the women elsewhere on TV: young, perfectly groomed, always smiling, never complaining, demure, eager to please, eager to consume. Unlike Katy Winters, who urged us to be cool, calm, and collected in all those revolting Secret commercials, these women were angry; they yelled, argued, and accused; they raised their fists and shook them; and they mounted a full-scale attack against Madison Avenue and the prevailing media stereotypes of women. They violated the nation's most sacred conceits about love, marriage, the family, and femininity. They denounced illegal, back-alley abortions, a previously taboo subject, as a form of butchery that had to stop. They talked back to men, invaded their bars and clubs, and even challenged the very fabric of American language, coining terms such as *sexism* and *male chauvinism* while exposing the gender biases in the words *mankind, chairman,* and *chick,* to name just a few. They insisted that "the personal is political," that motherhood, marriage, sexual behavior, and dress codes all had to be considered symptoms of a broader political and social system that kept women down.[3] *This* was news. After 1970, there was simply no going back.

Consider what happened in this one year.[4] Women charged *Newsweek* magazine with sex discrimination in hiring and promotion, and their sisters over at the competition filed a similar suit with the New York State Division of Human Rights against Time Inc. In March alone, over one hundred feminists staged an eleven-hour sit-in at the *Ladies' Home Journal,* NBC and CBS each ran a multipart series on the women's movement on their nightly newscasts, *Time* printed a special report called "The War on 'Sexism' " (they still felt compelled to put the offending word in quotation marks), and *The New York Times Magazine* ran a major article by Susan Brownmiller titled "Sisterhood Is Powerful." The *Times* magazine also ran articles that year on the Equal Rights Amendment, on Betty Friedan, and on whether there were biologically determined sex differences between men and women. Kate Millett's *Sexual Politics* became the most talked about best-seller of the year, and Millett herself appeared on the cover of *Time*.

August was another landmark month. On the third, the U.S. Justice Department, prodded by outraged female workers, filed suit against the Libbey-Owens-Ford Company of Toledo, Ohio—the department's first suit against sex discrimination in the workplace. A week later, on August 10, the House of Representatives, prompted by the brilliant tactical work of Representative Martha Griffiths (D-Michigan), passed the ERA. Two weeks after that, on August 26, the Women's Strike for Equality took place in cities around the country. And the *Ladies' Home Journal* included in its August issue an eight-page supplement titled "The New Feminism," written by some of the women who had occupied the *Journal*'s offices five months earlier. Stickers reading "This Ad Insults Women" appeared on billboards, subway posters, and the sides of buses. Bella Abzug was elected to Congress; Shirley Chisholm was reelected. Hawaii and New York State liberalized their abortion laws. Feminists began appearing on talk shows, Gloria Steinem or Germaine Greer debating the likes of Hugh Hefner or William F. Buckley, Jr. And *The Mary Tyler Moore Show* premiered in September, noteworthy because, despite its overly accommodating and compliant heroine who said "oh geez, oh golly" too much (not to mention "Oh, Mr. Grant"), it actually featured a single woman on her own without a steady boyfriend and with a steady job.

The watershed year of 1970 actually began in November 1969, when *Time* became the first mass magazine to feature a major article on the movement.[5] It was written by Ruth Brine, one of the few female contributing editors at the magazine, who was also (the publisher's note hastened to emphasize) a mother of three, as if this ensured her objectivity and immunized her against contamination from this latest ideological plague. Headlined "The New Feminists: Revolt Against 'Sexism'" and placed in the "Behavior" section of the magazine, the article oscillated wildly between dismissive ridicule and legitimation of certain feminist grievances. Thus it was typical of the schizoid coverage of feminism. Brine suggested that the movement was highly derivative, its activities and its charges of oppression "all borrowed, of course, from the fiery rhetoric of today's militant black and student movements." The implication, often repeated elsewhere, was that this was a copycat movement, a frivolous imitation, with no genuine basis in true oppression, true hardship.

Labeling feminists as, simply, "the angries," Brine observed, "Many of the new feminists are surprisingly violent in mood, and seem to be trying, in fact, to repel other women rather than attract them." It went without saying—and so, of course, it had to be said—that feminists "burn brassieres." The most prominent image of feminism, a seemingly required illustration for any article on the topic, and one brandished here, was a photograph of women learning karate, to signify the movement's deadly seriousness and its hostility toward men and femininity. This was a familiar, and deliberate, journalistic strategy. As the journalist Susan Brownmiller described it, male editors would insist, succinctly, "Get the bra burning and the karate up front."[6] "Soon," Brine predicted, "we may expect legions of female firemen, airline pilots, sanitation men and front-line soldiers (although anthopologist Margaret Mead thinks that they would be too fierce.)" Yet despite this alleged fierceness, the article emphasized that "women themselves do not, in truth, have a record of soaring achievement." The message was clear: women were, by nature, a bunch of incompetents who, if you gave them just a little power, would turn into megalomaniacs and become as lethal as Snow White's wicked stepmother.

The story also suggested that women had to be brainwashed in order to become part of the movement. This, too, was a common theme, that feminists, like the pods in *Invasion of the Body Snatchers,* cannibalized perfectly happy women and turned them into inhuman aliens. Young women were especially "fertile ground for the seeds of discontent" that were sown in consciousness-raising groups. According to *Time,* these were "rap sessions" in which women "drum their second-class status into each other by testifying to various indignities." Radical feminists "soon attracted a number of women who otherwise had no radical leanings at all. The latest recruits include factory workers, high school girls, a number of discontented housewives, and even a coven [!] or two of grandmothers." The discourse of invasion recurred over and over again, resonating with the still powerful anti-Communist rhetoric of the cold war. Brine described the "radical wing of Women's Liberation" as consisting of "groups, or cells, which constantly split and multiply in a sort of mitosis." One could readily imagine a sci-fi horror film, "Invasion of the Mutant Feminist Bitches" against whom conventional male weaponry was helpless.

At the same time, and in less suggestive language, the article acknowledged that feminists "have also drawn attention to some real problems," such as the wage gap between men and women, the lack of decent day care, and the fact that two-thirds of the women who worked did so because they needed the money. In a small sidebar, highlighted in pink, *Time* listed a series of statistics documenting women's low salaries and their underrepresentation in business, the professions, and politics. Like virtually every other mainstream news organization, *Time* legitimated liberal feminism's charges about economic discrimination. For one thing, the statistics were irrefutable. But, also, the news media embraced the conceit that the United States was a society of equal opportunity, and where it wasn't it had to change, especially after prodding from a sanctimonious, and often hypocritical, press. "Equal pay for equal work" was a slogan quickly accepted by many journalists as a reasonable and moderate goal; it was a concrete, measurable reform, it built on the rhetoric of democracy, and it suggested that women *could* be integrated into male jobs without insisting that they *would*. "Equal pay for equal work" was also handy for journalists: they could affirm it to show they weren't sexists, then use that support to marginalize other, more sweeping feminist critiques as deviant and extreme.

Four months later, in March 1970, *Newsweek* featured its own "Special Report" story, "Women in Revolt." The cover illustration featured a silhouette of a naked woman, her arm raised and fist clenched, breaking through the circle and cross symbol for woman, cracking the circle in half. The article, "Women's Lib: The War on 'Sexism,' " was initially assigned to Lynn Young, an assistant editor at the magazine, who claimed that her male colleagues attacked it for not being objective enough. One editor asserted, "Only a man could portray 'the ludicrous soul of this story,' " and had a man rewrite her article. The piece was reportedly rewritten every week for two months before her editors decided not to run it. Then *Newsweek* hired Helen Dudar, the wife of one of its senior editors and a writer for the *New York Post,* to write the piece.[7]

Dudar's article was surprisingly sympathetic, although she reinforced existing metaphors, like the one that cast feminism as a science project gone berserk. She wrote that "women's lib groups have multiplied like freaked-out amebas," and she found the feminists' hostility "gravely infectious." But she also provided one of the least sensationalized accounts of radical feminism and wrote about women's second-class status with passion. As a newcomer to feminism, she recorded her own reactions to her topic. "As I sat with many of the women I have discussed here, I was struck by how distorting the printed word can be. On paper, most of them have sounded cold, remote, surly, tough, and sometimes a bit daft. On encounter, they usually turned out to be friendly, helpful, and attractive. Meeting the more eccentric theoreticians, I found myself remembering that today's fanatics are sometimes tomorrow's prophets." At the end of the article she admitted that she had gotten a real education, that she'd had to question some very basic assumptions about her own position in life, and that the process was deeply unsettling. Nonetheless, "the ambivalence is gone; the distance is gone. What is left is a sense of pride and kinship with all those women who have been asking all the hard questions. I thank them and so, I think, will a lot of other women."

To balance this out, *Newsweek* featured a one-page insert titled, "Other Voices: How Social Scientists See Women's Lib."[8] This piece was filled with the typically pompous comments of primarily male "experts" who endorsed equal pay for equal work, but cited a range of studies to show that, in a host of areas, feminists were simply ignorant, wrongheaded, and misguided women prone to hyperbole. (Marilyn Goldstein of *Newsday* revealed to a fellow journalist in 1970 that whenever her paper covered the movement, one of her editors instructed reporters to "get out there and find an authority who'll say this is all a crock of shit.")[9] *Newsweek's* assortment of dispassionate blowholes asserted that men and women really were biologically different, that girls were by nature more nurturing and passive, boys more active and aggressive. Each expert was introduced as someone "famous," "eminent," "distinguished," and "the most knowledgeable" in his field about sex roles. Dr. Abram Kardiner of Columbia maintained, "From what I've seen of the liberationists, their most conspicuous feature is self-hatred. I see tremendous vituperativeness and lack of feeling." Dr. Mary Calderone, "distinguished for her work on sex education," denounced the movement "because the women in it are militant, unpleasant and unfeminine."

This same mixture, grudging acknowledgment of a few feminist critiques infused by a disdain for feminists themselves, characterized TV's equally schizophrenic coverage. The CBS network began its three-part evening news series on "the blossoming of the feminist movement" on March 3, choosing David Culhane to cover the story. The first installment focused on economic discrimination against women, pointing out that their median salary was $4,000 a year, about half that for men. Culhane noted that women were confined to "women's jobs," such as teacher, secretary, or nurse, and discouraged from entering the professions. He added that there were fewer women holding Ph.D.'s in 1970 than there were in 1940. Although women made up 51 percent of the population, they were an "oppressed majority," a position backed up by an interview with Betty Friedan. Then the story cut to a women's meeting in Northridge, California, in which moderate middle-class women, young and middle-aged, calmly discussed the dilemmas they faced. "Most women are going to have to work as head of households to support an entire household and taxed the same as a man," explained one woman, "and yet paid one-third as much for identical work. How do we make the public understand that this woman can't compete . . . she can't compete in the labor market enough to feed her children?" In this story we learned that women had a legitimate point about their second-class economic status.

But when women, especially young women, showed their anger, this was less acceptable. The story cut to Senate hearings on the safety of the birth control pill, which younger, more "militant" women had "disrupted" by standing up and yelling at committee members. "Women are not going to sit quietly any longer—you are murdering us for your profit and convenience," yelled one young woman. Added another, "I'd like to know why is it that scientists and drug companies are perfectly willing to use women as guinea pigs, but as soon as a woman gets pregnant in one of these experiments she's treated like a common criminal." When the chairman asked the young women to sit down, one shot back, "*No,* we aren't going to sit down—why don't you give us some solid answers to our questions?"

Whatever the intended effect of this footage, young women like me, watching this on TV, were yelling, "Right on!" because it was so thrilling to see women my age taking on these bloated, self-righteous senators who thought girls should be quiet, smile, and serve tea. The story moved on to other disorderly women demonstrating against sex-segregated bars, and as they angrily confronted a bar's owner, they equated having a "men only" bar with having "whites only" facilities. After one woman was attacked by a male patron of the bar, the women discussed their need to learn how to defend themselves physically. The last scene showed what reporters repeatedly referred to as "militant feminists" learning judo and karate. The final image of the story was of a woman hurling a man to the floor and pinning him there. No one could miss the point. "Militant feminists," meaning anyone more outspoken than Pat Nixon, favored brass knuckles and Molotov cocktails as the only way to achieve women's liberation.

The second installment opened with Walter Cronkite sitting in front of a picture of Sigmund Freud. Those of us already sick of being told that we suffered from "penis envy" and that our biology was our destiny, braced ourselves for the worst whenever we saw Freud invoked, and we were not to be disappointed here, as Cronkite intoned, "Sigmund Freud, an expert on women if there ever was one, said that despite his thirty years of research, he was unable to answer one great question: What does a woman want?" (Well, Walter, he might have found out if he'd actually *listened* to them.) Freud might be even more confused today, opined Cronkite, if he saw the current "militant demonstrations" staged by women. Culhane then opened his story with footage of the Miss America demonstration, a protest that was anything but "militant." While he cited Playboy Clubs as a special target of feminists, the camera zoomed in on the jiggling cleavage of a particularly well-endowed bunny, and Culhane described these watering holes as places "where men come to observe remarkable displays of female pulchritude," thereby embracing the objectification of women that feminists deplored and suggesting that it was, in fact, harmless. He hastened to add, however, that it wasn't just "sour grapes" that led feminists to protest the objectification of women's bodies. "They can and indeed have won beauty contests," he reported, as if it was newsworthy—and shocking—to think that a feminist would be anything but hideously ugly, then cut to an interview with Alice Denham, a former model and playmate of the month who had become a feminist.

Just when you wanted to punch Culhane in the snout, he changed tone, reporting quite movingly on Jean Temple, a college-educated divorced mother of four in her forties who was agitating for child-care centers because she was "unable to work and take care of her children at the same time." Speaking of her constant worry about her children while she was at work, and about how her family was always on the verge of poverty, Temple said simply, "My children now have to bring themselves up." Here Culhane demonstrated how male journalists got it about the oppression of economic discrimination and didn't get it at all about the bondage of sexual objectification. He closed the story by delineating the differences between liberal and radical feminism. The moderates wanted "equal job opportunities, equal pay with men for the same jobs, child-care centers, and more or less unrestricted abortion." The more militant feminist groups, however, "say even these goals are not enough." He promised that the next report would look at the "revolutionary views of these radical women," the word *radical* receiving especially heavy emphasis.

The final segment pulled out all the stops. Several radical feminists, including Ti-Grace Atkinson, Shulamith Firestone, and Anselma dell'Olio, were interviewed by a female reporter, Conchita Pierce. The sections of the interviews the network chose to air focused on these women's critiques of marriage and the family as institutions that can't help but oppress women. As Atkinson asserted, "If you had equality between men and women, you couldn't have marriage." "What would you substitute for marriage?" asked Pierce. "What would you substitute for cancer?" Atkinson replied. Firestone argued that "pregnancy is barbaric" and that women should not have to bear the burden of reproduction alone. Scientific research should be directed toward what Culhane paraphrased as "the so-called bottled baby. . . . That, of course, is one of the most radical visions of feminism."

Here we see how vexed the relationship was between radical feminism and the mainstream media. What radical feminists presented as revolutionary and utopian, the mainstream media saw as a bad acid trip. Some radical feminists refused to cooperate at all with anyone in the media, alienating women journalists who wanted to give their views a wider hearing. Yet radical feminists were right to be wary of media that delighted in the superficial and the shocking because this approach endorsed reformism rather than a complete break with the past. Ti-Grace Atkinson became a media darling because she gave great sound bites like "Marriage means rape" or "Love has to be destroyed." But the coverage she received used such disembodied quotations to make radical feminists seem like crazed freaks. Now it's true, most radical feminists were over the top in their condemnation of patriarchy, and their pronouncements were outside mainstream thought. But rarely did any reporter acknowledge the thoughtful analysis, or the painful realities for many women, that led to such conclusions.

Culhane concluded the series in a typical way, pitting women against women and acting as if male sexism was a completely insignificant barrier to change: "So far, the women's rights movement has had one fundamental problem; not so much to persuade men, but to convince the majority of American women that there is something basically wrong with their position in life." After some final footage of women singing a feminist version of the "Battle Hymn of the Republic," the camera cut to a smirking Walter Cronkite, eyebrows raised in amusement, as he softly chuckled, "And that's the way it is."

Two weeks after the CBS series ended, NBC weighed in with its own, which turned out to be one of the most sympathetic pieces done on the movement. This point of view was due in no small part to the firmness and persuasiveness of NBC's female reporters—Liz Trotta, Norma Quarles, and Aline Saarinen—who covered the story. In Saarinen's first report, a rapid-sequence montage of Barbie dolls, fashion models, women in print ads, and footage from a Virginia Slims commercial drove home how women are victimized by "degrading stereotypes." And Saarinen was one of the few to high-light feminists' emphasis on personal choice, by reporting their insistence that "domesticity and motherhood should be one option among many options." In just a few minutes, Saarinen had acknowledged the legitimacy of the major points underlying the 1968 Miss America protest and broadcast them to millions.

Liz Trotta followed up this report with a review of society's sexist attitudes toward girls. "Discrimination begins early in a girl's life," noted Trotta, as she interviewed expectant fathers in a hospital waiting room, all of whom hoped they would be getting boys. Over footage of children playing, she pointed out that the girl "learns that her place is in the home. The boy learns his place is not in the home." Trotta then went to Austin, Minnesota, and asserted that "by the time she's in high school, a girl has been brainwashed." She then aired a classroom debate among high school students over women's rights, in which the boys claimed that girls only go to college to find a husband and that girls are inferior and simply want an easy life. As one young man summed it up, "Like, my mother, she went to college, you know, she got some dietary deal, and she doesn't know anything." (I wonder what kind of a reception he got from his know-nothing mom that night.) Trotta let these retrograde comments speak for themselves. She concluded, "There are young girls here who are bright, enthusiastic, and full of hopes, but, like most women, they'll go out in the world knowing their place, and that place is secondary to men." This was powerful and persuasive stuff.

Norma Quarles covered economic discrimination against women, offering such statistics as "only 1 percent of the 31 million working women earn $10,000 or more." Some "exceptional" women can make it, but they will "be fighting man's prejudice all the way." In an especially savvy and effective ploy, Quarles edited together, on the audio track, a series of quotations by men about how women can't concentrate like men, aren't levelheaded, can't be aggressive at work, and are basically domestic. These she played over footage of women working with computers, in banks, in heavy industry, and in offices, images that directly contradicted the men's dismissive comments and dramatized the ignorance and stupidity of sexism.

In the final report, Saarinen conveyed the richness and diversity of feminism, describing movement members as ranging from "reformers to revolutionaries." She showed women in demonstrations getting arrested and being dragged to police vans. Cutting to footage of a demonstration by the Women's International Terrorist Conspiracy from Hell (WITCH), Saarinen described the "flashier, more original" WITCH as "uniquely satirical and witty in a movement that, like all crusades, is rather humorless." This was one of the few moments when a journalist laughed with, not at, radical feminists and understood what they were poking fun at, and why. Saarinen concluded, "There's a group for every taste, from militant man-haters and lesbians to happily mated." While acknowledging that there were disagreements among these groups, she emphasized that "the strength of the movement lies in what the groups hold in common," their determined fight against discrimination. She closed with a powerful plea from suffragist Alice Paul, then in her eighties, who asked, "Mr. President, how long must women wait for liberty?" Viewers of the NBC series saw an extremely convincing and sympathetic account of the pressing need for women's liberation, an account that would soon be pooh-poohed elsewhere.

The biggest story of the year, and the one that received the most coverage, was the Women's Strike for Equality on August 26, to commemorate the fiftieth anniversary of the ratification of the Nineteenth Amendment. Women were urged to drop their stenographer's pads, their laundry baskets, and their compliant, nurturing demeanor, to strike for a day in protest of sexism in the United States. Organizers of the strike agreed on the following demands, which you can read with a wistful sigh, since none of them has been achieved: equal opportunity for women in employment and education, twenty-four-hour child-care centers, and abortion on demand. To drive home the role played by the media in reinforcing women's oppression, organizers also urged women to boycott four products whose advertising was offensive and degrading to women: *Cosmopolitan* magazine, Silva Thins cigarettes, Ivory Liquid, and Pristeen, the infamous "feminine hygiene" spray. The strike was probably the most important public action of the movement, and given the number of women who participated, and the even larger number who were converted to feminism, it was a huge success. But you would never have guessed that from the news.

Newsweek described the movement as a "shaky coalition of disparate groups" and asserted that "there is plenty of reason to doubt that [it] will ever be able to unite women as a mass force. Certainly it has not done so yet."[10] What Aline Saarinen of NBC had characterized as a strength—the fact that the movement sustained a wide spectrum of groups with different ideological positions—was cast by *Newsweek* as an insurmountable weakness. *Time* opened its story with the world-weary, oh-what-we-boys-must-endure quip "These are the times that try men's souls, and they are likely to get much worse before they get better."[11] Women had better button their lips and keep their anger to themselves, *Time* warned, quoting no less an authority than Margaret Mead: " 'Women's Liberation has to be terribly conscious about the danger of provoking men to kill women. You have quite literally driven them mad.' " Noting that the movement "has not produced much humor," the article cited *Sexual Politics* as the new bible for feminists and described Kate Millett as "the Mao Tse-Tung of women's liberation," "a brilliant misfit in a man's world" who lived in a dashiki and work pants and didn't wash her hair enough. Reading *Sexual Politics,* warned Millett's doctoral-thesis adviser, "is like sitting with your testicles in a nutcracker."

Commentary on television before the strike mingled amused condescension with outright contempt, and no network was more notorious than ABC and its virulently sexist anchormen Harry Reasoner, Howard K. Smith, and Frank Reynolds. On August 11, in his commentary, Reynolds observed that now there were "lady" jockeys, "lady" generals, and a female president of the U.N. General Assembly, and that "even the House of Representatives has finally decided that women are entitled to the same rights as men." The first major implication of the ERA Reynolds chose to highlight was that women might be required to pay alimony, which, he noted sarcastically, "would restore the ancient and honorable profession of gigolo to its rightful glory." The second implication of the ERA was that women would be subject to the draft, which would decidedly end "America's role of world policeman." He explained why with a chuckle. "Female draftees would presumably retain at least some of their civilian prerogatives, so it would be obviously impossible to fly a regiment halfway around the world at a moment's notice when at least one-half the regiment could simply never be ready on time. It is not that there is anything inherently unequal about women in such matters, it is just that they are, well, different." Oh, Frankie, such a wit.

On August 25, Reynolds's colleague Howard K. Smith weighed in with his thoughts on women's liberation. "Like the majority of Americans," Smith said, he was "weary of the abrasive type of group protest." While sympathetic to "Indians and Negroes," who had been "genuinely mistreated," Smith confessed to a "modified *un*sympathy with women's liberation." He found "a few of their demands," such as equal pay, equal access to "some jobs," and child-care centers, to be "good." He suggested women were already more than equal, since they constituted 53 percent of the population and "they get the most money, inherited from worn-out husbands." He derided what he saw as a demand for "sameness," which he denounced as "abhorrent." Then, in a bizarre non sequitur, Smith observed that European cities traditionally have had more charm than those in America. "But when American women adopted the miniskirt, displaying much more woman, it was the biggest advance in urban beautification since Central Park was created in Manhattan." Winding down from such lyrical heights, Smith said, "To me, women's lib has that in common with the midi, which is now threatening us—that it is a kind of defeminization." Praising the differences between men and women, Smith concluded, "Vive la différence!" This, I remind you, passed for journalistic analysis in 1970.

When August 26 arrived, there were marches and rallies in most major cities, and in New York the day's events culminated in a march down Fifth Avenue, followed by speeches and a rally behind the New

York Public Library. The police had cordoned off one lane for the parade, but the barricades got pushed aside as somewhere between 20,000 and 50,000 marchers filled all the lanes of Fifth Avenue. Although few women actually went on strike during the day, thousands participated in lunchtime and after-work demonstrations.

Not every female reporter was as sympathetic as the women at NBC. Linda Charlton reported for *The New York Times,* "In New York, as elsewhere in the country, the impact of the day of demonstrations beyond those already involved or interested in the women's liberation movement appeared to be minimal."[12] I hasten to emphasize that there were no featured interviews—zero—with any of the thousands of women who participated in the march, and whose lives may indeed have been changed by the experience. A small sidebar piece next to the article was headlined "Leading Feminist Puts Hairdo Before Strike."[13] Girls will be girls, of course, and it was eminently newsworthy that Betty Friedan was no exception: she was twenty minutes late for her first scheduled appearance because of a "last minute emergency appointment with her hairdresser." A larger story on the same page, by Grace Lichtenstein, was titled "For Most Women, 'Strike' Day Was Just a Topic of Conversation."[14] The story began, "For the vast majority of women, yesterday was a day simply to go about one's business—whether that meant going to a job, attending a Broadway matinee, having one's hair done or washing the baby's diapers." A female employee of Doyle, Dane and Bernbach was described as spending the day in "the most liberated way possible. She took off to play golf." A spokesman for the Equitable Life Assurance Society told Lichtenstein, "The movement is regarded with some ridicule here." A typist for the company added, "I'm against the whole equality thing. . . . I'm afraid of being drafted." Lichtenstein also interviewed suburban women. As one folded diapers, she said, "Women's liberation? Never thought much about it, really." But those who *had* thought about it apparently eluded the reportorial staff of the nation's newspaper of record.

One of my favorite pieces on the strike was another story in *The Times* titled "Traditional Groups Prefer to Ignore Women's Lib."[15] The Daughters of the American Revolution, the Women's Christian Temperance Union, and the Junior League, which were described as "traditional groups" that had "for decades championed women's rights," were cast as "facing a challenge from a movement that many consider bizarre, alien, and totally unacceptable." The traditionalists, according to the article, considered women of the movement "ridiculous exhibitionists, a 'band of wild lesbians,' " or "communists." Mrs. Saul Schary, incoming president of the National Council of Women, asserted, "There's no discrimination against women like they say there is . . . women themselves are just self-limiting. It's in their nature and they shouldn't blame it on society or men." After describing the women in the movement as self-seeking exhibitionists, she added, "And so many of them are just so unattractive. . . . I wonder if they're completely well."

This was a consistent media device: to have "refined" women denounce "grotesque" women. In its leading editorial on August 27, *The Times* echoed Mrs. Schary's remarks, condemning the demonstrations as "publicity seeking exhibitionism" and "attention getting antics."[16] The newsmagazines were no better. *Time* snickered that the Fifth Avenue march provided "some of the best sidewalk ogling in years" but seemed disappointed that there were no "charred bras."[17] *Newsweek* emphasized that "lib supporters came up short" in getting women out in the streets, except for "small detachments" who formed "unstructured battalions" of presumably warlike, fearsome commandos ready to nuke sexist men and housewives to kingdom come.[18]

On television, the three networks used varying approaches in their coverage. But they had one thing in common: they *all* showcased the Jennings Randolph "bra-less bubblehead quip," giving this bonehead more coverage than any woman involved in the strike. On NBC, the advances of the Saarinen-Quarles-Trotta series were forgotten, as not-so-subtle editing strategies delivered a new message: that the movement was filled with preposterous exaggerations and thus was naturally off-putting to more sensible gals. In the network's footage on strike activities in Washington, DC, viewers saw and heard a black woman in a park singing, "And before I'll be a slave, I'll be buried in my grave. . . . Yes, goodbye slavery, hello freedom." As the woman sang these powerful lyrics about the oppression of slavery, the camera cut to white women in dresses and pearls lounging lazily on the lawn and languorously eating ice cream in the sun while they listened. The striking juxtaposition of the song's lyrics and the images of extremely comfortable women enjoying a leisurely picnic put the lie to claims that women were "oppressed" in any way like other groups had been. In its report on Los Angeles,. NBC showed marchers chanting repeatedly, "Sisterhood is powerful, join us now," as they punched the air with clenched fists. On the words "join us now," the camera zoomed in on two waitresses watching the march who scurried back to safety behind the doors of the restaurant. Again, in pictures alone, without any commentary, NBC conveyed the gap between feminists and "real" women. In his commentary at the end of the program, Frank McGee derided the "nonsense being mouthed today by some of the more extreme members of the current women's liberation movement" and scolded them for trying to make wives and mothers feel inferior. But it was usually McGee and other male commentators, not feminists, who pushed this equation between being a housewife and being inferior.

The coverage on CBS was, not surprisingly, in line with that network's earlier news reports. Right after an ad for Playtex bras, Walter Cronkite introduced the protest by calling its participants a "militant minority of women's liberationists." Of the four stories about the strike from around the country, three were by male reporters, and they discounted the strike and thus the movement as ridiculous, inconsequential, and having little bearing on most women's lives. Bob Schakne in New York opened his story over footage of a small group of women carrying placards with this introduction: "It turned out there weren't a lot of would-be liberated women willing to stop their work for the day in New York. Early demonstrations tended to be small, and the onlookers were by no means always sympathetic." When the film cut to the march on Fifth Avenue, which Schakne severely underrepresented by saying it drew "several thousand people," viewers nonetheless saw an enormous crowd of marchers jamming the street, arm in arm, some with raised fists, some with signs. Schakne noted that "the tone of the protest stayed moderate and orderly. The radical feminists of the movement attempted no confrontation," as if viewers should have expected women in fatigues, firing bazookas.

Bill Kurtis, reporting from Los Angeles that "several hundred" women's liberationists "shared the spotlight with an opposing group," focused on the confrontation between the two groups. As men holding signs reading "Viva la Différence" heckled the feminists, the women turned on them, chanting, "Go do the dishes! Go do the dishes!" Then several women grabbed the signs from the men, tore them in pieces, and threw them back in the men's faces. The strike was thus cast as nothing more elevated than a playground spat. The story then cut to Richard Threlkeld in San Francisco, who announced, "Women's liberation day went largely unnoticed in San Francisco's middle-class neighborhoods, where housewives were too busy just being housewives to pay it all much mind." He interviewed a woman in a supermarket parking lot, who said, "I think it's ridiculous," which evoked a loud and approving chuckle from Threlkeld. She continued, "I think it's stupid. I don't think women should just stay home all the time, but I don't think they belong out either." (Say what?) Another woman, carrying her shopping bags out of the store, said she was a happy housewife and a happy mother, and a third woman echoed this sentiment.

This juxtaposition—in which women with complaints were shown only in highly charged, dramatic, public demonstrations, yelling loudly and tussling with men, while women without complaints were in more tranquil, everyday settings—made women

shoppers opposed to the movement appear more thoughtful, ratio-
nal, and persuasive than their feminist counterparts. The visual positioning of them, in places such as supermarket parking lots, suggested
these women were much more connected to the fabric of daily life.
The juxtaposition also suggested that women had only two choices
of how to be and where to be: compliant, calm, and sexually
rewarded in private; or aggressive, strident, and sexually mocked
in public. The network's pattern of framing the story, especially
Threlkeld's segment, suggested that most women were quite contented with their lot, were well treated financially and emotionally,
and simply could not comprehend a series of complaints that seemed
exaggerated and irrelevant to their lives.

After a commercial break, Eric Sevareid offered his commentary
on the day's events. He dismissed the notion that women were
oppressed, cast women's liberation as a minority movement, and
echoed the feminism-as-disease metaphor by suggesting that it spread
by "contagion" as women's libbers indoctrinated previously happy
women. Yet Sevareid endorsed "three practical aims with which a
great many men also agree: equal opportunities in employment and
education, abortion on demand, and child-care centers. Nor does
this end the list of realistic inequities." So even in the midst of his
pompous dismissal of female oppression, Sevareid put his seal of
approval on three revolutionary feminist goals. How could viewers
not feel torn about feminism when commentators like this kept trying to have it both ways?

Not surprisingly, some of the most smirking coverage came from
ABC, those wonderful folks who gave us Spiro Agnew as the latest
authority on women. Bill Brannigan, reporting from the New York
Stock Exchange, assumed the pose of a man trying very hard to keep
a straight face and struggling, for the sake of "objectivity," to restrain
his sarcasm. "Trading, inside, was not affected by women's liberation.
But outside, there was a bemused sort of traffic congestion. The two
dozen pickets appeared a little unsure of themselves. It was only
when policemen, who outnumbered the pickets, stepped in to sepa-

"Whoa, Mom!
Can't you take it?"

BABY: Shame, mom! You said you'd like to have a baby's easy life—but now that we've changed places, you fuss!

MOM: D'you blame me, lamb? These straps! This wriggling around! If I'm uncomfortable, how does your tender skin stand it?

BABY: Stand it? Mommy, I'm miserable! And now you know, too, why babies need Johnson's Baby Oil and Johnson's Baby Powder!

MOM: Honey, I'll get 'em—quick! Then what do I do?

BABY: Just this, Mom. After my bath

protect my skin all over with pure, gentle Johnson's Baby Oil. And don't forget to use it at diaper changes, to help prevent what my doctor calls "urine irritation!"

Other times, I'll thank you for soft, soothing sprinkles of Johnson's Baby Powder, to help keep chafes and prickles away!

MOM: I haven't been a careful mother, have I? Watch me reform!

BABY: Watch me reform too! With Johnson's to take care of my skin, I won't have half as many howls coming!

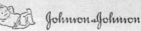Johnson's Baby Oil
Johnson's Baby Powder

Johnson & Johnson

Designed to give every mother nightmares: one of Johnson & Johnson's "Giant Baby" ads, as it appeared in *Life* in 1947. No ad campaign, apparently, was too bizarre when it came to terrorizing our mothers into concentrating all their energies on baby sputum and talcum powder. (*Collection of the author.*)

Jacqueline Kennedy redefined femininity for baby boom girls coming of age in the early 1960s. She was a fashion plate who knew the Greek origin of the word *ostracize*, a wife who knew more languages than her husband, and an American princess with feet twice the size of Cinderella's. (*AP/Wide World Photos.*)

A Summer Place and *Susan Slade* were classic pregnancy melodramas in which "good" girls gave the double standard a giant raspberry. Sandra Dee and Troy Donahue (*above*, in *A Summer Place*) and Connie Stevens and Grant Williams (*below*, in *Susan Slade*) embark here on an unwitting first stage of family planning. (*Courtesy of Movie Still Archives.*)

Don't let these innocent poses fool you. With their number one hit "Will You Love Me Tomorrow?" the Shirelles were the first girl group to give voice to teen-girl sexual desire and spoke to a whole generation of adolescents who were wondering, "Should I? Or shouldn't I?" (*Courtesy of Movie Still Archives.*)

While some girl groups tried to look like good girls, other groups looked bad. With their ratted-up hairdos and don't-mess-with-me black eyeliner, the Ronettes expressed teen-girl rebellion against middle-class suburban mores. (*Courtesy of Movie Still Archives.*)

We screamed, we pulled our hair out, and we breached police barricades throughout the land. But Beatlemania was not some empty-headed mass hysteria; for girls in the mid-sixties, it was a collective jailbreak. (*AP/Wide World Photos.*)

As Holly Golightly in *Breakfast at Tiffany's*, Audrey Hepburn made female bohemianism, a disdain for marriage, and flat-chestedness the height of glamour in the early 1960s. (*Courtesy of Movie Still Archives.*)

As Cricket Blade in *Hawaiian Eye*, Connie Stevens didn't dust furniture or pack lunches like Donna Reed. She got to ride in convertibles with hunky detectives and sing duets with Edd "Kookie" Byrnes, which seemed like a lot more fun than vacuuming. Pictured here with Connie are (*left to right*) Anthony Eisley, Robert Conrad, and Poncie Ponce. (*Courtesy of Movie Still Archives.*)

After her success in *The Miracle Worker*, Patty Duke got stuck with this TV turkey classic, *The Patty Duke Show*, in which she had to convince us that it was genetically and emotionally possible to have an identical cousin. Cathy, the drip, not pictured, though Mom and Dad (Jean Byron and William Schallert) make the cut. (*Courtesy of Movie Still Archives.*)

Sally Field, in her cunning bolero outfit, and flanked by her teddy bear, surfboard, and jaunty musket, as TV's terminally perky Gidget. Perkiness, while at times nauseating, also allowed girls to take control, initiate action, and have some fun—even, at times, at the expense of boys. (*Courtesy of Movie Still Archives.*)

It doesn't take a shrink to decipher why Jeannie's bottle was shaped the way it was, or why Major Nelson was happiest when she was safely contained in it. This woman's power was so formidable that it disrupted the entire manned space program in America. And in this unretouched photograph, Barbara Eden's belly button is visible just above her waistband. (*Courtesy of Movie Still Archives.*)

Beginning with the smash hit *Bewitched* in 1964, women on TV suddenly had magical powers, which men begged them not to use. Despite her dorky husband Darrin, Samantha did get to zap her house clean and turn troublesome men into French poodles, often with the help of her mutinous mother, Endora. (*From left*, Elizabeth Montgomery, Agnes Moorehead, and Dick York.) (*Courtesy of Movie Still Archives.*)

Dismissed by the media as "bra-less bubbleheads," "ridiculous exhibitionists," and "man-haters," feminists organized the first major demonstration for women's liberation at the 1968 Miss America Pageant, when they charged that each contestant was reduced to nothing more than a piece of meat. Women responded in droves, increasing the ranks of women's organizations around the country four-hundred-fold by 1974. (*AP/Wide World Photos.*)

As the feminist the media loved to hate, Kate Millett found herself on the cover of *Time*, artistically rendered as a grim, ball-busting ninja from hell. The article inside noted that Millett didn't wash her hair enough. (*Copyright © 1970 Time Inc. Reprinted by permission.*)

August 16, 1971 / 50 cents

Newsweek

The New Woman

Gloria Steinem

By contrast, Gloria Steinem was adulated by a news media more obsessed with her hair and legs than with her ideas. What stupefied the press was why a woman men slavered over would *ever* become a feminist. *(Copyright © 1971 Newsweek, Inc. All rights reserved. Reprinted by permission.)*

The flouncy hair and string bikinis prompted charges of sexism. But in *Charlie's Angels*, with its unlikely trio of feminist heroines (*from left*, Jaclyn Smith, Farrah Fawcett-Majors, and Kate Jackson), women worked together, for the first time on television, to get the bad guys, not a few of whom were identified in the dialogue as "male chauvinist pigs." (*Courtesy of Movie Still Archives*.)

The mid-seventies brought us countless superwomen who could lift tanks, stop bullets with their bracelets, and run 35 miles per hour. In case you missed the message that women had to be more like men, there was always a thick, knotted Tarzan swing to remind you, here modeled by the Bionic Woman (Lindsay Wagner). (*Courtesy of Movie Still Archives*.)

The wealthy attorney and right-wing activist who portrayed herself as "just a housewife," Phyllis Schlafly helped defeat the ERA by charging that its main purpose was to force women into unisex urinals and infantry units instead of letting them be wives and moms. (*AP/Wide World Photos.*)

Tussling in reflecting pools, wrestling in the mud, and hurling cold cream at each other, Krystle (Linda Evans) and Alexis (Joan Collins) in their legendary catfights on *Dynasty* enacted the pitched battle between feminism and antifeminism that raged throughout the mass media in the 1970s and '80s. (*Courtesy of Movie Still Archives.*)

With their reliance on fake French names, accents and circumflexes run amok, and references to "collagen fibers" and "molecular structures," the cosmetics industry in the 1980s marshaled science and snobbery to declare war on the new woman's most lethal enemy, wrinkles. (*Collection of the author.*)

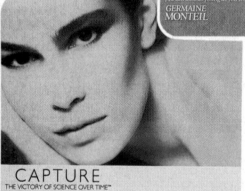

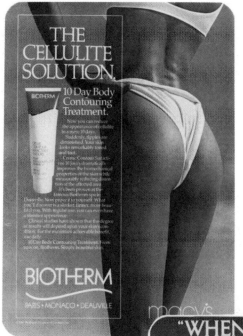

The cosmetics industry invented "cellulite" in the 1970s to describe that portion of the female body between the knee and the waist. To achieve the "buns of steel" that the upscale female workaholic was supposed to have, you could either spend half your life in a health club or slop some Biotherm on your thighs. (*Collection of the author.*)

The media superwoman of the 1980s had a much bigger drill than any man—than any mastodon, for that matter—and used it to obliterate the gaping contradictions surrounding the real women of America, who didn't want to live up to some superhuman standard and, instead, just wanted a break. (*Collection of the author.*)

They packed a piece *and* wore mascara, and if you messed with them you were dead meat. The perfect antidote to *Monday Night Football*, *Cagney and Lacey* (Sharon Gless, *left*, and Tyne Daly) attracted millions of devoted viewers who knew that women could wear makeup and still be tough and successful. (*Courtesy of Movie Still Archives.*)

No longer forced to keep her lips zipped and bake cookies, Hillary Rodham Clinton has galvanized millions of women by blending femininity and feminism. When this brainy and attractive First Lady testified before Congress on behalf of universal health care in September 1993, senators were stupefied to discover that a feminist could wear nice clothes and could even have a sense of humor. (*AP/Wide World Photos.*)

rate demonstrators from pedestrians, that the picket line actually took shape. The chanting was restrained." Over footage of one of these male onlookers helping one of the demonstrators pick up some papers she had dropped, Brannigan observed, "Even though male chauvinism is under attack, chivalry, it appears, is not dead." Not one of the women demonstrators was interviewed.

Then the story switched to Bill Wordham in Los Angeles, who also did not talk with any women involved in the strike but instead gave airtime to a counterdemonstration organized by Jacque Davison, a young, busty bleached blonde in a tight sweater, her hair teased, curled, and varnished, identified on the screen as "anti-women's lib." Here was a story made in heaven for the boys at ABC—a rootin', tootin' catfight. Wordham asked Davison, a housewife with seven children and "proud of it," why she was demonstrating against women's liberation. She responded, "I like being a girl. It's fun. We are free . . . we're freer than you men. I'm sorry to tell you, fellas, but we're freer than you are." Wordham ended, "A few hard-core liberationists [Qu'est-ce que c'est, "hard-core"?] joined the march and there was some pushing and shoving and shouting." The final image from Los Angeles was the catfight between Davison and a feminist demonstrator.

One of the most striking, though hardly surprising, aspects of the media coverage of the women's movement is the way that news organizations repeatedly—almost desperately, one is tempted to note—ignored, erased, and dismissed male opposition to women's liberation. Male commentators and reporters, positioning themselves as the wise, dispassionate onlookers, used their alleged endorsement of equal pay for equal work, or their appreciation of women's thighs, to demonstrate that *they* weren't male chauvinist pigs and to suggest that their other attacks on feminism stemmed not from sexism but from simple common sense. Male observers of the movement weren't hostile; they were "amused." Opposition to the women's movement, reporters insisted, came from women, not men, and they included plenty of interviews with unsympathetic women to prove their point. Rarely, however, were there interviews with male attorneys, college professors, doctors, or corporate executives, let alone with shop foremen, union stewards, or construction workers, about why they had so few women co-workers and how they would regard the entrance of women into their ranks. Men were simply not put on the spot, nor were their attitudes flushed out.

Instead, women with no economic or political power were used as stand-ins for men who opposed feminism. Through this tactic, male journalists could ask why men should support changes even most women didn't want, and they could smirk over one of their favorite events, the catfight, while smiling knowingly and maintaining that women *were* different from men, and weren't the differences cute and delightful. Thus was misogyny naturalized, transformed into a kind of world-weary tolerance of what everyone understood to be women's inherent foibles.

Even if most women *did* want a liberation movement, its success was doomed, according to news accounts, because women were constitutionally incapable of cooperating with one another. Certainly there were real divisions within what was broadly termed the women's movement. Yet by playing up such divisions, the news media reinforced the stereotype that women were completely incompetent as politicians, tacticians, and organizers and had proved, once again, that they didn't deserve to be active anywhere but in the kitchen, the bedroom, and the nursery.

Possibly the most important legacy of such media coverage was its carving up of the women's movement into legitimate feminism and illegitimate feminism. Mainstream journalists, most of whom were men, endorsed a narrow, white, upper-middle-class slice of liberal feminism and cast the rest off as irresponsible, misguided, and deviant. Nearly every story and editorial about the women's movement acknowledged that women really did suffer from economic discrimination and approved of "equal pay for equal work." Many also endorsed child-care centers and the legalization of abortion. They supported, in other words, going through the courts and legislatures

for redress and establishing one or two new institutions to help working mothers. Feminism, in this view, should only redraw the workplace, and this only slightly. Other regions of society, like a man's
home, his marriage, his family, should be cordoned off from feminist
surveyors. Yet for young women like me, these issues were exactly
the locus of the movement: we got it that the personal was indeed
political. While inequities in employment were carefully documented, neither the print media nor television devoted news time to
inequities in marriage, divorce, and child rearing. Critiques of marriage and the family were much too explosive, and hit too close to
home, for male journalists to be comfortable analyzing them. But
since such criticisms were, in 1970, articulated primarily by radical
feminists, they were easy to dismiss as loony and bizarre. This reinforced the media's insistence that the personal was *still* the personal
and should never be politicized. The overall message was that women
had no business trying to imagine wholesale social change; that was
man's work.

Perhaps the biggest difficulty for feminists was that the most basic
and pernicious forms of female oppression did not lend themselves to
visual documentation. Women's real grievances—the burdens, frustrations, and inequities in their lives—occurred behind closed doors.
Unlike the civil rights movement, there were no protesters being
hosed down or attacked by dogs. There was no war footage, or photographs of napalm burning people's skin. There were just these
women, most of whom looked OK on the outside but who were, on
the inside, being torn apart. Feminists had to make the private public, the invisible visible, and the personal political. This was an
extremely difficult assignment, especially with a media increasingly
hooked on dramatic, violent pictures.

Time and again the media emphasized that members of the
women's liberation movement were completely out of touch with,
hostile to, and rejected by most American women, when, in fact,
many women's attitudes toward feminism were much more compli-
cated and were constantly moving toward support. And the move-

ment was much broader-based than the images revealed. No black feminists, with the exception of Shirley Chisholm, appeared in these news stories, even though Florynce Kennedy, Frances Beal, and Eleanor Holmes Norton, to name just a few, were already active in the movement.

The news media's ambivalent representation of feminism was simultaneously empowering and crippling, for it legitimated middle-class, liberal feminism and applauded legalistic reform at the same time that it dramatized the severe psychological and emotional costs to women who challenged patriarchal versions of female sexuality and who publicly violated the boundary between the public (male) and private (female) spheres. The word *militant* was tossed around all too loosely to marginalize any woman who wanted more than a few legislative reforms and served to demonize female behavior that refused to remain friendly, accommodating, compliant, docile, and obsequious. Women, in other words, might get pay raises and child-care centers if they just asked nicely and kept smiling at men. Karate images, which overflowed with anxieties about female anger, male castration, and the possible dissolution of amicable heterosexual relations, marked "militant feminism" as a potentially deadly trend. And the repeated use of *militant* as an adjective imparted to many feminists attitudes from female separatism to a love of violence that they did not, in fact, embrace.

But let's consider what else we did see and hear, and why such coverage may have been empowering to some women viewers. The media did enable us to hear speakers on television attack the sexual objectification of women and the impossible beauty standards imposed by advertisers. They provided a platform for women furious over their inability to control their own bodies and their reproductive lives. They showed us women challenging men in the streets, chanting at them to "go do the dishes." I remember being initially intrigued and repelled by what I saw. At the age of twenty, I had just discovered how much fun boys could really be, and now this? At first I bought into the media dismissal that comfy young women like me couldn't possibly be oppressed. And the reduction of sophisticated feminist critiques into "man-hating" made me wary. But, like millions, I stayed tuned; I read *The Female Eunuch* and *The Golden Notebook;* and I woke up. The messages from feminists I saw and heard in the news resonated with my own experiences, while the representation of women in ads and TV shows undermined my aspirations and ambitions. So when Harry Reasoner trashed the women's movement from his privileged podium on ABC, it made me even more angry, more committed to feminism, and more determined than ever to hurl a series of expletives—or whatever else was handy—at the next paunchy, middle-aged man I met (and I met too many of them) who treated me as if I couldn't possibly be serious about having a career of my own.

While the coverage repudiated feminists as ugly, humorless, disorderly man-haters in desperate need of some Nair, it also endorsed selected feminist principles, particularly those premised on equality of opportunity. It showed that while women who got together in the public sphere were subject to male derision, they could also change society. And at the same time that radical feminists and their often shocking pronouncements were marginalized, portions of their vision were folded into the mainstream, thus reconfiguring what constituted the middle ground.

The news coverage pinioned women between the same messages we had grown up with, only now the stakes were higher. On the one hand, by endorsing a few liberal reforms like equal pay, the media reinforced the message that women had every right to expect to be treated as equal citizens, with the same rights, responsibilities, and opportunities as men. On the other hand, by mocking and dismissing the way feminist activists looked and behaved, and by marginalizing many of their critiques of society, the media also endorsed the notion that in some cases female subordination and sexual objectification were not only fine but desirable. In one moment, the media exhorted women to be equal and active; in the next, they urged them to be subordinate and passive. Sound familiar? We had been hearing it all our lives.

What was different now was that many women, especially young women, were aware of these contradictions and pointed to them in their demonstrations, newsletters, and speeches, holding them up as untenable. Understanding that the internal conflicts we faced weren't our own lonely struggle but resulted from being raised female in America was, in the language of the times, mind-blowing, and, as such, a colossal relief. Finally, the demonstrators and the female reporters said, out loud, on television, that women were in an absolutely impossible situation because they couldn't ever live up to the mutually exclusive traits society demanded. Women like me started to seek some kind of satisfactory resolution to these contradictions, not in ourselves but in society. We had become conscious not only of our inequality but also of how our identities had been fragmented. The warring pieces, we saw, were virtually impossible to hold together without constant posing, dissembling, and the abandonment of our own needs and desires.

There were other blind spots in the media coverage that worked to women's advantage. The media failed to convey the exhilaration of participating in the women's movement. Yes, there were divisions, battles, and internecine strife. But there was also a compelling utopian vision, a great unity of purpose, and a respect for diversity. Once a woman experienced the sheer joy of uniting with her sisters to effect personal and societal change, only to see on television and in the press an image of grimness and humorlessness, it was hard to trust the media again. The antidote to this was the consciousness-raising group, which spread rapidly throughout the country, forming an alternative, behind-the-spotlight communications center for women to discuss what the news ignored or belittled. These underground networks were quite consciously independent of and often at odds with the dominant media. Here, working through their ambivalent positions, women came to appreciate how they had been socialized—especially by the media—to be all things to all people. Now, when we went back and forth between the girl talk of our groups and the mostly boy talk of the news, we understood more clearly why much of what we had grown up with on TV, and what we still saw, made us uncomfortable, insecure, and furious. We learned—and loved—the power of rejecting media pronouncements and of giving guys like Howard K. Smith a big Bronx cheer. We also learned that feminism itself, unlike the one-dimensional caricature we saw in the media, was many things to different women. It was becoming apparent that there were as many ways to adopt a feminist perspective as there were ways to be a woman. Most important, we realized that it was within our power to accept or resist the new stereotypes, picking up some shards, kicking away others. Feminism, like womanhood itself, became a pastiche.

While the media helped spread the word about feminism, producing converts and enemies, they had one particularly pernicious, lasting effect. By demonizing prominent feminists like Kate Millett, the media effectively gutted one of feminism's most basic challenges to gender roles: that women should be taken seriously and treated with respect regardless of whether they were conventionally "attractive." The media countermanded this heresy, not only in the news but through entertainment shows in the 1970s that offered up Charlie's Angels and the Bionic Woman as the new exemplars of the liberated woman. The media representation of feminism reinforced the division between the acceptable and the deviant, between the refined and the grotesque, between deserving ladies and disorderly dogs. This false dichotomy helped to reaffirm, more than ever, the importance of female attractiveness to female success, and the utter folly of taking to the streets. Even as the media attention accelerated the spread of the women's movement throughout the country, it stunted the movement's most liberatory potential, a handicap that cripples all of us, women and men alike, to this day.

CHAPTER 9

The Rise of the Bionic Bimbo

OK, you want to talk backlash, let's talk backlash. Not to take anything away from the 1980s, which brought us *Fatal Attraction* and news stories about women over thirty-five being more likely to receive a terrorist's bullet than a marriage proposal, but the backlash that accompanied the women's liberation movement suggests that testosterone poisoning reached epidemic proportions in the early 1970s. Backlash didn't need time to build up; backlash didn't wait for feminism to settle in. Backlash was there from the moment women took to the streets, barking and nipping at their heels. The war between feminism and antifeminism in the early 1970s raged throughout the media in an explicit, no-holds-barred action. For at the same time that the news media were bringing feminism—including radical feminism—into people's living rooms and thus helping, despite the negative coverage, produce more converts to the cause, the entertainment media were trying to figure out how to capitalize on feminism while containing it.

This ideological warfare about woman's proper place was the prevailing subtext of American popular culture in the 1970s, and the backlash against feminism showed spectators like me how very right feminists were about the persistence and immobility of sexism. This backlash made me more committed to feminism than ever, and eager to shed many—but not all—of the holdover trappings of 1960s femininity. At the same time, however, the backlash was filled with cautionary tales about what happens to women who are too angry, are too outspoken, and get too much freedom. These new media tales recycled the familiar female caricatures, updating the age-old drama about how assertive a woman could be and still be approved by men.

The pop culture versions of the liberated woman were meant, it seems in retrospect, to be a compromise between the demands of feminists and the resistance of antifeminists. But they were also a powerful tool for managing an extremely threatening, even revolutionary, social movement. Now, as I've said before, it wasn't that six white guys with cigars and white loafers conspired together to repackage feminism so it would help sell Lestoil or Oil of Olay. But media moguls work in a highly insulated environment, trusting their "guts" as much as, or often more than, the market research they get.[1] Given their insularity and the rampant sexism of the industry in the 1970s, it's not surprising that they came up with similar responses— a mix of concessions liberally larded with dire warnings.

What was different, however, about the 1970s was that now millions of women had a sense that it was their right and responsibility to deconstruct these images even as they felt their pull. Nearly every pseudofeminist gambit on television, from *The Mary Tyler Moore Show* to *Charlie's Angels,* produced a host of public analyses and attacks by women who agreed that imagery and symbolism mattered to our everyday lives and our political futures.

To taste just a few samples of backlash 1970s style, let's begin with my favorite newscasters, those highly objective, dispassionate types over at ABC News. Harry Reasoner, who had already made his views about the women's movement perfectly clear, became rabid over the publication of that pioneering feminist magazine many of us eagerly awaited, *Ms.* The magazine was first published as a forty-page insert in the December 20, 1971, issue of *New York,* then as a magazine all its own a month later.

I still recall the visceral fury I felt when watching Reasoner's commentary on December 21. He opened by describing the magazine as "pretty sad" because "it is so clearly just another in the great but irrelevant tradition of American shock magazines" that do things like "expose the chemical composition of Coca-Cola" or publish nude photos of Marilyn Monroe. Such magazines "usually last about three issues," the fate he confidently predicted for *Ms.* To succeed, magazines need someone of H. L. Mencken's caliber, "but there is no sign in *Ms.*—or indeed in the whole women's movement—of an H. L. Mencken," since how could any woman be as smart or sardonic as the Bard of Baltimore? Reasoner acknowledged that "the girls who are putting together *Ms.* are prettier and probably brighter than Ralph Ginsberg, who seems to publish most of the shock magazines. But the only thing they are more than H. L. Mencken is prettier."

After equating *Ms.* with pornography and tabloid journalism, he went on to an assessment of the first issue itself. "There isn't an article in *Ms.* that wouldn't look perfectly all right in one of the standard women's magazines, and has probably already been there, only somewhat better written," he sniped cattily. But the main problem for the editors and writers of *Ms.* was that "they've said it all in the first little issue. I can imagine some stark, antisexist editorial meeting trying to decide what to do next." He and several of his friends had discussed betting on the magazine's longevity, but none of them would put money on its lasting more than five issues. Pronouncing the magazine DOA, Reasoner ended his commentary with "I'm sorry—I'm sorry," the tone indicating the girls were dreaming if they hoped for the magazine actually to last.

But ABC couldn't let even this level of fulmination lie. Harry apparently got his colleague Howard K. Smith so exercised that the next night he, too, had to weigh in on the women's movement. "Among the multitude of causes in this cause-ridden age, one that has not, to me at least, made its case is women's lib," he began, echoing his line at the time of the Women's Strike for Equality. He admitted that there was prejudice against women in some fields, including journalism, but, he hastened to note, "there are prejudices against every class of human," including TV reporters, "but they aren't about to make a federal case out of it," as if there was any correspondence between people's irritation with guys like him and the legal and social discrimination women faced every day. The real truth, according to Smith, was that we lived in a matriarchy that was getting stronger and more fearsome every minute. "Women dominate our elections; they probably own most of the nation's capital wealth; any man who thinks he, and not his wife, runs his family is dreaming," he asserted falsely, then described Bella Abzug as "the politician I would least dare to make an enemy of, excepting, perhaps, Shirley Chisholm." To prove that there was no such thing as inequality and discrimination against women, that women were already plenty liberated, he cited Indira Gandhi and Golda Meir, known for their "toughness." "So I'm not persuaded by women's lib—indeed, there may be a case for man's lib."

Smith apparently was ignorant of the following facts, which his commentary erased but which help explain why *Ms.* did not meet the fate Harry Reasoner so glibly predicted for it. In 1970, women earned 58 percent of what men did, and forty-three states limited the number of hours women could work, generally to eight a day, meaning overtime and other job opportunities were forbidden to them by law. Some states restricted the amount of weight a woman could carry on the job—anywhere from ten to thirty-five pounds, in other words, the weight of a child from infancy to kindergarten. Most women in 1970 found it impossible to get a mortgage or a credit card in their own names, and in many states a woman's income and property were legally under her husband's control.[2] So much for the matriarchy theory. On January 25, 1972, the first full issue of *Ms.* appeared, and I remember running to the newsstand to get my copy. Apparently, so did thousands of others—250,000 issues were sold out in eight days, and 35,000 women sent in subscription cards.[3] Blow that up your shorts, Harry.

But backlash was hardly restricted to the news media. The women's liberation movement also provided fodder for TV shows from *The Beverly Hillbillies* to *All in the Family,* and you will hardly be surprised to learn that the portrait of feminism in these quarters was less than charitable. Ridicule often took the form of placing feminist rhetoric in the mouths of ridiculous sitcom characters. I mean, how can you take complaints about oppression seriously when they're uttered by Ellie May, let alone Granny, the rolling pin–wielding, karate-chopping matriarch who terrorized men? In a scene from one *Beverly Hillbillies* episode titled, simply enough, "Women's Lib," Granny and Ellie May are parading around the kitchen with placards. When Jethro comes in and sees the one reading "Free Women," he yelps, "I'm gonna git me one of them!" to the delight of the laugh track. Archie Bunker's daughter, Gloria, the Kewpie doll on *All in the Family*, yells to Archie after having scanned a book on feminism, "We're tired of being exploited by men—tired of you holding us down and keeping us back. And if you continue to exploit us, we're gonna rise up against you someday like our black sisters and our Chicano sisters and I don't even know what I'm saying anymore." So much for feminism being anchored in lived experience and genuine conviction.

Not to be outdone, *Green Acres*, with Eva Gabor and Eddie Albert, featured "The Liberation Movement." Lisa (Gabor) attends her women's club meeting to hear a guest speaker from the Women's Liberation League, which Oliver (Albert) refers to as "one of those bra-burning groups." When she returns from the meeting, she has been transformed into an enraged, jargon-spouting feminazi who yells at Oliver, "All men treat women as second-class citizens because they're afraid to give them equal status. You make me look like a fool in front of my friends. Men are afraid of women, that they'll take over the world because they are smarter." She continues, "From now on, I am not going to walk four paces behind you in bare feet with a laundry bag on my head." Now, since Lisa spent much of her time flouncing around in chiffon, ostrich feathers, and gemstones the size of Fig Newtons, completely unable to cook or manage the household, the viewer saw immediately that feminist generalizations about domestic life certainly didn't apply here, and therefore, they might not apply elsewhere. Oliver insists, "Lisa, you already have equal rights." She is unmoved. "You should do the housework one day, and

I the next, and we will live happily ever after." By now, Oliver is pissed. "Is that what that nut woman told you? Don't you women realize what a nice, soft touch you've got the way it is? All you have to do is vacuum a rug, make a bed, do a few dishes." Lisa shoots back, "You're leaving out the *hard* part." Here Lisa itemizes the true nature of women's oppression. "Have you ever waited for an hour and a half for your nails to dry? Have you ever tried to make an appointment at a beauty parlor before a holiday? Have you ever put on a red dress and found that you don't have shoes to match?"

Lisa decides she wants to reverse sex roles and be called Max. She insists that any woman can do the "man's work" around the house as easily as any man. She appears for this work in skintight blue satin overalls. She quickly discovers, however, that fixing the shed and other chores are quite beyond her, so she secretly hires handymen to do the tasks for her but leads Oliver to believe that she has done them herself. She also discovers that Oliver doesn't really want to sleep with her now that she's liberated. Finally she admits, "I'm not too happy about this liberation thing. Tomorrow why don't I go back to being the woman and you the man?" She immediately regains her desirability. "Why do we have to wait until tomorrow?" Oliver asks slyly.

The episode's message is transparent. Feminism comes from outside the home, from initially persuasive but shallow propaganda that infects women and turns them into something they're not. There is no basis for feminism in women's everyday, lived experiences, because women aren't truly oppressed. To be equal to men, and to be able to do what men do, women have to pretend and lie, since equality is impossible. Plus, if men and women really were equal, men could never get it up again since women would no longer be attractive.

Even teen romance comics, the ones filled with busty, red-lipped girls who cry their eyes out in one panel and kiss some guy named Chad or Dusty in the next, got into the act. As with the notorious "headlight" comics of the late 1940s, comics in the early 1970s were a key repository of antifeminism. Comics like "Our Love Story," "Girls' Love," "Young Romance," and "Falling in Love" featured story lines in which young women think that what they want is a career, only to discover that this ambition makes them repulsive to men and no fun to be with. In one story, a misguided girl named Pam learns that she won't get the promotion she wants, in part because her clothes are frumpy. "You're probably a pretty girl when you're not wearing those business suits or that sack you've got on!" her boss tells her at a party. (This was before women had a name for such power-tripping drivel, sexual harassment.) Pam ducks into the ladies' room and strips down to the foxy little hot pants number she couldn't resist wearing under her dowdy feminist costume, and now the reception is quite different. Her boss exclaims, "Pamela! Like WOW!" while the male co-worker she had been competing with for the promotion looks at her in quite a different light. In the final frame, as the two of them kiss that comic book kiss, the balloon over Pam's closed eyes reads, "The moment our lips met . . . I knew! My preoccupation with women's lib had ended. . . . I was surrendering!"[4]

This backlash, however, began to mingle with deep confusion in the entertainment industry. Just what were they going to do about women, anyhow, especially if some of them followed Gloria Steinem while others were lining up behind Phyllis Schlafly, who emerged in 1973 as the George Patton of antifeminism? More to the point, feminists in academia had begun cranking out hundreds of studies of how women were depicted in ads, soap operas, comic books, women's magazines, movies, and sitcoms, and the results of many of these studies were published in popular magazines. Caroline Bird critiqued the portrayal of women in "What's Television Doing for 50.9 Percent of Americans?" in a 1971 issue of *TV Guide,* charging, "Television . . . does not provide human models for a bright thirteen-year-old girl who would like to grow up to be something other than an ecstatic floor waxer." Leonard Gross, also in *TV Guide,* charged the networks with bias against women.[5] Other articles, like "TV's Women Are Dingbats," "Women Get the Short End of the Shtick," and "Same Time, Same Station, Same Sexism," documented that despite the superficial appearance of change on TV with shows like *The Mary Tyler Moore Show* and *Police Woman,* the medium was as sexist as, possibly even more sexist, than in the days of *Our Miss Brooks, Oh, Susanna,* and *I Love Lucy.*[6]

Study after study showed that women were severely underrepresented on television, and that the ones we saw were exceptionally attractive, slim, sociable, accommodating, dependent, helpless, incompetent, and under thirty-five. They almost always smiled. Seventy percent of all TV characters in the early 1970s were male; 40 percent of these boys were over forty, but only 15 percent of the girls were. Women continued to be typecast as homemakers, secretaries, nurses, and, with increasing frequency, crime victims. Single and working women were especially likely to take it in the chops, while married women who didn't work received the most favorable treatment in TV land.[7] Three-quarters of those television commercials that featured women were for products to make you, your bathroom, or your clothes stop smelling bad; women were rarely used in ads for cars or gasoline, which most women used with more frequency than they did Lysol. But whether an ad featured women or not, the sales pitch had to be clinched by the male voice of authority: men accounted for nearly 90 percent of all voice-overs in TV ads.[8] In print ads, female models were frequently posed to look like children: wide-eyed, often in a puckish, clowning pose, being carried piggyback by some guy or kicking their legs in the air, and, in general, doing things you would never see a male model doing. Gazing up at men, physically leaning on men, and regularly pictured lying on floors, rugs, beds, and sofas, the display of women's bodies in ads was defined by submission, passivity, incompetence, and deference to male authority.[9] It wasn't just radical feminists who read about and believed these studies. As early as 1972, 75 percent of the 120,000 respondents to a questionnaire in *Redbook* agreed that "the media degrades women by portraying them as mindless dolls."[10]

The women's liberation movement, and the studies like this that it generated, threw TV producers, news organizations, and filmmakers into a complete tizzy. Women were the major consumers of much of this media, yet there, on the news and in the pages of *Ms.*, *Redbook*, *The New York Times*, and even *TV Guide*, feminists were attacking media imagery of women with a vengeance—and an accuracy—that hit home for millions of us. "What to do, what to do?" you could hear media executives asking themselves, not wanting to alienate "traditional women" yet desperate not to lose the young upscale women receptive to feminism (an enormous chunk of the market). They knew they had to react—but had yet to figure out how. Plus, there was schizophrenia among producers themselves. Some were hard-core male chauvinists who thought acting, for women, consisted of wearing a G-string and a smile, but others were persuaded by some versions of women's liberation and knew their audience was too. All this marketing uncertainty and ambivalence added to the contradictory media reaction to and co-optation of feminism in the 1970s.

Hollywood's solution was simple: Hey, let's just pretend women don't exist for a few years while all this blows over. Good parts for women in films became scarcer than circle pins. Instead, we got road movies, buddy pictures, or some combination of both: *Easy Rider*, *Butch Cassidy and the Sundance Kid*, *Midnight Cowboy*, *M*A*S*H*, *Deliverance*, *The Sting*, and *The Last Detail*. The prize roles for women were Jane Fonda as a prostitute in *Klute* and Diana Ross as a victimized drug addict in the biopic about Billie Holliday, *Lady Sings the Blues*. Females, especially pushy ones, got to be deranged slashers, as in *Play Misty for Me*, screeching, hysterical victims trapped in a sinking ocean liner in *The Poseidon Adventure*, or possessed Antichrists who spewed split pea soup at Mom and a few priests. Or, as in *Last Tango in Paris*, they got to take all their clothes off and be sodomized with the help of some Land O'Lakes while the bloated male lead was protected from the certain embarrassment of having to strip down.

And, of course, in films like the blockbuster *Billy Jack,* they got to be tied up spread-eagle to stakes and raped. But mostly, in the early and mid-1970s, women were invisible in the movies. The medium that had responded most rapidly to changing sexual mores in the late 1950s and early 1960s was one of the slowest to respond to the changing status of women in the early 1970s. Women having sex they could deal with; women having aspirations, hey, that was something else.

By contrast, television, which in the late 1950s and early '60s pretended there was no such thing as sex, responded almost immediately to feminism and sought to manage and contain the threat it posed while seeming to accommodate it. After the initial backlash of 1970 and 1971, television became a highly contested terrain in the struggle not just between feminism and antifeminism but over what type of feminism was going to become accepted into the mainstream. The first sitcom with an avowedly feminist character came in a spin-off from *All in the Family. Maude,* which debuted in September 1972 and was an instant hit, became the fourth highest rated show of the 1972–73 season. Most men I knew hated the show; nearly every woman I knew loved it. Maude, played with relish by Bea Arthur, was not young, or skinny, or conventionally "pretty," which was, in many ways safe, because it would have been much too threatening to have a sweet young thing say—and do—what Maude did. At five feet eleven inches, she was as tall as, or taller than, most men, and *Time* described her as having "the voice of a diesel truck in second gear."[11]

Outspoken, sharp-tongued, and sarcastic, eager to take on any man in a debate about politics and especially about the status of women, Maude said all the things you wished you had said when, at 2:00 A.M., you reviewed how badly you'd handled your day, and how you had failed to stand up, verbally, to men you wanted to kill. The deep pitch of her voice and her willingness to yell and to engage in verbal fisticuffs were central to the show's big joke: women who had not severed the cords between their opinions, needs, and desires and their voice boxes were so unusual that they were, well, funny. When visiting Edith Bunker, her cousin, Maude refuses to cater to Archie's expectation that he will be waited on hand and foot, and even has the effrontery to sit in his chair. After he fails to respond to her call that breakfast is ready, she goes upstairs, pulls the pillow out from under him, and announces, "Are you waiting for a special invitation? I said breakfast is on the table. . . . You can either come to the table and eat or lie there and feed off your own fat." In another episode, as she waits next to an examining table for her gynecologist, she places her hands deliberately on the stirrups and sighs, "Just once, I'd love to get a doctor in these." When her mother describes her love for her husband as "biting my tongue and standing behind him right or wrong," Maude counters, "If you think that's love, then you're a horse's patootie."

Maude was a thrilling catharsis—a woman with a mouth on her—and probably what was most thrilling about her was her refusal to compromise or to take on any of the conventional guises of femininity. The most heated controversy of the 1972–73 television season was the two-part show "Maude's Dilemma," when Maude, discovering herself pregnant at age forty-seven, decides to get an abortion. No sitcom woman had ever done this before.

But Maude was also fearsome, an often unyielding battle-ax, a caricature herself of the older, privileged American woman who constantly castrates her little worm of a husband. At the same time that Maude ridiculed sexism and male privilege, she reinforced the stereotype of the feminist as a strident, loud, unfeminine bruiser who could afford to be a feminist because she was older, less needy of male approval, and financially comfortable. She was contrasted to her neighbor Vivian (Rue McClanahan), an overly accommodating, hyperfeminized ditz. Were these our choices, the ball-busting harridan or the doormat? Hey, hadn't we seen these choices before? We wanted to speak our minds, to reconnect our voices to *all* of our inner selves, not just the polite ones. But *Maude,* liberal politics and all, suggested that if we did—if we really did—we'd be as feared and as laughed at as Maude. Younger viewers like me felt that compromise was still a way of life. And we wanted to see these compromises on TV and in the movies, but in a way that preserved female dignity. With a few isolated exceptions, we were to be sorely disappointed.

Black women fared no better, and it's certainly easy to argue that they fared worse. After decades of invisibility on television, punctuated by the overly sappy *Julia,* in which Diahann Carroll broke the color barrier by getting a lead in a sitcom, black women began to get roles, but most often as oversized, forbidding matriarchs whose dialogue consisted primarily of yelling at men and ridiculing their husbands. The black female voice on TV was even more forbidding than Maude's. The most terrifying was Aunt Esther (LaWanda Page) of *Sanford and Son,* who threatened Fred Sanford with warnings like "I'm gonna jump down your throat and stomp on your liver" while she chased after him brandishing an umbrella or other weapon, ready to strike. In return, he constantly insulted her appearance, driving home how hideous women become once they are older and have some opinions. In *Good Times* (itself a spin-off from *Maude*), Esther Rolle was infinitely more sympathetic as a strong and caring wife and mother, but many of the same stereotypes clung to her, as they did to Louise Jefferson in *The Jeffersons.* Black female characters in the early 1970s fell into either the stereotype of the hefty, asexual, loud-mouthed, castrating, domineering woman who wasn't really a woman at all—like Flip Wilson's drag character Geraldine—or the exotic tigress much more sexualized than her white sisters. Even as black women on TV were given louder and more demanding voices, the media further negated and silenced them.

Other sitcoms in the early 1970s participated in the drama of the struggle for the female voice, how it should be used and what it should and should not say. *The Mary Tyler Moore Show* and its spin-offs *Rhoda* and *Phyllis* showed women of varying marital status working outside the home, and *The Mary Tyler Moore Show* was held up both as a sign of progress and as an example of recalcitrant sexism in the representation of women's lives. Because it was, when it first aired in 1970, the only major TV show with a single woman in the title role, it became a lightning rod for feminist criticisms and aspirations. And few shows embodied more perfectly the intertwining of traditional femininity with new feminist ambitions. In a masterful balancing act, the show spoke powerfully to women yet domesticated feminism at the same time.[12] Sure, Mary Richards was out on her own working in a good job and, in contrast to her man-chasing friend Rhoda with the New York accent, not slavering to give up that job to get married. She called up men for dates, and she fended off men she didn't like. She made it clear that solitude was vastly preferable to spending time with some oaf, just because he was a man. But why, asked feminists, did a TV producer call her male boss Mr. Grant when everyone else in the entire office building called him Lou and he, like everyone else, took the liberty of calling her Mary? Why, if she really was a producer, was she most frequently seen typing, serving as Ann Landers to other staffers, and replacing the flower in the vase on her desk? Why, demanded feminists, must the media always take away with one hand what they had just given us with the other?

These criticisms point to the major conflict for women, particularly middle-class women, that *The Mary Tyler Moore Show* addressed: just how assertive could, or should, the "new woman" be? The logo for the show's production company said it all: the familiar MGM wreath, but instead of a roaring lion in the middle, there was a mewing kitten, finally at center stage, but never, ever, able to roar. Much of the commentary on *MTM* at the time misread the show, I think, taking one snapshot of it at a particular moment and making pronouncements about its cultural significance. Either it was retrograde (no TV producer did the menial jobs Mary did) or it was progressive (she was independent, lived alone, and had a career). These wildly varying responses simply illustrate how open this show, and Moore's performance in it, were to various readings by different women.

Mary's struggle to blend assertiveness with submission and diplomacy was best exemplified by her gestures, her facial expressions, and, especially, her language. Simultaneously feisty and meek, Mary often took one step forward and two steps back as she sought to find the middle ground for herself between traditional femininity and the new womanhood. The part of her body most engaged in this struggle was her larynx. At times, in fact, it seemed as if Moore was caricaturing the way women repeatedly use words and phrases like "maybe," "perhaps," "have you considered," and "I don't know how to say this, but . . ." to cushion the impact of a request, demand, or refusal. She also stuttered, paused, and let her voice trail off when she was being pressed to tell some boor what she really thought of him or to assert a position at work. Mary used her voice to dramatize the ongoing struggle for women to speak their minds, even after the women's movement. As soon as she raised her voice, she muted it. It was as if her vocal cords alternated between femininity and feminism.

In the first episode, when Lou Grant interviews Mary for a job, he starts asking her what religion she is and whether she's married. She responds, "I don't know how to say this, but you're not allowed to ask that when someone's applying for a job." She then blurts out the answers to the personal questions. As Grant persists, she stands up as if to leave, raising her voice slightly and saying, with a quaver, "You've been asking a lot of personal questions that don't have a thing to do with my qualifications for the job." It's clear this was not easy for Mary Richards to say, but she did say it. Yet right after this defiance, as soon as she is hired for the job, she almost cants her head and, eyes down, gives every indication she will be an obedient employee. In the same episode, when Rhoda asserts that the apartment Mary expects to move into is really hers and that Mary should get out, Mary protests, "You think I'm a pushover, don't you? Well, if you push me, I might have to push back—and hard." Rhoda doesn't buy this for a minute and scoffs, "You can't carry that off," to which a deflated Mary admits, as her voice slides down several octaves and decibels, "I know." Yet Mary keeps the apartment. She also insists that her breakup with her boyfriend of two years was "my choice," and when he comes to town to try to rekindle their romance, she appreciates, yet again, that he's not committed enough to her and tells him good-bye. When he tells her to take care of herself, she answers, "I think I just did."

At times Mary Richards was completely compliant, a lady, putting herself through contortions to spare others' feelings. At other times she was absolutely definite, standing up for her rights as a woman and a worker. Most frequently, she asserted herself with one phrase or sentence but couched the assertion in such a stuttering, roundabout manner that it hardly seemed like an assertion at all. Mary's specialty was this deployment of linguistic camouflage, using verbal decoys of compliance to achieve what she wanted. Through Mary, women's desires for independence, autonomy, and respect were expressed and validated, yet also choked off, swallowed, muted. We identified powerfully with this pas de deux, for few real-life dramas for women in the 1970s were more difficult than the tension between speaking the truth and hedging it, or even, in the end, keeping quiet.

As the show progressed into the mid- and late 1970s, the Mary Richards character evolved as well, becoming more assured, more sarcastic, more authoritative. Without ever being explicitly feminist—the writers deliberately avoided women's rights issues[13]—the show subtly dramatized the ideological molting process that young women were experiencing as the decade wore on. The Mary we first met after the theme song asked "How will you make it on your own?" lived on her own and liked it, and was "gonna make it after all." But she also smiled too much, was too eager to please, and usually couldn't say no to job demands or to needy friends. As the seasons passed, however, she became less concerned about sparing people's feelings and more assertive about protecting her independence—all diplomatically, of course. The show, then, validated the struggle of many working women to make the workplace more humane, shaped as much by traditional "female" values of nurturance, praise, and mutual support as by traditional "male" values of cutthroat competition, criticism, and individualism.

The men in the show offered caricatures of patriarchy. Ted Baxter, the self-important, narcissistic anchorman, showed that behind the distinguished silver hair and baritone voice of the news announcer who told us the way it was there was a shallow, ignorant, preening imbecile who understood nothing. The gruff and insensitive Lou Grant couldn't express his feelings and had an impoverished personal life. Murray Slaughter was a eunuch, forced to write copy for Ted Baxter and disappointed in his own ambitions. Mary was the most balanced, sensible, and happy of them all. But there was the inevitable unspoken warning: don't aspire to too much success or power—look what it does to men, think of what it would do to a woman. More important, Mary was idealized by all three men, each of whom had a bit of a crush on her and who, in one episode, even fantasized about marrying her. We were reminded, week in and week out, that this adulation came from Mary's traits as a caring, nurturing, ever-supportive, smiling woman who would never be too pushy or demand too much, a woman who didn't raise her voice, a woman who knew how to ask for things without seeming like she wanted anything for herself. Old contradictions never die; they just get new outfits.

There was also another unfolding drama, this one about female friendship and sisterhood. In the first four seasons, Mary lived in an apartment building that resembled a female dorm. Rhoda was upstairs, Phyllis was downstairs, and the three often met in Mary's apartment to talk about their work, their lives, and men. The woman's world of Mary's apartment balanced the man's world of work. But when Rhoda and Phyllis were "spun off" into series of their own in 1974 and 1975, Mary no longer had her sisterly support group.[14] Now the only women in her life were Georgette, Ted Baxter's ditzy wife, and Sue Ann Nivens, the female barracuda who ate men—and little girls like Mary—for breakfast. These women weren't sisters, and Sue Ann made it quite clear that she could regard Mary only as competition. When one of Mary's female relatives, her Aunt Flo, a seasoned journalist, appeared, we saw an older, high-powered, insensitive, overly aggressive career woman who made Mary feel inadequate. This move from the female camaraderie of the show to Mary's isolation from women and increased alliance with men mirrored other subtle, and not so subtle, negations of sisterhood elsewhere in the mass media as the 1970s progressed.

In these years, television was wrestling with what to do not only with women's voices but with their bodies as well. The conflict over women's new sexual freedom was staged, most frequently, on cop shows. The 1974–75 season saw the debut of two new trends on television, one the mirror image of the other. In *Police Woman,* starring Angie Dickinson as Sgt. Pepper Anderson, and *Get Christie Love,* with Teresa Graves, the barrier against women having the title role in a cop show was broken. (*Get Christie Love* was meant to break the color barrier as well, but the show only lasted one season, possibly because viewers didn't quite buy a female cop who smirked suggestively to criminals, "You're under arrest, sugah.") And so women wouldn't get too cocky, another barrier, a long-held TV taboo, was also broken in that season. It was now OK to discuss and portray the crime of rape, and soon women were getting raped everywhere, especially on shows like *Police Woman.* George Gerbner, then dean of the Annenberg School of Communication and a leading authority on television violence, decried the "counterattack on the women's movement" that involved such "tactics of terror" as "the institutionalization of rape."[15] But the counterattack escalated in *The Streets of San Francisco, Kojak, Mannix,* and other detective/cop shows, where we often got to see and/or overhear the woman gasp, cry, and whimper as she was violated for the viewing audiences' supposed pleasure. Ironically, it was on shows like *Police Woman*—allegedly a sop to women, but created, produced, and written by men—that we saw the height of the backlash.

First, let's consider the character "Pepper," her name neither masculine nor feminine, but one you might give to your cat. Angie Dickinson proposed the name herself, saying, "Somehow I can't imagine a woman police officer named 'Lisa.' "[16] The opening

sequence of the show, which juxtaposes shots of her legs descending
a staircase, action shots of her with gun in hand, images of her face
frozen with fear as she's being attacked, and close-ups of her breasts,
established the centrality of her sexuality to her success on the job.
The gorgeous, blond, and husky-voiced Pepper's main job as a cop
was to go undercover as a prostitute, stripper, gangster's moll, or
aspiring porno queen to set the black widow's trap. But she wasn't
the predator, she was the prey. As the sexy, luscious bait, in her low-
cut, fringed sheath or jumpsuit, Pepper was invariably found out by
the bad guys and always had to be rescued by the white, male cavalry,
the *real* cops headed by Lt. Bill Crowley (Earl Holliman). Often she
was rescued just as she was about to be raped or sexually violated in
some other way. So the audience got to fantasize briefly about a
woman who dared to do a "man's job" getting her just deserts. But
the threat of Pepper's unleashed sexuality also got contained just in
time. Episodes had titles like "Warning to All Wives," "Anatomy of
Rapes," and "Bondage." Crowley and others urged Pepper to use her
sex appeal in all aspects of her work, like when trying to secure
authorization for a wiretap from a lecherous judge. Often she would
receive this advice while getting her male compatriots a cup of coffee. Her gun was always smaller than theirs, just a little snub-nosed
thing with hardly any range or power at all compared with what the
boys had. But at least it fit into her purse.

The first episode of *Police Woman,* about a bank robbery, contained a rape. Invariably, the rape victims in these episodes were
young and single, and their occupational choices usually meant that
they were "asking for it." They were nude models, or strippers, or
actresses willing to star in porno movies. For the purposes of viewer
titillation, these women were humiliated in some way, either forced
to do a striptease at gunpoint before being murdered or tied up with
leather straps and threatened with an iron poker. In another episode,
when a nude model is found raped and bludgeoned to death, one cop
dismisses the crime by noting that the victim is "not exactly the kind
of chick who'd have to have her arm twisted." Later, after examining

the body, the coroner tells Pepper and Crowley, "There are indications that the lady had herself *quite* an evening," as if there were portions of the assault she had welcomed.

The sexual liberation of women, in other words, became an excuse to terrorize them and to reinforce the most offensive stereotypes about which kinds of women get raped and why. In this same episode, an older, married white woman accuses a black man of raping her; in the end, she confesses she was lying. When women like that claim they've been raped—women who are not young, gorgeous, and scantily dressed—who can believe them? At the very time when feminists were beginning to attack rape laws and the way rape victims were treated by police and the legal system, shows like this, under the guise of feminism, reinforced every negative stereotype about rape that perpetuated the system. Women kept seeing themselves as helpless victims, as being both responsible for male rage and violence and unable to escape from it without the help of other, better men. Some women at the time praised *Police Woman* because it featured a strong female lead. But I remember this show well, a kind of TV noir with sexually provocative and rapacious women needing either extermination or rescuing by men, and I remember how little pleasure and how much anger it brought to me.

Then there was the drama about women and power. In 1976 came television's most ingenious resolution to the tension between feminism and antifeminism. What we got was the bionic bimbo, the superhuman woman with lots of power, maybe even a gun, flouncy hair, a mellifluous voice, and erect nipples. She was the immediate forerunner of the superwoman, the size-six CEO with a Ph.D., two perfect children, a doting husband, not a line on her face, and the ability to rebuild the car's engine on the weekend. She sang to us, as the Enjoli woman did, "I can bring home the bacon, fry it up in the pan, and never, ever let you forget you're a man." Later, she appeared in ads as the no-nonsense businesswoman in stiletto pumps who could best any man. In one example of subliminal seduction gone awry, the new superwoman CEO was pictured holding a really, really big drill which, presumably, she would use to drive any competition into the pavement.

In 1976, we saw the debut of *The Bionic Woman, Wonder Woman,* and, of course, *Charlie's Angels.* Few shows drew more instantaneous criticism from feminists than *Charlie's Angels.* Judith Coburn, a journalist, called it "one of the most misogynist shows the networks have produced recently. Supposedly about strong women, it perpetuates the myth most damaging to women's struggle to gain professional equality: that women always use sex to get what they want, even on the job." She cast the program as "a version of the pimp and his girls. Charlie dispatches his streetwise girls to use their sexual wiles on the world while he reaps the profits."[17] And feminists weren't alone. Virtually everyone trashed the show as a piece of sexist soft-core porn that drove television to new lows. *Time* described the show as "mediocre" and "aesthetically ridiculous," adding, "Brightly lit and crudely shot, the visual style indeed reminds one of comic art at its least sophisticated level."[18]

Since I had been glued to ABC that summer, watching the Olympics, I, like millions of others, knew *Charlie's Angels* was coming: ABC took advantage of the huge Olympic-viewing audience to hype the show ad nauseam. By then, I was in graduate school studying the media and teaching about it, and, well, I had an excuse; watching *Charlie's Angels* was part of my "work." (Hey, it's a dirty job, but somebody's got to do it.) And when I first saw the show, I was as outraged as other feminists over its objectification of women and its celebration of patriarchy through the use of invisible Charlie's instructing voice. But you know what? I watched it regularly, and not just for work. At the same time that I hated it, I loved it. Unlike *Police Woman,* this show did something I certainly wasn't supposed to admit, then or now: it gave me pleasure. And I had plenty of company. On Wednesday nights at 10:00 P.M., a staggering 59 percent of all TV sets in use were tuned to Farrah, Jaclyn, and Kate, which meant 23 million households watched *Charlie's Angels* every week. And these viewers weren't just slavering fourteen-year-old boys or people with single-digit IQs: the show ranked seventh among college graduates and those who earned over $20,000 a year. It was popular with women and with men, although often for different reasons.

There is no doubt that the show was escapist rot of the first order, combining plots a three-year-old could follow with plenty of cheesecake. But neither its sexual titillation nor its See-Spot-Run plotlines adequately explain why this show, at this time, became the media and cultural phenomenon that it did. Looking back on *Charlie's Angels* after nearly twenty years, we find some interesting and pleasant surprises mixed in with the string bikinis and those hideous bellbottoms, so try to hold your nose and bear with me.

The reason *Charlie's Angels* was such a hit was that it exploited, perfectly, the tensions between antifeminism and feminism. The opening sequence established this tension immediately. We hear the voice of the great white patriarch, Charlie, announcing, "Once upon a time, there were three little girls who went to the police academy." But what we see aren't three little girls. We see three buxom women grimly shooting guns, using judo to flip men over their heads and onto the ground, and writing traffic tickets. Then Charlie says sarcastically, "And they were each assigned very hazardous duties," as we see them stuck in the kinds of dead-end jobs women usually get confined to: doing clerical work and serving as crossing guards for schoolchildren instead of working as real cops. Distancing himself from the retrograde and unenlightened bureaucracies that fail to take advantage of the talents of smart, accomplished women, Charlie announces proudly, "But I took them away from all that, and now they work for me. My name is Charlie."

Then, as the lush theme song, a cross between the James Bond theme and the music from *South Pacific,* fills the soundtrack, we see the angels in their new job, driving race cars at a hundred miles an hour, brandishing guns and commanding, "Freeze!," chasing and being chased by villains, and flipping their voluminous hair across their faces. They now get to do what men do, but they are still very much women. Charlie, a sophisticated and enlightened man, is the agent of liberation for these women, suggesting that it is smart, modern men who will set women free. But Charlie is also instantly recognizable as a traditional patriarch—commanding, unseen, permeating everything, issuing orders and instructions the girls must obey. He is also a complete lech, a trait we're meant to find endearing. Charlie couldn't possibly supervise the angels face-to-face—he'd be too busy chasing them around the office to get anything done. Instead, he has a eunuch, Bosley, supervising the harem; Bosley is an office manager who poses no sexual threat and who, as the butt of countless jokes and incessant teasing, affirms that some men are quite easy to make fools of and dominate.

The plots were pretty standard. At the beginning of each show, Charlie informed the angels about someone, usually a young woman, who had been victimized in some way; often they then met the girl, instantly bonded with her, and told her not to worry, they would help. To do so, they had to go undercover to expose and thwart the bad guys. And here's where things get interesting. In the first season they went undercover as prison inmates, WACs in basic training, and roller derby queens. The girl they were helping was almost always from what was called "a simple background," meaning less sophisticated and of a lower socioeconomic class than they, although the angels' class was somewhat indeterminate. So they didn't just go undercover into an occupation not theirs, they also went undercover into another class, coming to the aid of a less fortunate sister who didn't have their resources, their training, or their chutzpah. The angels were always extremely sympathetic and helpful to these girls, suggesting a female bond across class barriers that many feminists were trying to achieve in real life. These absolutely preposterous situations spoke to a fantasy about women being able to help other women against brutish, oppressive men, and they affirmed the importance of sisterly love.

Once the angels were given the case and their undercover roles, they usually acted independently of Charlie. What we saw, as the case progressed, were three women working together, sharing information, tips, and hunches, using inductive and deductive reasoning to piece together the solution to the crime. They tested their perceptions and ideas against one another, and if one fell too easily for some man's explanation of things, the others razzed her for being too soft. The term *male chauvinist pig* was a regular part of their vocabulary. They conspired together against bad men, one posing as bait while one or both of the others snuck up behind and nailed the bastard. Unlike Pepper Anderson, who was always getting bailed out by her male compatriots, the angels saved themselves and one another, often with their guns, always with their wits. It was watching this—women working together to solve a problem and capture, and sometimes kill, really awful, sadistic men, while having great hairdos and clothes— that engaged our desire.

Nor did the angels always have to use their sexuality to get what they wanted. It's true, their looks never hurt, and the endless bikinis, décolletage, and wet T-shirts, which prompted libidinous comments from the appreciative male characters, reemphasized to women viewers the importance of looking like a *Playboy* centerfold if you're really going to get what you want. No doubt this made it more palatable when they talked back to bad guys, which they did all the time and with plenty of conviction, looking some chunky, menacing beefalo straight in the eye and saying, "I don't believe you. You're a liar."

They also took on bad women, and here negative stereotypes of the lesbian as a menacing, bull dyke dominatrix abounded, as it was made clear that the angels, despite their guns and defiance of men, were still real girls. These bitch villainesses cared not a whit for human life or decency, and they specialized in victimizing young women. In one episode with the titillating S & M title "Angels in Chains," the girls have to go undercover into a women's prison, only to run into a warden named Max(ine), who instructs them to "strip to your birthday suits" and eyes them appreciatively as she douses them with disinfectant. Corrupt dyke roller derby queens are just as bad, and Jill (Farrah) knees one in the stomach and pounds her on the head as part of what she refers to as "unfinished business." Women like this got no empathy; they got cold-cocked—and not by men, but by other women.

When they went undercover, the angels often cross-dressed, and we saw them in army fatigues, prison work shirts and jeans, or race car driver jumpsuits and helmets. Women in men's clothing look smaller than men in men's clothes, reminding us that women aren't as big and strong as men: there is a fantasy of easy domination and conquest here. But this cross-dressing also challenged conventional gender roles, emphasizing that the angels could assume masculine roles with a great degree of success. And when these women with their perfect makeup, voluptuous bodies, and huge hairdos wore men's clothes, they showed that masculinity, like femininity, was a put-on, a masquerade, something these girls, with their wits and guns, could indeed impersonate without becoming too manly or corrupted by male desires for power and domination.[19]

Charlie's Angels pulled off a neat trick: while it reinforced traditional male power through Charlie's faceless voice and agenda-setting instructions, it also tried to pretend that there was no such thing as patriarchy, at least the way feminists had characterized it. Instead, there were just a few bad men, isolated deviants, and if only these guys were exterminated or locked up, women would have nothing to fear. There wasn't a system that oppressed women, only a few power-hungry bad guys. And if women worked together to ferret them out, all would be fine. But despite this repudiation of feminist analyses, I must admit I enjoyed seeing women in nice clothes and great hair brandishing guns to put certain boys in their place, and to kill them if need be. Here feminism and antifeminism stood in perfect suspension. In seeking to have it both ways—to espouse female liberation and to promote the objectification of women's bodies—*Charlie's Angels* offered a compromise with empowering and thwarting effects.

But I wasn't sure what to make of *Wonder Woman* and *The Bionic Woman*. Having grown up with *Bewitched* and *The Flying Nun,* and hoping stupidly that maybe, now, we'd get something a little more realistic than a woman whose power lies in her bracelets, we got, instead, more far-fetched, metaphorical cartoons in which women, without special effects, were powerless. The campiest of the bionic bimbos was Wonder Woman, played by the statuesque, voluptuous former beauty queen Lynda Carter. The show's theme song contained the best lyrics ever written: "In your satin tights, fighting for your rights, and the old red, white, and blue." Wonder Woman was an Amazon princess from an all-female island somewhere near the Bermuda Triangle; she wasn't supposed to like or need men, but then she met one and kinda lost her resolve.

At first the show was set during World War II, when Wonder Woman fought Nazis, but in 1977 the scene changed to contemporary America. In both incarnations, Diana Prince put on glasses and worked as a secretary in low-cut dresses, and her boss, the dark-haired, FM-voiced Steve Trevor, had no idea she was Wonder Woman. Whenever Steve, or American national security, was in danger, Diana dashed off to a private room and started spinning. As she spun, an orange explosion emanated from her navel, and, when the sparks had cleared, there she was in her gold-braided, red satin bustier, her star-studded blue satin short shorts, and her knee-high, high-heeled, red satin boots, which must have been real easy to run and jump in. Once she was in this outfit, there was nothing she couldn't do. She stopped tanks with her bare hands, snapped assault rifles in two as if they were toothpicks, lifted up trucks, hurled bad guys through the air, and leaped tall buildings in a single bound—all in her red spikes. She could knock down a steel door with one kick, and her golden bracelets deflected all bullets, all this to the sound of beating tympanies and screeching synthesizers. At the same time that Wonder Woman's breasts seemed constantly poised to burst forth from their Playboy bunny–type container, Wonder Woman reasoned calmly with Steve about the crime in question and gave him ideas, suggestions, and solutions for how to foil the bad guys. This girl used her brains and her body. But as tough and powerful as she was, Wonder Woman never used her powers to advance her own interests, and she never spoke of her own goals and ambitions. She had power, all right, but it was always put to altruistic ends, to save the man she secretly cared for (a desire she couldn't admit to) and to save her country. With Steve she was as soft-spoken, pleasant, and diplomatic as Samantha Stevens. As Diana Prince, her powers were hidden, kept secret. As in 1964, female power was still a secret power, kept under wraps, never discussed, used only in emergencies, never used for self-advancement. Unlike in 1964, this power wasn't supposed to be confined to the domestic sphere. It could, and should, be used in public, in the service of good and evil, and to preserve national security itself.

The same was true for Jaime Sommers (Lindsay Wagner), the Bionic Woman. She was the least kitschy of them all. She didn't have a costume, was not constantly seen in bikinis or wet T-shirts, and didn't giggle all the time, although she did eventually get a bionic dog, Max. When she was introduced to the viewing public as the Six Million Dollar Man's fiancée, she was a tennis pro, one of the top-ranked women players in the world. But when she got her own series, her cover was the more femininely appropriate role of schoolteacher. Jaime Sommers had bionic legs that allowed her to run thirty-five miles per hour and jump from rooftops, a bionic right arm that was capable of ripping open steel doors and the like, and a bionic ear that allowed her to crack safes, overhear dastardly plots, and anticipate the arrival of UFOs. Like the angels, she often went undercover, assuming, by turns, the role of nun, lady wrestler, and the perennial favorite, roller derby queen. Like the angels, she took her orders from a man, although this one was visible. Unlike the angels, she worked alone, her best friend not another woman but a dog.

Behind the bionic limbs and Old Glory short shorts, the flouncy hair and snub-nosed guns, behind Maude's yelling and Mary's partially swallowed words, was a media compromise with feminism. They would show us women with power, but only in comic book settings that could never be mistaken for reality. This power had to be kept secret, as the women who possessed it masqueraded as regular women, as lower-class women, as women with absolutely no power at all.

Given their power, it was critical that the women be hyperfeminized, with large, gravity-defying breasts and perfectly souffléed hair.

The dramas we witnessed in the 1970s, about our being severed from while trying to reclaim our voices, our sexuality, our agency in the world, urged us to rewrite Helen Reddy's song and, instead, to murmur, as we watched the cute-as-a-button MTM logo, "I am woman, hear me purr." Women *could* have it all, but the levels of accomplishment we were offered were impossible for mere mortals to attain. As with *Bewitched* nearly ten years earlier, women's emerging power—their political power, their sexual independence, their growing individual assertiveness—was either too scary or simply too incomprehensible to portray with any realism. So, once again, we got metaphors and kitsch: women with magical, superhuman powers made possible, the viewer knew, not by the woman herself but through the wizardry of special effects, designed and controlled by men. We saw Jaime Sommers leap buildings in a single bound, accompanied by great sound effects, and Wonder Woman zap bad guys with her magic bracelets. But in the early 1970s, when approximately 45 percent of women were working outside the home, many of them married with children, we still didn't see women's real heroism on TV: women juggling it all with virtually no support from any quarter and demands coming in from everywhere.

Ricocheting between the various representations of feminism and pseudofeminism we saw on TV in the 1970s, we realized we would have to reinvent ourselves yet again. Now there were a few women on TV with steel oblongs of their own, although they were decidedly smaller than what dangled provocatively under the armpits of their male counterparts. These stubby, truncated phalluses, wielded by braless women with leonine hair, signified woman's new power—her new, stubby, truncated power. It wasn't much, but it was a start.

CHAPTER 10

The ERA as Catfight

L adies and gentlemen! In this corner, we have Gloria Steinem, a beautiful, single, and childless career woman in a miniskirt, who likens marriage to prostitution and insists that "if men could get pregnant, abortion would be a sacrament." In this corner, we have Phyllis Schlafly, an attractive, successful wife and mother of six in a shirtwaist, who claims that feminism will enslave women and calls feminists a "bunch of bitter women seeking a constitutional cure for their personal problems." OK, girls, the gong has sounded, have at it.

In the 1970s, while Joe Frazier and Muhammad Ali were pounding the crap out of each other around the globe, we had our own feminist Thrilla in Manila right here in America. This was what the debates about feminism got reduced to in the mass media: a catfight between two women. Still unknown to most Americans in 1970, when the media spotlight was on Betty Friedan, Kate Millett, and Shirley Chisholm, by the mid-1970s Gloria Steinem and Phyllis Schlafly personified the stark and supposedly mutually exclusive choices before us. It will come as no surprise that their elevation to these positions says more about the media's response to feminism than it does about either feminism or antifeminism.

The catfight is a staple of American pop culture, and by the 1970s it had evolved into various forms of especially sloppy faux combat between women, like female mud wrestling or Jell-O wrestling. In its purest form, it features two women, one usually a traditional wife (blond), the other a grasping, craven careerist (brunette), who slug it out on a veranda, in a lily pond, or during a mud slide. Usually they fight over men or children. Sometimes, as in *The Turning Point,* they just hit each other with their little purses. Other times, as in the incessant catfights in *Dynasty,* Krystle got to slop a big, gushy glob of cold cream in Alexis's face, or Alexis got to throw pond scum down Krystle's blouse.[1]

The catfight—which in the 1960s we only got to see in B movies like Russ Meyer's *Faster Pussycat! Kill! Kill!*—made it into the mainstream in the 1970s and '80s. We tend to think of the catfight as a staple of the nighttime soaps, and the daytime soaps as well. So it's worth reminding ourselves that the catfight was first revived not in prime time but through a more respectable venue, the news media. We can trace those mud-wrestling scenes on *Dynasty* back to the hissing and clawing on the nightly news. For all too many baby boomers, raised with Cinderella and Gidget, now coming of age with Bella Abzug and Germaine Greer, the 1970s was a tough decade, and not just because of polyester pantsuits or the fact that every number one hit in the country seemed to be by John Denver. Reeling between two very different visions of how women should behave and what they should aspire to, we searched for a resolution that gave us power but didn't cost us love. In this struggle, we got little help from the mass media, which seemed, when it came to women, only able to provide caricatures of extremists on each side. Yet we took what we got—Steinem versus Schlafly, Alexis versus Krystle—and drew pieces from each as we continued puzzling through what now seemed like the impossible task of forging a new identity. The media gave us plenty of warnings about feminism while acknowledging that there was no going back. The compromise we would have to jerry-rig for ourselves.

Throughout the 1970s, I was struggling big time with which feminism, or feminisms, I was going to assume. Going to graduate school helped consolidate my transformation; work or marriage to someone who thought women should be seen but not heard did it for others. The academic department I was first in was so sexist I transferred out after a few weeks. It had never, to my knowledge, graduated a woman Ph.D. and, of course, had no women on its faculty except one visiting professor. With a few key exceptions, the rest of the department was larded with one self-satisfied, pompous fathead after the next who did things like wink at me during academic advising meetings and ask me what I was going to cook for dinner that night. Other women I knew got comments on their seminar papers telling them how cute they were. Mostly, the professors treated women with complete contempt, waiting for them to drop out so they could type some man's seminar papers. This was the first time I had run smack into so inhospitable a male establishment, and I decided one thing right away—if I made it out of there alive, I was never going to be like them, callous, condescending, elitist swine. So one thing feminism came to mean for me, right away, was a repudiation of how men like this conducted business. But how, exactly, should women be instead? Many women who tried to enter male enclaves in the 1970s have stories like this, and knew that whatever the news media was suggesting, the struggle wasn't between women, it was between women and men. And just at this point, the biggest catfight of them all began on the TV screens and in the newspapers and magazines of America, the battle over the Equal Rights Amendment.

As a metaphor for the struggle between feminism and antifeminism, the catfight provided a symbolic catharsis of woman's internal conflict between the desire for liberation and the longing for security. It was also a spectacle: two women, often opposites, locked in a death grip that brought them both crashing down into the muck. Both women were sullied; no one won. Meanwhile, the men, dry, clean, and tidy, were off in some wood-paneled den relaxing, having a drink and a smoke, and being reasonable.

The catfight served two critically important ideological functions: it put the lie to feminists' claims about sisterhood and reasserted, in its place, competitive individualism in which women, like other Americans, duked it out with each other. The notion that all women were "sisters," bound together across ethnic, class, generational, and regional lines by their common experiences as an oppressed group, was the most powerful, utopian, and, therefore, threatening concept feminists advanced in the 1970s. The best-selling book *Sisterhood Is Powerful;* the signs and banners that read "Women of the World Unite"; the rapid spread of consciousness-raising groups in which women found common cause; the articles and editorials advancing sisterhood in *Ms.;* the sight, on the news, of tens of thousands of women marching together arm-in-arm—all these suggested that maybe enough women *would* form a political and cultural sisterhood. Of all the concepts and principles that feminists advanced, none was more dangerous to the status quo than the concept of sisterhood. Hence, the absolute importance of the catfight to demonstrate as simply and vividly as possible that sisterhood was, in fact, a crock of shit. Through the catfight, the threat that feminism posed could be contained and turned back on itself.

We had been raised to compete over men and to scrutinize ourselves and other women to see who was thinner, younger, sexier, nicer, prettier. And we had grown up with a notion of a female hierarchy in which some women—the Waspy, wealthy, young, and beautiful—were at the top of the pyramid and other women—the poor, the dark-skinned, the ugly, the old, the fat—were at the bottom. Multimillion-dollar industries were built on this foundation of female competition, and it was a notion wired into our sense of self. The competitive spirit was what animated individualism, and it is hard to think of an American value more enduring than rugged individualism. Each of us was special and unique; each of us had a shot at being distinctive in some way; each of us was encouraged to imagine herself as apart from the herd, as someone people somewhere, someday, would notice stood out. So many women greeted the sisterhood concept with ambivalence, a combination of euphoria and discomfiture.

In the 1970s, millions of women of all ages struggled with the tensions between embracing sisterhood and clinging to that bulwark of American ideology, democratic individualism. I remember walking around New York or Boston in the early 1970s in my work shirt and jeans, looking at fifty-year-old women dripping with gold jewelry, fur coats, and a few poodles and wondering whether I really could get behind the idea that these women were my sisters. At the same time, I was a social worker for a while and felt enormous empathy with and admiration for—sisterhood, if you will—the working-class women I met who did things like handcuff the fathers of their babies to their hospital gurneys so the fathers, in violation of hospital policy, would be in the delivery room when their babies were born.

And here lies the dirty little secret about sisterhood. It was easy to feel sisterhood with those "beneath" you or lateral to you in class, wealth, or appearance. But to feel it with those "above" you—hey, that little insecure, catty voice kicked in, those weren't your sisters, they were the competition, the ones getting more than you got, the ones who had won, the ones you could never beat. The news media, TV shows, and ads nurtured this worm burrowing through the apple of sisterhood, personifying and dramatizing female competition wherever possible, erasing or simply refusing to represent (with a few exceptions) the power of female friendship, cooperation, and love. In a decade suffocating under the weight of male buddy movies and male buddy cop shows, we got a total of one major movie about female friendship, *Julia*. Whereas many in the women's movement sought to highlight sisterhood and dismiss differences among women, the mainstream media became obsessed with those differences, emphasizing all the things that kept women divided and apart. Even *Ms.*, with a different agenda from the nightly news or TV shows, was riddled with the tensions between sisterhood and individualism. Articles about how to start consciousness-raising groups or join feminist pressure groups coexisted with articles promoting individual transformation and advancement and profiles of self-made women.[2] Once again, we were at the crossroads of an irreconcilable conflict. *Ms.* suggested we could have both communalism and individualism, but the mainstream media were more definite. The major subtext of the 1970s was this: sisterhood, you fools, is both impossible and undesirable.

By the early 1970s, the catfight had become the dominant news peg about the progress of the women's movement, and the campaign to ratify the Equal Rights Amendment was cast as the catfight par excellence. The stakes were higher than who got the boy, but we were back to the same old story we grew up with: Tinker Bell versus Wendy, Betty versus Veronica, the impossibility of female cooperation. And this is the primary reason we lost the ERA: if women themselves were so hopelessly divided over the amendment, why should it pass? While it's true that some women were deeply threatened by and anxious about the ERA and lobbied strenuously to defeat it, polls throughout the decade showed that they were the minority.[3] The main struggle was between ERA proponents and male legislators, and behind-the-scenes corporate lobbyists, but this is not the struggle we saw on the nightly news. What we saw was the catfight.

"Women Versus Women" was how the debate over the ERA was headlined in news articles, TV shows, interviews, and documentaries. All the news media's initial responses to the women's movement—the demonizing of feminists as out of the mainstream, the exaggeration of the movement's internal divisions, the erasure of male opposition to feminism—became even more pronounced during the coverage of the ERA. And the media's addiction to "official" spokespersons and leaders reinforced America's long-standing cult of individualism.[4] Focusing on leaders implied that not all women shared the same talents or the same plight—some were more, or less, equal than others. In the sifting process of identifying leaders, and ultimately certifying the ones who would be legitimate and the ones who would not, we saw, again, the caricature of the female grotesque, of the older or unattractive woman who had "stepped into the limelight out of turn" and was quickly rushed offstage in favor of less physically and politically unruly women.[5] While other social movements went through this tango with the media, in which one or two people emerged as the leaders or spokesmen, it was only in the women's movement that a spokesperson's reception in the press depended on the degree to which she resembled a model in a Maidenform or a Duncan Hines ad.

It is, of course, a commonplace to note how much more important appearance is for women than for men. But there was more to it than this. Of all the social movements of the 1960s and '70s, none was more explicitly anticonsumerist than the women's movement. Feminists had attacked the ad campaigns for products like Pristeen and Silva Thins, and by rejecting makeup, fashion, and the need for spotless floors, repudiated the very need to buy certain products at all. Now I'm sorry, but attacks like these simply cannot be tolerated in a nation whose main cultural activity is shopping. Yes, there was sexism in the relentless overemphasis on feminists' appearance, but more than gender privilege was at stake. By ridiculing how feminists looked, the American media insisted that consumerism, especially by women, had to remain both a central pastime and a religion. This, too, the catfight would reinforce.

Competition between women—not over their ideas but over their looks and behavior, and especially their sexuality—defined the first stage of the catfight, the selection of the head felines. Conflict, after all, requires combatants. When feminists refused to single out a spokeswoman, the media anointed their own.[6] Their choice? The glamorous, successful, articulate journalist with her choice of male escorts and a leonine mane of hair, Gloria Steinem.

A close-up of a smiling, sunny-faced Steinem appeared on the cover of the August 16, 1971, issue of *Newsweek* under the headline "The New Woman." Since Steinem had done virtually no organizational work in the movement until 1971, her selection as feminist poster girl was distressing to activists who had been in there pitching for nearly half a decade. The magazine made it clear that this, thank God, was no Kate Millett. The entire first paragraph focused on her appearance, "her long, blond-streaked hair falling just so above each breast" and her "most incredibly perfect body." Steinem was something most feminists allegedly weren't: sexy and extremely attractive to men. As *Newsweek* put it, "one of the basic assumptions" about feminists is that they "must be losers." Steinem, however, presumably could get laid whenever she wanted to and was *still* a feminist. This dumbfounded *Newsweek*. But because of her "emphatic sexuality," *Newsweek* emphasized, "Steinem is looked upon with suspicion and envy by many of the sisters," especially, the article noted, women like Friedan.[7] Here was the catfight again. By 1972, Steinem's canonization was complete: there she was, on the January cover of *McCall's* under a headline that might sound familiar, "Year of the Woman."

Steinem was used to displace all those other women male media moguls apparently didn't want to look at or listen to, like Kate Millett, Betty Friedan, and Bella Abzug. Millett had emerged, against her will, as one of the first media-anointed feminist leaders in the summer of 1970, especially when *Sexual Politics* became a runaway best-seller.[8] She found herself on the August 31 cover of *Time* as an unsmiling, thick-eyebrowed sphinx with emerging eye bags and a laser beam stare that could melt testicles from fifty yards away. Four months later, in December, the stereotyping of Millett as the brawny, repellent feminist had reached new lows. In fact, the artist Aslan, known for his loving drawings of peach-toned, inviting pinups in *Esquire,* drew a caricature of "the feminist," clearly with Millett in mind, and *Time* duly reprinted the image with the caption "A splenetic frenzy of hatred." Saggy-breasted, beefy, and scowling, one fist on her hip, the other holding up a bra in flames, wearing sandals favored by Roman centurions and a button reading "WITCH," this woman clearly hated men, no doubt because she had been rejected by them so many times. *Time* used the drawing to illustrate its article "Women's Lib: A Second Look," in which Irving Howe quipped about *Sexual Politics,* "There are times one feels the book was written by a female impersonator." As it turned out, the worst strike against Millett was her admission that she was bisexual, a disclosure, in *Time's* words, that "is bound to discredit her as a spokeswoman for her cause, cast further doubt on her theories, and reinforce the views of those skeptics who routinely dismiss all liberationists as lesbians."[9] Within six months, Millett had been projected onto a leadership role she didn't seek and banished to the fringes of legitimacy.[10] Women like me took note of what happened to this successful intellectual: she was chewed up and spit out, her private life ripped apart, her fate a morality tale for us all.

Steinem also knocked Betty Friedan out of the spotlight. The founder of NOW and a woman more than happy to be regarded as a feminist leader, Friedan found herself marginalized by the news media, in no small part because of her age and appearance. In a *New York Times Magazine* article titled "Mother Superior to Women's Lib," Paul Wilkes obsessed on her looks and described the young Friedan sitting on "a lonesome perch by the weed-filled, abandoned cemetery," "her eyes glistening with tears" because "Betty wasn't an attractive girl." She would "happily have traded 30 points on the IQ scale for a modicum of good looks and popularity." She had grown up to become "a vision of somebody's eccentric, middle-aged aunt, her hair a swirl of cowlicks, her face deeply lined, [and with a] double chin," a woman with "her clothing in disarray" who carried "a leather purse the size and shape of a horse's feedbag." Surely a woman like this—sagging, wrinkled, disheveled, disappointed in love—couldn't really show women the road to happiness. The article then pitted Friedan against other feminist leaders, using captioned photos of "Women's Libbers" saying things like "Betty's greatest strength—her aggressiveness—is also her greatest weakness" or that Betty championed women's liberation "so that her own emotional needs can be fulfilled."[11] Meow. Then there was the feminist billed by *Time* as "Bellacose Abzug," nicknamed in the press "battling Bella" and described, variously, as "a sumo liberal," "a lady wrestler," "an interoffice tyrant undreamt of since Caligula," and "a rhinoceros," whose voice Norman Mailer said "could boil the fat off a taxi driver's neck."[12]

Were these real women or oddities? With the women's movement cast as a bizarre carnival, filled with disorderly, parading
women—freaks of nature—in forbidding, scary masks, bursting into
previously peaceful, harmonious male enclaves, it is not surprising
that questions of imposture would arise. By refusing or failing to conform to prevailing notions of prettiness and demureness, these
women sought to gain strength from such defiance. But this failure
was used against women deemed grotesque: if a woman wasn't attractive to men, then she could not be a leader of women.

Steinem, by contrast, became extremely effective as the exemplar
of the new, liberated young woman; she was the compromise the
news media had been looking for, a feminist who looked like a fashion model. I remember my own ambivalence about Steinem in the
early 1970s and the hostility she evoked from other feminists. She
seemed an opportunist, someone who stepped in after other women
had done all the organizing and taken all the flak. And Steinem was
often used symbolically as a rebuke to women less talented, less beautiful, less autonomous, and less successful than she. Steinem was the
woman you competed against and lost to, the woman you hoped
wasn't working in your husband's office, the one you hoped your
boyfriend never met, the one you never wanted to run into on the
beach with both of you in bathing suits. It wasn't easy to feel sisterhood with a media star like this.

But Steinem was also one of the best things for the women's
movement, because she nullified many of the dismissive comments
about feminism and feminists, as did Germaine Greer, author of the
best-selling *The Female Eunuch*. Precisely because they were tall, slim,
and beautiful, they got away with saying things Friedan didn't dare
utter. So, while Friedan, who was much more accommodating to
men in her speeches and her politics, got cast as a man-hater,
Steinem, who constantly spoke out against the ruling elite of white,
upper-middle-class males, did not.[13] The word *strident,* repeatedly
used to describe Friedan in news stories, was rarely used about

Steinem, even though she was more radical. When she denounced marriage because it "makes you half a person" and turns women into "slaves," she wasn't ridiculed as an alien or a lunatic. Because of her beauty, Steinem was able to smuggle radical critiques of the status of women into mainstream discourse and gradually get them discussed and even accepted. And she did this by appearing on dozens of talk shows acting as if nothing could be more sensible or self-evident for all women than feminism.

But Steinem also found herself stereotyped as the exception, as the woman who could speak only for the gorgeous, fiercely independent, talented few. Despite her pleas for sisterhood, other women eyed her suspiciously. Despite her efforts to showcase black feminists by lecturing in tandem with either Dorothy Pitman Hughes or Florynce Kennedy, the sound bites, and the pictures, were of her.[14] Steinem was young, childless, and single by choice. Although she criticized the inequities of marriage, she also defended housewives and advocated repeatedly and passionately that they be paid what they were worth. (But when she sought to calculate all the services that a husband and father would have to buy if he didn't have a wife—housecleaning, cooking, baby-sitting, chauffeuring—she also included prostitution, which offended many wives, who hardly thought of themselves as hookers.) Here was one personification of feminism, the beautiful career girl, indifferent to marriage and children, so confident, successful, and fulfilled she didn't need a husband or even a steady boyfriend. She embodied a kind of voluntary separatism from men that I wasn't able to accept or interested in embracing. Did that mean I was a weenie, a sellout, not a "real" feminist? The other personifications, like Abzug or Friedan, were variously typecast as combative, shrill, unattractive, and humorless, suggesting that for women to get the opportunities they wanted, they had to abandon their socialization as helpmates, nurturers, and sex objects overnight. (And this even though Abzug and Friedan were wives and mothers.) As the battle over the ERA heated up in the 1970s, these were the media archetypes for us to embrace or reject. These were your choices, female grotesque or femme fatale, the one unappealing, the other unattainable.

As we oscillated between Germaine Greer and Kate Millett, Gloria Steinem and Bella Abzug, the mind-set of feminism itself became one of ambivalence. We had no choice but to read between the lines, to take what strength we could from Friedan, Millett, and Abzug, despite their stereotyping as has-been harridans. Many of us were deeply emboldened by what these women said and wrote, even if we were not completely ready, ourselves, to "boil the fat off a taxi driver's neck." I took what I could from Steinem, too, the permission she and Greer gave me to continue to shave my legs, wear mascara, covet nice clothes, sleep with men, and still be a feminist. Steinem and Greer made me feel that women could cobble together elements of the codes of femininity they were unable to expunge with a feminism they were eager to adopt.

And then another woman appeared on the national scene in 1973, a woman eager to serve the media's need for an opposing feline in the catfight to come. To women like me, who supported the Equal Rights Amendment, Phyllis Schlafly made the Wicked Witch of the West look like Mary Poppins. There have been few women, if any, more publicly cynical than Schlafly, who using the pretense of helping women made it perfectly acceptable to keep them under the great boot of patriarchy. But you had to hand it to Phyllis. She was an incredibly shrewd activist and demagogue, and it is no exaggeration to credit her and her Stop ERA campaign with singlehandedly defeating the amendment.

Schlafly headed a highly effective grass-roots organizing project that quickly developed enormous political clout. Congress had finally passed the Equal Rights Amendment in March 1972, and within a year twenty-eight states had approved the new amendment: ratification seemed a foregone conclusion. But then the tide turned, and as early as 1973 the ERA was in trouble. By 1975, thirty-four states had ratified the ERA, but after that date only one more state voted yes (Indiana in 1977), and several states that had passed the amendment voted to rescind approval. After a ten-year fight to the finish, the ERA died in July 1982, only three states shy of the number required for ratification.[15] Schlafly achieved this victory, in part, because she was brilliant at exploiting media routines, biases, and stereotypes to make the ERA seem both dangerous and unnecessary. She became a media celebrity, and the media became her most powerful weapon.

Schlafly understood that conflict, especially between women, was automatically newsworthy, and that if one side consisted of everyday, "normal" moms, that side would automatically receive more favorable coverage, especially if the "other side" was "women's libbers." She understood that simple but incendiary statements—especially those that conjured up a wholesale destruction of sex roles and the family as we knew them—made great sound bites. She milked the negative stereotypes of the feminist for all they were worth. Given that feminism had been cast repeatedly as a minority movement that represented very few women, no one challenged Schlafly's authority to speak for the "typical" American woman. When she said things like "The overwhelming majority of women do not want ERA" and "The women's lib movement is not relevant to most women," she was convincing. Drawing heavily from the cult of individualism, Schlafly suggested that the ERA would force conformity on all women. Most of all, she appreciated that by organizing women to oppose the ERA, she automatically gave men, who held the overwhelming majorities in every state legislature in the country, permission to oppose women's liberation without looking like sexist pigs. Phyllis Schlafly knew she couldn't lose once she transformed the ERA from a struggle between women and a male-dominated political system into a catfight between the girls. And that's just what Schlafly, queen tigress of them all, did. More to the point, the media bought it.

The text of the ERA sounded innocent enough: "Equality of rights under the law shall not be denied or abridged by the United

States or by any State on account of sex." Hold your horses, cried Schlafly. This may *sound* simple, but you'd better read between the lines. Assuming the role of schoolmarm, Schlafly urged her students not to take things at face value, especially when dealing with the government. With sex roles, conventional marriage, the U.S. economy, and the presidency itself under assault (it was, after all, the time of Watergate), Schlafly had a climate of uncertainty to exploit, and she did so with the persistence, and the subtlety, of a battering ram.

The ERA didn't mean equality for women, she warned. On the contrary, it meant servitude and increased vulnerability. Sounding, for just a second, like Abbie Hoffman, she denounced the ERA as "a big rip-off" for American homemakers. Mothers would no longer be able to count on their husbands or ex-husbands for support of their children. Why, the ERA could force all women, whether they wanted to or not, to get jobs, no matter how menial, and to consign their children to day-care centers, just like in all those Commie countries. Women would be drafted into the army just like men, and have to be slaughtered in combat, just like men. Her favorite verb was "wipe out," as in "The ERA will wipe out our right to have single-sex schools and colleges." Prisons would be coed, and churches would be required to have female priests and ministers. The ERA automatically legalized—why, it even encouraged—marriage between homosexuals, who would now rush to become grammar school teachers. Worst of all, the ERA meant that when you had to go to the bathroom in a restaurant or bus station, you'd be compelled to do it right next to some strange, lascivious man with his penis hanging out peeing in a smelly urinal while he watched you wipe yourself. Is *this* what you want? demanded Schlafly.

While feminist leaders who debated Schlafly (like Eleanor Smeal and Jill Ruckelshaus) often spoke in the conditional—the ERA "might" or "may" or "could" do this or that depending on how the courts interpreted the "legislative intent" of Congress, Schlafly spoke in ironclad certainties, always using the verb *will* and speaking confidently about "devastating effects." And she successfully changed the terms of the debate by acknowledging the feminist goals the news media had endorsed—equal pay for equal work and increased opportunities for women—and pointing out that the Equal Employment Opportunity Act of 1972 and the Equal Credit Opportunity Act of 1974 had already taken care of these inequalities. The ERA was no longer about discrimination in housing, education, or employment. The ERA was no longer about equal rights, a concept most Americans favored. The ERA was about unisex urinals and coed penitentiaries. In a nutshell, Schlafly made the anti-ERA campaign more newsworthy, and, dare I say it, more sexy, than the campaign for ratification.

She also repeated and amplified stereotypes about feminists, which the press duly reprinted. Feminists were "petty . . . and vindictive" and "think it is unequal that mothers have to take care of their babies."[16] Feminists "just don't want to be nice. They want to be ugly."[17] On a 1977 ABC special, hosted by none other than Howard K. Smith and titled, predictably enough, "ERA: The War Between the Women," Smith asked her about the feminist charge that she was affiliated with the John Birch Society. (Schlafly attended Birch Society rallies and proclaimed the atomic bomb to be "a marvelous gift that was given to our country by a wise God," so you be the judge.)[18] Schlafly smiled patronizingly and said, "I think those attacks just show the poverty of the arguments on the other side. I don't spend my time going around telling you all the lesbian organizations that are pushing ERA, although I could. I like to argue it on the merits of the question." Schlafly repeatedly used the word *reasonable* to describe her incessant ad hominem attacks on the ERA's supporters. The fact that she always looked, as *Time* put it, "crisp and composed" in her shirtwaist dresses and that her "upswept blond hair" was always "perfectly in place" signified orderliness, containment, and rationality. One *Time* headline read, "Feminine but forceful, Phyllis Schlafly is a very liberated woman."[19] Now here was a certified leader.

In 1977, the catfight turned into a stand-off, and this was the year that the women's movement began to decline as an ongoing news story. The movement's last gasp was the National Women's Conference, which took place that November in Houston with approximately 14,000 in attendance. The three-day conference produced a National Plan of Action consisting of twenty-five separate recommendations to be forwarded to President Jimmy Carter and Congress. Read them and weep. They advocated government-funded battered women's shelters; national health insurance for all Americans with provisions for women's special needs; government funding for day-care centers; rape prevention programs and programs for victims of child abuse; and extension of Social Security benefits to housewives. Since as of this writing, over fifteen years later, America has three times as many animal shelters as it does battered women's shelters, no national health insurance plan, no federal funding for day-care centers, and a rape rate that is terrifying, any one of these provisions could be thought of as revolutionary.

But the news media focused on the three most controversial resolutions—calls for passage of the ERA, federal funding for abortions for low-income women, and an end to discrimination against lesbians—as if the others didn't exist. All three networks and the newsmagazines ignored the calls for national health insurance and child-care centers and zeroed in on "lesbian rights," without reporting, for example, that a woman could lose custody of her children if she was revealed to be a lesbian, a barbaric policy that still exists in some parts of America. Lesbians' concerns—even their existence as a group—were finally being recognized, but only in a way that used their sexuality to demonize feminism and attack other women. The other main dramas the news media hammered away at were the conflicts between feminists and antifeminists within the conference, and between those women at the conference and the thousands of other women who attended a counterrally across town headed by Schlafly. Erik Engberg of CBS summed up Houston this way: "The battle between feminists who control the convention and the antifeminists yelling foul was in full swing." Here were the girls slogging it out in the mud again.

Even worse, in the long run, were the televised images of the conference itself. Thousands of jostling women in a convention-cum-circus atmosphere presented an indelible image of disarray. It's not like there wasn't dissent and disagreement at the convention; there was. But the overwhelming sense of sisterhood that many women left with was deemed neither newsworthy nor photogenic. When ERA supporters at the conference did a snake dance through the convention hall to celebrate the passage of the ERA resolution, it looked, on the TV screen, contrived, childish, disorderly. No doubt it felt quite a bit different. But television cameras make such spontaneous outbursts of camaraderie and joy look extremely silly. This is not always by design; it's just that TV cameras are incapable of conveying the spirit behind public demonstrations and the infectious sense of communal resolve that animates them. So these were the final messages of Houston. Sisterhood was impossible, and when you saw female unity, it meant it had been forced under duress. Worse, sisterhood was moronic and made you sound naive and look like a jerk. Sisterhood had women making spectacles of themselves on national television. Meanwhile, through Schlafly's efforts, and the media's complicity, male opposition to the ERA became invisible. Hardly any attention was ever paid to the hundreds of male legislators or the male-dominated organizations that helped fund Schlafly's Stop ERA, and they were the real ones to block the amendment, and to benefit from its defeat.

But what the catfight inspired in most people, including feminist women, was resignation and a desire to retreat from politics. By 1977, the ERA looked doomed; in fact, political activism looked doomed. The zeitgeist of the late 1970s emphasized self-improvement and personal fulfillment over political reform and the betterment of the community. Best-selling advice books like *The Managerial Woman, Dress for Success,* and *When I Say No I Feel Guilty* stressed individual strategies for individual women—usually more privileged women—to get ahead. Women had to learn how to be assertive, but not too assertive, to become team players at work, to dress in female versions of the pin-striped suit with blouses that had ties at the neck. Women had to make their peace with patriarchy and learn how to fit in. They had to compete with men and with other women if they were going to fulfill their feminist aspirations.

This is the message that underscored two of the most popular TV series of the late 1970s and early 1980s, *Dallas* and its imitator, *Dynasty.* It is no surprise that these shows appeared when they did, when the ERA was ready for extreme unction. Here we saw women competing with women in a variety of venues rarely staged on prime-time TV, and women arguing with each other about what kind of woman to be in the post-ERA era. Just so women wouldn't miss the point, the female characters couldn't even trust their own biological sisters, let alone those not connected by blood. But these shows also enacted feminist critiques of the status quo. Ostensibly about power, wealth, and the intrigues of the oil industry, both shows replayed, week in and week out, the simultaneous disintegration and resilience of the American family, symbol, of course, of America itself.

In *Dallas,* patriarchal capitalism, personified by the stupendously venal J. R. Ewing, was corrupt, inhumane, cynical, and destructive, especially of women and weak men. This was fully acknowledged and pushed, in fact, for all it was worth. But *Dallas* and *Dynasty* reaffirmed that patriarchal capitalism was the only game in town, the only imaginable way to organize society, and that it was impossible for women, whether they were traditional wives or ambitious vixens, to put forward an alternative.

Both shows quickly developed enormous audiences, both in the United States and abroad, and many of the series' most avid fans were women, including feminists like me. It is customary to dismiss entertainment popular with women as garbage, and soaps are probably the prime example, although how these are inferior to, say, a broadcast of men with skeleton masks and ice skates chasing a black disk and beating each other up with sticks is beyond me. Trashed for years as contaminated bilge ingested by passive and victimized women, especially homemakers, soaps have seemed, to some, like the ultimate in antifeminist propaganda. This attitude certainly greeted the night-time soaps. But like *Bewitched* and *Charlie's Angels,* these shows spoke volumes about our inner contradictions and gave us pleasure at the same time.

First of all, the in-your-face, self-conscious kitschiness of both shows allowed people like me—aspiring professionals—to feel superior to them and to make fun of their incredibly bald narrative strategies at the same time that we were completely sucked in. In those early years, missing *Dallas* on Friday nights or *Dynasty* on Wednesday nights was simply out of the question. Imitators and spin-offs like *Knots Landing* and *Falcon Crest* also addicted millions. Many people watched these shows, especially *Dallas,* in groups, as a sort of end-of-the-week party. It was almost as if you couldn't resist the powerful undertow of *Dallas* without a few friends around to act as lifeguards. But together, people laughed, hooted, and screamed at the show, gave the characters nicknames, and both imagined and predicted plotlines. In this way, viewers were simultaneously engaged with yet distanced from this highly feminized, and therefore despised, Venus's-flytrap of pop culture. These viewing strategies, the laughter especially, allowed me to pretend I was impervious to the pull of *Dallas* and gave me permission to indulge in this hedonistic, completely unredeeming pastime seemingly designed for the brain dead and the politically bankrupt. Being, in 1979, both a freshly minted Ph.D. and a new wife, I had to use the show as a constant affirmation of my own cultural superiority. Who was I kidding, besides myself?

The pleasure of immersing yourself in these absurd, antifeminist melodramas, in which women were crushed, pitted against each other, and objectified—yet resisted patriarchy in a variety of ways while wearing lilac chiffon gowns and tons of jewelry—was total. Feminists like me were supposed to know better, and at first I felt I shouldn't have taken the delight I did in the conflicts between Sue Ellen and Pam or the catfights between Krystle and Alexis. But I did, and so did other feminists.[20] As we came to understand, it was precisely our contradictory stance as viewers, our disdain for the show yet our absorption in it, that gave us so much satisfaction.

These shows affirmed what I knew about patriarchy: men controlled everything, and some of them, like the caricature J.R., were the worst sexist pigs you could imagine, cheating on their wives, regarding them as baby machines and sex objects, squashing even their most puny aspirations. But they also dramatized the tensions between traditional womanhood and the "new" woman and did something the male-dominated cop and detective shows didn't do: they let us into the subjective worlds of the female characters. Sue Ellen Ewing was a real favorite with viewers, especially female viewers, and there were good reasons for this. Through Sue Ellen's spats and conversations with Pam, her monologues to her shrink, Dr. Ellby, and her confessions to her series of lovers, we hear her analysis of her situation. And her analysis is that women unfortunate enough to be ensnared in the world of Southfork are trapped and doomed.

Despite the differences between herself and her sister-in-law Pam, Sue Ellen, who's been around, insists that their situations are the same—that they are united and similarly positioned whether they like it or not—because they are both Ewing wives. Sue Ellen is a fatalist who thinks that the notions of individualism and free will for women are a cruel hoax. Against Pam's repeated protestations (after all, she has her own career and, at the beginning of the series, a happy marriage, and Sue Ellen has neither), Sue Ellen reiterates in various episodes that "all Ewing men are the same. . . . And for you to survive you have two choices. You can either get out, or you can play by their rules." Pam refuses to see things in such totalizing terms, asserting, "I will never accept the fact that Bobby and J.R. are the same." In another episode, Sue Ellen warns that it doesn't matter which Ewing you're married to: "In a couple of years they'll look at you in the same way: as property. And you'd better be wrapped up in a pretty little package."[21] Wasn't this what the New York Radical Women warned us about in Atlantic City in 1968?

This was one of the central debates between these two—whether men were all alike, meaning selfish, brutish, oppressive pigs, or not. It was a debate about whether patriarchy could ever be "feminized," infused with some degree of tenderness, empathy, and egalitarianism between the sexes. It was the same debate that had occurred in "Sweet Talkin' Guy" twenty years earlier. And the show provided different answers, sometimes suggesting the pigs *were* all alike, and other times suggesting they weren't alike at all. By giving women viewers several positions to inhabit, either exclusively or alternatively, the show spoke to women's ambivalence about loving and needing men yet feeling trapped in the seeming inevitability of patriarchy. And it spoke to women who, in the morning at work, might indeed feel that all men were alike—pigs—and who, at night with their boyfriends or husbands, made an exception.

Pam and Sue Ellen were in constant competition, over their status in the household, over the approval of the great matriarch Miss Ellie (who suggested that strong women had it easier in earlier, prefeminist times), over their clothes, and over whose choice—to work or not to work—was wiser. They competed not outside the home but squarely in the domestic sphere, and consumerism was central to the contest. Whose clothes were nicer, anyway, and who bought too much and who bought too little? Few shows provided a more powerful rebuke to the anticonsumerist stance of feminism than *Dallas,* with its constant emphasis on the joys of shopping, driving fancy new cars, and going to spas.

Dynasty upped the ante even more. These women had great clothes and a level of opulence unmatched since Versailles. And we got *real* opposites and *real* catfights. On one side was blond, stay-at-home Krystle Carrington (Linda Evans), the Mother Teresa of soaps, endlessly empathetic and supportive, always willing to listen and care, beloved by her servants, an incredibly irritating, goody-two-shoes throwback I wanted to throw a pie at myself. In the other corner was the most delicious bitch ever seen on television, the dark-haired, scheming, duplicitous, supremely self-centered and self-assured career vixen Alexis Carrington Colby whatever (Joan Collins). Krystle just wanted to make her husband happy; Alexis wanted to control the world. How could you not love a catfight between these two?

This was the Battle of the Titans, the final duke out between the traditional wife and mom and the feminist bitch from hell. Since each woman was such a flagrant caricature, it wasn't easy to identify with either, or, for that matter, with the white trash sex kitten Sammy Jo; the nearly mute, whiny victim Kirby; or the mentally unstable Claudia. But what we could identify with as Alexis and Krystle slugged it out in some reflecting pool was what lay between these characters, the compromised space we inhabited that seemed vastly superior to the extremes they had chosen.

Watching the catfights, we could see, enacted before our eyes, our own, never-ending struggles between that portion of our psyches still tethered to prefeminism and the other portion firmly hitched to feminism. What did it mean to be a woman, and, in the wake of the women's movement, what kind of women should we be? How assertive and ambitious should we be and how accommodating to men? These and other questions bedeviled us constantly, so watching Krystle and Alexis grapple with them, metaphorically, in the mud provided a powerful catharsis for the terminally conflicted American woman.

What many women identified with, then, was this conflict, this tension, this ambivalence. We were starting to realize, as we approached our thirties and forties, that the one constant in our lives was, in fact, contradiction itself. Different women, of course, watched and used these shows in very different ways, but it would be a mistake to think we were all just passive viewers. Many women sat in their living rooms egging the female characters on, urging Sue Ellen or Krystle to do something, to act, to get a job or leave the bastard or both. And many of us, watching Alexis, tried on the bitchy personality for size, and found that sometimes we liked the fit.[22] Women viewers in their sweat suits, jeans, or flannel bathrobes could still feel superior to these women dripping with silk and emeralds because they felt that their solutions, their compromises, their blending of feminism and traditional womanhood were vastly superior to the monolithic approaches taken by—or forced upon—Krystle, Sue Ellen, and Alexis. To those viewers still trapped in dictatorial relationships or low-paying, traditionally female jobs, the shows allowed fantasies about revolt, and rebellion, if only vicariously. But vicarious rebellion sometimes leads to something else.

Although we don't see as many catfights on prime-time TV today as we used to, the catfight remains an extremely popular way for the news media to represent women's struggles for equality and power. In 1987, when Mikhail Gorbachev came to Washington for an arms control summit, the first lady mud wrestling between traditional wife and mom Nancy Reagan and careerist, intellectual bitch Raisa Gorbachev blew the boys right off the front pages of America. Lead-story coverage was given to the shoving match that occurred when Nancy gave Raisa a tour of the White House and Raisa sought, as *The New York Times* noted, to "upstage" her hostess by talking too much to the press and hogging the limelight. Neither *The Times* nor *USA Today* would let Raisa get away with this: they exposed her grotesque diplomatic faux pas of wearing a black cocktail dress and—how low can you go?—sagging black stockings with rhinestones on them during the day. Raisa wasn't very ladylike at all; instead, revealed *The Times,* she was "just assertive enough to give some listeners the impression that she was sparring." She cattily dismissed the White House as a museum (what a dig!) and assumed a "schoolteacher tone" as she "peppered Mrs. Reagan with questions as if the First Lady were a graduate student facing an oral examination." This kind of coverage made us think (hope?) that what we'd get next, instead of some boring old negotiations between a bunch of men about world disarmament, would be a knockdown, drag-out, hair-pulling, eye-scratching wrastling match for world peace. A defeminized, Marxist comrade-in-arms and a hyperfeminized capitalist mannequin get along? Never!

In the 1992 campaign, the contests between Barbara Bush and Marilyn Quayle in one corner, and Hillary Clinton in the other, showed that when it comes to conveying the multilayered complexities women have faced as they have negotiated through work, marriage, motherhood, and politics, the news media will opt for the simplistic yet coercive metaphor of woman-on-woman violence whenever possible. The reason Camille Paglia has become such a media darling, despite an ego the size of Australia and two books that don't make a lick of sense, is that she loves to trash feminists—or, at least, her particular caricature of feminists. Ditto for Katie Roiphe, whose attacks on women twice her age who work in rape crisis centers or battered women's shelters have helped to make her famous. The mainstream media's love of the catfight has made it hard for feminists who value debate and dislike orthodoxy to welcome such debate. (And despite what Paglia and Roiphe think, not all feminists are Stalinists.) All too many feminists feel they must maintain a united front, like it or not, because disagreements among some feminists are simply used to cast all women as face-clawing, eye-scratching hysterics.

Nonetheless, whether on the nightly news or in prime time, the battles between the simpering, sheltered wife and mother on the one side and the ambitious, independent, outspoken bitch on the other pulled women in the audience to the middle, to the space between the two archetypes. The space in the middle was not passive and helpless, nor was it masculinity in drag. This space inside our heads and our hearts was filled with elements of each side, with compromises, with inner conflicts as well as possible resolutions. The media referees insist on putting feminism in one corner and antifeminism in the other, as if feminism could never be in the middle, but what they fail to recognize is that feminism *is* this middle ground. It may be filled with ambivalence and compromise, tradition and rebellion, but the space between the two cats—the space where we, the girls, are— is what feminism is all about.

CHAPTER 11

Narcissism as Liberation

"I'm worth it," insists Cybill Shepherd in her brattiest, na-na-na-poo-poo voice as she swirls her blond hair in my face. Since I have to be restrained, physically, from hatcheting my television set to death whenever this ad appears (and every woman I know has the same reaction), it is amazing to think it actually sells hair dye. But it must, since this campaign has been harassing us for nearly a decade. "I'm worth it" became the motto for the 1980s woman we saw in television and magazines ads. Endless images of women lounging on tiled verandas, or snuggling with their white angora cats while wearing white silk pajamas, exhorted us to be self-indulgent, self-centered, private, hedonistic. In stark contrast to the selfless wife and mom of *The Feminine Mystique,* not to mention those hideous, loudmouthed feminists who thought sisterhood and political activism mattered, women of the 1980s were urged to take care of themselves, and to do so *for* themselves. An ad for Charles of the Ritz, featuring a gorgeous model dripping with pearls and staring off into space, summed up women's recent history. "I'm not the girl I used to be. Now I want to surround myself with beautiful things. And I want to look beautiful too. I've discovered that it's easier to face the world when I like what I see in the mirror."

By the 1980s, advertising agencies had figured out how to make feminism—and antifeminism—work for them. There had been a few clumsy starts in the 1970s, like the Virginia Slims "You've Come a Long Way, Baby" campaign, which equated liberation with the freedom to give yourself lung cancer. And feminine hygiene sprays like Massengill's pictured the product with a political button reading "Freedom Now" and touted the crotch rot in the can as "The Freedom Spray." But the approaches got more subtle and certainly more invidious as America's multibazillion-dollar cosmetics industry realized that all those kids who once bought Clearasil and Stri-Dex were now getting something even worse than acne—wrinkles. Here was an enormous market—the women who grew up with, who in fact made possible, a youth culture—now getting old. You could almost hear the skin cream moguls in their boardrooms yelling yippie-kiyo-kiyay.

The appropriation of feminist desires and feminist rhetoric by Revlon, Lancôme, and other major corporations was nothing short of spectacular. Women's liberation metamorphosed into female narcissism unchained as political concepts and goals like liberation and equality were collapsed into distinctly personal, private desires. Women's liberation became equated with women's ability to do whatever they wanted for themselves, whenever they wanted, no matter what the expense. These ads were geared to the woman who had made it in a man's world, or who hoped she would, and the message was Reward yourself, you deserve it. There was enormous emphasis on luxury, and on separating oneself from the less enlightened, less privileged herd. The ability to spend time and money on one's appearance was a sign of personal success and of breaking away from the old roles and rules that had held women down in the past. Break free from those old conventions, the ads urged, and get *truly* liberated: put yourself first.

Narcissism was more in for women than ever, and the ability to indulge oneself, pamper oneself, and focus at length on oneself without having to listen to the needy voices of others was the mark of upscale female achievement. These were the years when we were supposed to put the naive, idealistic, antimaterialistic 1960s behind us and, instead, go to polo matches and wash our hair with bottled water from the Alps. Ralph Lauren, in his ads for sheets and oxford cloth shirts, used manor houses, antique furniture, riding boots, and safari gear to make us long for the days when the sun never set on the British Empire, when natives (and women) knew their place, and robber barons ran America. Huge museum exhibits celebrated England's "Treasure Houses" and the gowns favored by Marie Antoinette and her pals, each of which represented the work of 213 starving peasant seamstresses.[1] *The Big Chill* suggested that even radical baby boomers had sold out to Wall Street, a move portrayed as inevitable and perfectly understandable.

For women in the age of Reagan, elitism and narcissism merged in a perfect appeal to forget the political already, and get back to the personal, which you might be able to do something about. But let's not forget the most ubiquitous and oppressive anatomical symbol of the new woman's achievement that came into its own in the 1980s: the perfectly sculpted, dimple-free upper thigh and buttock. A tour through the land of smooth faces and even smoother buttocks and thighs makes one appreciate why the women of the 1980s who had reason to feel pride in their accomplishments still felt like worthless losers when they looked in the mirror or, horror of horrors, put on a bathing suit. Of course, these feelings were hardly confined to baby boomers. Nor are they confined to the past. Though I write about what emerged in the 1980s in the past tense, I feel awkward about doing so, because the ad strategies established then are still in high gear, and we watch their effects with sorrow, anger, and empathy. When I go to any number of college or university swimming pools, I see women twenty years younger than I, at their physical peak, healthy and trim, walk out to the pool with towels wrapped around their waists so their thighs will be exposed to the world only for the few nanoseconds it takes to drop the towel and dive into the pool. I have *never* seen a young man do this. Then they go back to the locker room and slather their sweet, twenty-year-old faces with Oil of Olay so they can fight getting old "every step of the way."

Advertisers in the 1980s, especially those targeting women, apparently had a new bible: Christopher Lasch's 1979 best-seller, *The*

Culture of Narcissism. Lasch identified what he saw as a new trend, the emergence of people who seemed self-centered and self-satisfied but were really deeply anxious about what others thought of them. Americans were becoming increasingly self-absorbed, he wrote, but not because they were conceited. On the contrary, Americans were desperately insecure, consumed by self-doubt and self-loathing, and totally obsessed with competing with other people for approval and acclaim. The "narcissistic personality," according to Lasch, was compulsively "other-directed" and consumed by self-doubt, even self-hatred. As a result, the narcissist craved approval and fantasized about adulation. Any sense of self-esteem was fleeting, hinging on things like whether someone looked at you funny or laughed at one of your jokes. This obsessive need for admiration prompted the narcissist to become skilled at managing impressions, at assuming different roles, and at developing a magnetic personality. Narcissists were always measuring themselves against others; being envied, for example, had become infinitely more important than being admired or respected. Narcissists had a strong belief in their right to be gratified and were constantly searching for heightened emotional experiences, for instant gratification, to stave off the fear that life is unreal, artificial, and meaningless. Narcissists were especially terrified of aging and death. Lasch particularly emphasized how the messages and ploys of American advertising had cultivated such narcissistic personalities.

When I read this book, I was struck by two things. First, Lasch kept using the pronoun *he* to talk about the narcissist, and this helped make the trend he was describing seem new. But for women, this wasn't so new, this was the story of our lives, of how we had been socialized since childhood. Second, it was in ads geared specifically to women, especially ads for cosmetics and other personal care items, that we saw advertisers applying, with a vengeance, the various insights of Lasch's book. Under the guise of addressing our purported new confidence and self-love, these ads really reinforced how we failed to measure up to others. Hanes, for example, in a classic campaign, skillfully resolved the tensions surrounding new womanhood in its series of ads titled "Reflections On . . ." A woman was pictured sitting across the arms of a leather chair, or in a wicker patio lounger, with her legs prominently displayed. She was usually dressed up in a glittery cocktail dress, exchanging smiles with a man in a tux. She was always white. In one ad, the admiring male voice said, "She messes up the punch line of every joke; can tell a Burgundy from a Bordeaux; and her legs . . . Oh yes, Joanna's legs." In another version, the copy read: "She does this flawless imitation of Groucho Marx; recites the most astonishing passages from Hemingway; ahh, and her legs . . . Emily's legs."

Joanna's and Emily's nonanatomical achievements were impressive—they knew things only elite men used to know, like how to select a wine, and their favorite writer wasn't Edith Wharton or Alice Walker, it was Mr. Macho himself. They didn't imitate Mae West (too threatening), they imitated a constantly lecherous man. They had cracked the male code, but, because of Hanes, they were still ladies. These women were huge successes at managing the impressions they gave to others, coming across as distinctive, nonconformist women who nonetheless conform perfectly to dominant standards of beauty. They were self-satisfied and self-assured, yet their value came from male admiration and approval. The ads suggested that without inner confidence, and a core self that is assured and discriminating (made possible, one can infer, by feminism), these women would not be the charmers they are today. But without male approval and admiration, they would not have the acclaim on which narcissistic self-esteem rests. It was in campaigns such as this that the appearance of female self-love and achievement was used to reinforce female dependence on male approval. If you wore Hanes, in other words, you would feel the contradictions between feminism and prefeminism thread together smoothly as you pulled them up over your legs and hips and then strode confidently out into the world.

The cult of narcissism Lasch saw in the 1970s exploded in the 1980s, nurtured by Reagan's me-first-and-to-hell-with-everyone-else political and moral philosophies. Under the guise of telling women, "You're worth it," advertisers suggested we weren't worth it at all but could feel we were, for a moment, if we bought the right product. Here we were again, same as it ever was, bombarded by the message that approval from others, especially men, means everything, and without it you are nothing, an outcast, unworthy and unloved. We were right back to Tinker Bell and Cinderella, urged to be narcissistic yet ridiculed if it was discovered that we were.

The narcissism as liberation campaign found its happiest home in certain television ads, such as those that sponsored shows like *Dynasty,* and in women's magazines like *Vogue, Harper's Bazaar, Mademoiselle, Glamour, Cosmopolitan,* and the aptly named *Self.* These magazines, with their emphasis on clothes, makeup, and dieting, were much more hospitable than *Ladies' Home Journal* or *McCall's,* which acknowledged that women couldn't be completely self-indulgent since they still were the ones responsible for pureeing bananas for the baby and getting dinner on the table at night. *Vogue* et al. didn't contaminate their pages with such gritty reminders of reality, thank God. Instead, they created a narcissistic paradise, a luxurious daydream, in which women focused on themselves and their appearance, and in which any change was possible, as long as it was personal.

Now, before I get on my high horse about cures for what the fashion magazines call "orange peel skin" and subdermal rehydrating systems, let me be perfectly honest about my own vulnerability to these really preposterous ploys. Like a lot of women, I look at ads for things like Elizabeth Arden's Ceramide Time Complex Capsules, little gelatinous spheres that look like a cross between a diaphragm and a UFO, which claim to—get this—"boost [the] skin's hydration level over 450% after one hour" because they are "supercharged with HCA, a unique alpha-hydroxy complex," and I think—or sometimes yell—would you puleeze get real here. I know that in 1987 the FDA had cracked down on cosmetics ads then in print because they were, to put it euphemistically, inflated in their claims. I know that putting collagen on your skin does nothing. Nevertheless, there's this perfectly airbrushed model, young, beautiful, and carefree, her eyebrows the only lines on her face, and I sigh a longing sigh. Even when we are fully able to deconstruct these pseudoscientific sales pitches, which would make any self-respecting snake oil salesman blush, there we are, a part of us still wanting to believe that we can look younger and that it's desirable to do so. I don't "read" *Vogue* or *Glamour;* if you'll pardon the masculine metaphor, I enter them. I escape into them, into a world where I have nothing more stressful to do than smooth on some skin cream, polish my toenails, and lie on the beach. But despite these soft spots, I'm here to say that deconstruction can make us strong, so let's be on with it.

In ads for personal care products in the 1980s, especially skin creams, makeup, and perfume, we confronted our ideal selves, eternally young, flawless, confident, assured of the envy of others, yet insulated from the needs of others. The Lutèce Bath, for example, created "your private world of luxury." In these ads, the contradictions that we'd lived with all our lives, the tensions between the need to be passive and the need to be active, were subtly and brilliantly resolved. Usually the women pictured were enjoying leisure moments, or what *Glamour* called "private time." They were sitting alone on their enormous porches, or reclining in beds of satin sheets, or soaking in bubble baths, sometimes with their eyes closed, in a state of relaxation and escape. In one of my favorites, an ad for something called Terme di Montecatini, we saw the profile of a woman at a spa, covered from forehead to rib cage with a kind of mud we assumed would make her even more beautiful while she just rested. Women like this are passive, inactive, supine. Yet make no mistake about it, these women are in complete control: they are dependent on no one, their time is their own, they are beyond the cares of the world, they long for nothing they don't already have. Those symbols of wealth—a huge veranda, the Riviera, art objects, unusual breeds of dogs, the omnipresent glass of white wine—convey comfort, luxury, insulation from the masses, and control.

It wasn't enough to put some Lubriderm on your face—my God, that was like consigning your skin to the soup kitchens of moisturizers. No, you had to spend money, and plenty of it, to be a discriminating, knowledgeable, accomplished woman. An ad for a product called Oligo-Major lectured, "No woman can afford to be without it." The cosmetics industry employed three main strategies to get women to buy the high-priced spreads for their faces instead of using the cheap shit, Pond's or Nivea—the building construction approach, the haute cuisine approach, and the high-tech approach, all intended to flatter the "new woman." They were designed to convey one basic message: you get what you pay for, and if you scrimp on skin-care products, you get what you deserve—crow's-feet, eye bags, turkey neck, the worst. Fail to spend $42.50 on one-thirty-second of an ounce of skin cream and the next time you look in the mirror, you'll see Lyndon Johnson in drag.

The building construction approach was best represented by a fabulous new product, Line Fill, a kind of Silly Putty for the face. Line Fill was also called skin Spackle—now we were supposed to think of ourselves as a slab of drywall—and was best used to "fill those character lines we can all do without." In the same age when "character," particularly for male politicians, became an obsession, women didn't dare look like they had any character at all. Chanel's Lift Sérum Anti-Wrinkle Complex relied on Plastoderm, which, despite its name, operated as a kind of hydraulic jack for sagging skin. "Wrinkles," informed the ad, "are 'lifted' by gentle upward pressure." The haute cuisine approach reached its apotheosis with "skin caviar," an "intensive concentration of vitamins, humectants, emollients and plant naturals." The assumption here was that aging skin was merely malnourished; so in a gesture reminiscent of our new heroine, Marie Antoinette, the truly discriminating woman should say, "Let it eat caviar."

But without doubt the most prevalent approach was the high-tech approach, the one that introduced us to "delivery systems," "collagen," and lots of words starting with *micro-* and *lipo-*. What women's liberation really meant was that now the labs of America would turn to our real concerns: our crow's-feet. Science and technology, those onetime villains that had brought us napalm, the bomb, Three Mile Island, Love Canal, and the Dalkon Shield, were themselves given a face-lift for women. They were rehabilitated as our allies and our minions. Science and technology were the most effective agents of luxurious narcissism, and the various forms of white goop that we slopped on our faces had amazing names that cloaked the products in mystery while keeping supposedly technophobic and techno-dumbo females engaged and credulous.

Here we see another clever twist on feminism. The women's health movement of the 1970s, as embodied in *Our Bodies, Ourselves,* insisted that doctors not treat women like morons but that they talk to us as adults, provide us with information and choices, and give us more control over our bodies. Advertisers said OK, you want technical, medical information, we'll give it to you. They got to have it both ways—they flattered the "new woman" with all this pseudoscientific jargon, suggesting that this was the kind of information she wanted, needed, and could easily understand, and they got to make the goop they were selling sound as if it had been developed at Cal Tech.

In the 1980s, in nearly every cosmetic ad we saw, science and technology were women's servants, and servants not just to expedite domestic chores (as in the bad, selfless old days) but through which women could remake themselves, conquer time, and conquer nature by overcoming their genetic heritage. Here women's desires for more control over and more autonomy in their lives were shrewdly co-opted. Naomi Wolf argues that the high-tech approach sought to speak to women whose work was increasingly dominated by computers and the microchip.[2] The words *performance, precision,* and *control* were used repeatedly, and products such as Swiss Performing Extract or Niosôme Système Anti-Age performed on you (you are passive) while performing for you (you are in command). One product's slogan was, simply, "The Victory of Science over Time." This product, like so many, contained "patented liposomes," which, in case you needed an explanation, were "micro-capsules of select ingredients of natural origin which fuse with the membrane restoring fluidity, promoting reactivation of cells in your skin." Niosôme produced "an exclusive action, 'Biomimitism.' " This was not supposed to make you think of conjugating spirogyra; it was supposed to make you feel privy to the world of the scientist. It was very important to feature microscopes, women in white lab jackets, and lots of footnotes about patents pending to suggest the weight of a scientific abstract.

As we read other ads for competing products (and there was no shortage of them), a pattern started to emerge. Nearly all the cosmetics companies referred to their products as "systems." These systems "penetrate" the "intercellular structure" of the skin, increasing "microcirculation." Using only the most advanced "delivery systems," presumably inspired by NASA, the Pentagon, and Star Wars, these creams and lotions deployed "advanced microcarriers" or "active anti-age agents," presumably trained by the CIA to terminate wrinkles with extreme prejudice. So cosmetics actually became weapons, and the word *defense* began to proliferate in ads at the same time, interestingly, that the Pentagon's budget was going through the roof.

In copy sounding as if it had been written by Alexander Haig, our skin was put in a bunker or, better yet, behind Reagan's version of Star Wars, as "protective barriers" and "invisible shields" deflected "external aggressors." These muscular products relied on the same high-tech weaponry we saw in *The Empire Strikes Back* and had straightforward names like Defense Cream and Skin Defender. You could almost see Luke Skywalker, backed up by the Green Berets, zapping those wrinkles back to kingdom come. Turning on its head the feminist argument that the emphasis on beauty undermines women's ability to be taken seriously and to gain control over their lives, advertisers now assured women that control *comes* from cosmetics. Cosmetics were sold as newly engineered tools, precision instruments you could use on yourself to gain more control than ever over the various masks and identities you as a woman must present to the world.

But lest all this high-tech talk alienate women, cosmetics firms also made sure to give their products European-, and especially French-sounding names. System was usually spelled *système;* concentrated became *concentré*. Accent signs became essential, as did the pronoun *Le*. Several product names simply went for broke, as in this little gem, Crème Multi Modelanté bio-suractiveé, or Lift Extrême Nutri-Collagène Concentré. What were brilliantly brought together were the seemingly opposite worlds of advanced, ever-changing, American engineering technology and laboratory science (traditionally the province of men) and the preindustrialist, timeless, beauty-oriented cultural authority of Europe (which caters to women). For new beauty products to sell, it seems, the ads had to refer to and unite recent scientific breakthroughs and the language of engineering with references to France, Switzerland, or Italy. The words *extract, serum,* and *molecular* suggested both the lab *and* elements found in nature. Thus Niosôme, from Lancôme, is an antiaging "system" with a French-sounding name that "recreates the structure of a young skin." Cosmetics ads straddled the Atlantic, linking American technology with European culture, and the traditions of the old world with the futurism of the new.

With the union of science and aesthetics, women now could draw from the achievements of men in a world in which science and technology did what we always wished they would do—slow the passage of time, provide us with cost-free luxury and convenience, and allow us to remake ourselves. It was through the female form, and the idealized female face in particular, that science and technology were made to seem altruistic, progressive, relevant to everyday needs, and responsive to women's desires. They were made humane and romantic, and allied with the realms of art, nature, and tradition.

At the same time, the pseudoscientific language not only legitimated cosmetic companies' claims but also assured women that these products were for discriminating, upscale consumers. The new woman was now sophisticated enough and privileged enough to benefit from a scientific enterprise designed specifically for elite white women. The linking of American science and technology with European cultural authority served to unite narcissism with elitism, to make elitism seem natural, legitimate, and inevitable, and to suggest that if you truly loved yourself, you had to aspire to the privileged, idle, self-indulgent world of the rich, who were the rightful beneficiaries of technology, and the true arbiters of high art. Here we had a new kind of magic. How could products that relied on herbal treatments, molecular biology, and chemistry fail to transform us into newer, better selves?

Of course, if you'd been derelict in your moisturizing duties, there were more heroic methods to combat the signs of aging. Article after article touted plastic surgery, so that no woman would ever have to go out in public again looking like Eleanor Roosevelt, Simone de Beauvoir, or Margaret Mead did in their later years. Experts from skin-care labs, their names trailed by twenty-eight initials signifying their degrees and affiliations, happily agreed to interviews for *Harper's Bazaar* and elsewhere, promoting the knife. They always said these really informative and logical things, like that the first part of the body people usually look at is the face, which is why you shouldn't have any lines on yours. So what if, after a few tucks, you were laid up for six weeks and looked like you'd gone eighteen rounds with George Foreman? It was true, some women did experience a little facial paralysis after a lift, and you might not look as Occidental as you used to or have enough skin to smile in quite the same way, but these concerns were all picky, picky, picky. Did you want to look like Cher, or not?

The other intermediate step was promoted in full-page ads by the Collagen Corporation. Here we met Sunny Griffin, "mother, building contractor, and former TV correspondent and model." Already I felt pretty inferior, but it quickly got worse. Sunny was ten years older than I and easily looked ten years younger. Sunny, it turned out, "didn't like those 'little commas' at the corners of her mouth, her crow's feet, or the lines on her forehead. So she did something about them." But, unlike me, she was a woman of action. She went to a doctor who stuck needles in her face, filling in those hideous lines with "injectable Zyderm© and Zyplast© Collagen." Now those wrinkles were "mere memories." Here were prefeminism and feminism beautifully reconciled in Sunny Griffin, Collagen poster girl. As a feminist, this superwoman had tackled male jobs and female jobs and combined them successfully with motherhood. This gave her permission to indulge her prefeminist side, the one still obsessed with little commas and crow's-feet, especially if she took decisive medical action to take control of her face and herself.

In the collagen ad, it was the beautiful, rich, and successful Sunny Griffin versus the rest of us. And that was the other important thrust of the narcissism as liberation campaign, the continuation of the catfight, the war between women. In all these ads, sisterhood was out, competitive individualism was in. It got worse if you actually fell for these ads (hey, I was in my thirties, what did I know?) and went out to buy some skin defender. If you've ever bought anything at a Clinique, Lancôme, or other such counter, you know what I mean. The saleswoman's face is made up like a Kabuki mask to put you off balance right away. And, clearly, all these women were trained wherever that awful secret place is that they train used car salesmen. Using a combination of intimidation, pressure, and highly uncharitable assessments of your existing skin-care regimen, these women sought to shame you into buying everything they had, which could come to the equivalent of a monthly car payment. The worst, and I mean the worst, thing you could say to one of these women was that you mixed products—you know, used a cleanser from one company and moisturizer from another. Then they'd nearly croak from exasperation at your stupidity and your self-destructive tendencies. Didn't you know, these cosmetic lines were *integrated* systems; each component worked with the other components as a unit. Mixing products was akin to putting a Chevy carburetor inside a Porsche engine and expecting the car to run. You'd wreck your face by mixing products;

you had to buy into the entire system or risk waking up one morning to discover your face turning into melting wax.

The notion of sisterhood being powerful seemed a real joke
under this onslaught. Fisticuffs seemed more appropriate. It took
work to remember that the salesclerks needed these jobs, that many
of them were supporting kids with their salaries, and that while we
squared off against each other across the glass-cased counter, the big
boys upstairs who didn't need face cream were getting ready for their
three-martini lunches and their affairs with women twenty years
younger than they.

Tensions between technology and nature, between feminism and
antifeminism, and between self-love and self-doubt were played out
not only on the terrain of the flawless female face. Everywhere we
looked, in the incessant "get-back-in-shape" TV ads and magazine
articles, on billboards, in the catalogs that jammed our mailboxes, and
in the endless diet soda and cereal ads on the airwaves, the perfectly
smooth, toned buttocks and thighs of models and actresses accosted
the women of America. They jutted out at us from the new, high-
cut, split-'em-in-two bathing suits and exercise outfits, challenging
us and humbling us, reminding all women that nothing in the world
is more repulsive and shameful than "orange peel skin," a.k.a. "cellulite." They provided women, whether black or white, rich or poor,
with a universal standard of achievement and success. They insisted
that the rest of us should feel only one thing when we put on a
bathing suit: profound mortification.

It's true that we also started seeing more female biceps, and every
few months *The New York Times* asserted that breasts were back "in."
But, still, it was the slim, dimple-free buttock and thigh that became,
in the 1980s and the 1990s, the ultimate signifier of female fitness,
beauty, and character. To make sure you couldn't hide them, the fashion industry gave us bathing suits with legs cut up to just below the
armpit. Trim, smug models were positioned with their knees bent or
their bodies curled so that their superhuman hindquarters were front
and center. And not just in *Vogue* or *Cosmo,* either: even in *The Village*

Voice, between the exposés on racism and government malfeasance, ads appeared for products like the videotape *Buns of Steel,* which promised, "Now you can have the buns you've always wanted." Saddlebag-busting products like Biotherm appeared, which actually suggested that if you just rubbed some cream on your buttocks, the dimples would go into remission.

Why this part of the body? Why were we suddenly but constantly confronted by these perfectly sculpted rumps? During the mammary mania of the 1950s and '60s, bust creams, exercisers, and padded bras suggested that women could compensate for what nature forgot. Yet while less-endowed women might buy such products, and bemoan their lack of voluptuousness, there was also a basic understanding that, short of surgery, there was little a woman could do to actually change the size of her breasts. The thigh was different: this body part could be yoked to another pathology of the 1980s, the yuppie work ethic. Thin thighs and dimple-free buttocks became instant, automatic evidence of discipline, self-denial, and control. You, too, the message went, can achieve perfect thighs through dieting and exercise. As Jane Fonda put it, "Discipline Is Liberation."[3]

Emphasis on the thigh, which still harasses us, stems from the fitness craze of the past fifteen years, when increasing numbers of women discovered the physical and psychic benefits of exercise. I learned in graduate school, for example, that if I swam sixty-seven laps in the pool I was less likely to strangle the pompous white male professors making my life miserable, and I'd also sort out some problem with my own work as well. Plus, for inspiration to get off your butt, there were women like Billie Jean King, one of my heroes, a fabulous athlete and a feminist, and the first woman athlete to earn more than $100,000 a year. When she beat the living crap out of Bobby Riggs in the much touted "Battle of the Sexes" in 1973, as women like me screamed with delight in our living rooms, she not only vindicated female athletes and feminism but also inspired many of us to get in shape—not because it would make us beautiful but because it would make us strong and healthy.

What too many of us forget is that the fitness movement began as a radical reaction against the degradation of food by huge conglomerates, and against the work routines and convenience technologies that encouraged us to be passive and sedentary. The organic health food movement was, initially, at its core, anticapitalist. The women's fitness movement, too, was a site of resistance, as women sought to break into sports previously restricted to men and other women simply sought to get strong. But one of capitalism's great strengths—perhaps its greatest—is its ability to co-opt and domesticate opposition, to transubstantiate criticism into a host of new, marketable products. And so it was with fitness.

Corporations saw immediately that there was gold in them thar thighs. The key to huge profits was to emphasize beauty over health, sexuality over fitness, and to equate thin thighs with wealth and status. What had worked so well in the past was to set up standards of perfection that were cast as unattainable yet somehow within reach if only the right product were purchased. So we got a new, even narrower ideal of beauty that continues to bombard us from every media outlet and serves the needs of a host of corporations.

Yet there was much more going on here than just the media capitalizing on a trend or the standard let's-make-'em-feel-inferior-so-they'll-buy-our-product routine. The flawless rump became *the* most important female body part of the 1980s because its cultivation and display fit in so well with the great myth of Reaganism: that superficial appearances really can be equated with a person's deepest character strengths and weaknesses. The emphasis on streamlined rumps allowed for a dramatic reshaping of feminist urgings that women take control of their bodies and their health. All we had to do was listen to Cher in those health spa ads, she'd tell us: thin thighs and dimple-free buttocks meant you worked hard, took yourself seriously, and were ready to compete with anyone. They were indicators of a woman's potential for success. Any woman, so the message went, could achieve perfect thighs through concentrated effort, self-denial, and deferred gratification, the basic tenets of the work ethic. All she had to do was apply herself and, of course, be a discriminating, upscale consumer. "You don't get this far by accident," proclaimed one sneaker ad displaying a tight, toned rump; "you've worked hard." Another magazine ad, this one for a spa, also spotlighted a machine-tooled hindquarter, intoning, "When you work at it, it shows." Meaning, if you've been slacking off, that will show too. Only "new women" had buns of steel; out-of-date women who had failed to have their consciousnesses raised didn't.

It didn't matter if you were healthy, exercised regularly, and weren't overweight. If wearing one of the new, ultrahigh-cut bathing suits would reveal too much roundness, a little fat (what the cosmetics industry christened "cellulite" in the 1970s), you would be dismissed as slothful and lacking moral fiber and self-respect, not to mention lazy, self-indulgent, insufficiently vigorous, lacking control, sedentary, and old. (The only acceptable sedentary indulgence was to lie on a chaise longue, slathered from head to toe in sludge, à la Terme di Montecatini.) No matter that the female hip area is naturally more fatty than the male (a function of reproduction), or that most women's jobs require constant sitting, two factors that tend to work against developing buns of steel. Over and again we were told that a real woman, whatever her age, would get off her butt and, by overcoming her sloth, not just get in shape but conquer genetics and history. Her buns of steel would instantly identify her as someone who subscribed to the new yuppie ethic that insisted that even in leisure hours, the truly tough, the truly deserving, never stopped working. The sleek, smooth, tight butt was—and is—a badge, a medal asserting that anal compulsiveness is an unalloyed virtue.

Perfect thighs, in other words, were an achievement, a product, and one to be admired and envied. They demonstrated that the woman had made something of herself, that she had character and class, that she was the master of her body and, thus, of her fate. If she had conquered her own adipose tissue, she could conquer anything. She was a new woman, liberated and in control. She had made her buttocks less fatty, more muscular, more, well . . . like a man's. So here we have one of the media's most popular—and pernicious—distortions of feminism: that ambitious women want, or should want, to be just like men. The woman whose upper thigh best approximated a fat-free male hindquarter was the woman most entitled to enjoy the same privileges as men. Orange-peel skin should be a source of shame, not only because it's "ugly," but also because it's inherently female. It indicates that, as a woman, you aren't working hard enough, aren't really taking responsibility for your own life. You aren't really liberated because you haven't overcome being a woman. A desirable woman doesn't look like a real woman looks; thus, one of the basic physical markers of femaleness is cast as hideous.

Yet well-toned, machine-tooled thighs suggested that women could compete with men while increasing their own desirability. Thighs, rather than breasts, became the focus in the 1980s because presumably everyone, the flat-chested and the stacked, men as well as women, could work toward buns of steel. Women could develop the same anatomical zones that men did, giving their muscles new definition, a definition meant to serve simultaneously as a warning and as an enticement to men. Buns of steel marked a woman as a desirable piece of ass, and as someone who could kick ass when necessary.

What made these thighs desirable was that, while they were fat-free, like men's, they also resembled the thighs of adolescent girls. The ideal rump bore none of the marks of age, responsibility, work, or motherhood. And the crotch-splitting, cut-up-to-the-waistline, impossible-to-swim-in bathing suits featured in such publications as the loathsome *Sports Illustrated* swimsuit issue could never reveal that other marker of adulthood, pubic hair. So, under the guise of female fitness and empowerment, of control over her own body, was an idealized image that infantilized women, an image that kept women in their place.

The upper thigh thus became freighted with meaning. The work ethic, the ethos of production and achievement, self-denial and deferred gratification was united there with egoism, vanity, self-absorption, and other-directedness. With the work ethic moved from the workplace to the private sphere, the greatest female achievement became, ironically, her body, her self. The message was that women were capable of remaking themselves and that this remaking required not only intelligent consumption but also hard work. Thus could women be, simultaneously, self-indulgent consumers, buying high-priced exercise shoes and spa memberships, and self-denying producers who were working hard to remake something—their bodies. They could be active subjects in control of their own images and passive objects judged by those images. They could be prefeminists and new women at the same time.

By the middle of the 1980s, these buttocks and thighs were making me and all the other women I knew really hostile and defensive. Their sleek, seemingly healthy surfaces really demanded that we all be pathological: compulsive, filled with self-hate, and schizophrenic, and we were already schizophrenic enough, thank you very much. Aside from the impossible standards of perfection they imposed, these buns of steel urged women to never stop and to be all things to all people: to be both competitive workaholics *and* sex objects, to be active workers in control of their bodies *and* passive ornaments for the pleasure of men, to be hard-as-nails superwomen *and* vulnerable, unthreatening, teenage beach bunnies. Straddling such contradictions, even on toned, fat-free, muscular legs is, in real life, impossible. And buns of steel were meant to separate the truly classy, deserving women from the rest of the lumpy female proletariat. Buns of steel, like a Pierre Cardin label, were a mark of well-earned exclusivity. Lumpy thighs were K mart thighs, not the thighs of Rodeo Drive.

The 1980s are over, but buns of steel are very much with us, in Diet Pepsi ads, Victoria's Secret catalogs, and women's magazines. A 1993 survey reported that while only 6 percent of women wished their breasts were either bigger or smaller, a whopping 72 percent wished they had "better thighs."[4] That same year, the cover of *Glamour* promised, in a two-inch headline, "A Better Butt, Fast!" The cover also promised to explain "Why 15 Million Women Own Guns."[5] I figure it's to shoot everyone involved in the campaign to make us think we need buns of steel. The article inside, titled euphoniously enough "The World-Class Butt," accompanied by exercise instructions and an enormous photo of a smooth, sixteen-year-old butt in white eyelet short shorts, lectured, "A toned, firm bottom has plenty to recommend it, as the photo on the right confirms." I also learned that the "flat bottom featured in those beach-blanket movies" was really out. "Now women want a defined, sculpted look with higher, rounder cheeks." Yep, this has been an overarching goal I've wanted to devote a lot of time to in the 1990s. But there's the same old hitch: "You have to work hard to firm them up. So get busy." No need to repeat which expletives I use when reading an exhortation such as this.

So where do these buttocks and thighs leave the rest of us, the real women of America who sit at desks or stand at sinks, who are over sixteen, and who don't have the time, money, personal trainer, or surgical team to help us forge our own buns of steel? Even nonoverweight women, and women who do and should know better, have been worked over so well that whenever we look at ourselves in the mirror or, worse, have to be seen in public in a bathing suit, all we can feel is disgust and shame. But it isn't just shame of our bodies. Buns of steel have taught us to be ashamed of the way we live our day-to-day lives; of the fact that whatever we're doing, we aren't working hard enough; that we don't have that badge of entitlement; that we don't really have enough self-respect and dignity; that we aren't enough like men; and, worst of all, that we're adult females in a culture that still prefers, by and large, little girls. All it takes is the slightest roundness, the smallest dimple, to mark a woman as a lazy, and therefore worthless, unattractive person whose thighs obliterate whatever other admirable traits or impressive accomplishments she might possess.

I'm tired of being told never to stop, and that some physical exertion, like pumping a Nautilus machine, is more valuable than some other exertion, such as chasing a two-year-old. I'm tired of Cher's rump, Christie Brinkley's thighs, and countless starved, airbrushed,

surgically enhanced hindquarters being shoved in my face. I'm tired
of being told that if I just exercise a lot more and eat a lot less, I, too,
can conquer biology, make my thighs less female, and thus not be
eyed with derision. I'm *real* tired of the marquis de Sade "bathing
suits" foisted on us by the fashion industry. Most of all, I'm tired of
the endless self-flagellation we women subject ourselves to because of
the way this latest, unattainable, physical ideal has been combined
with the yuppie work ethic.

And I'm not alone. Backlash works two ways, and women, especially cranky women my age, are really getting the fed-up-skis with
advertisers' obsession with machine-tooled faces and thighs. I think
that catalogs like Lands' End must be making a fortune on this backlash against buns of steel. They sell bathing suits that fit and that you
can actually swim in. If you make the mistake of waiting until late
June to order one, they're out of stock because furious women all
over the country now refuse to try on a glorified G-string under fluorescent lights that make you look like a very fat dead person.

At the same time that we can't exorcise such long-standing infe-
riority complexes about our bodies, we see women trying to reclaim
the fitness movement from Kellogg's, Diet Pepsi, Biotherm, and
all the rest of the buttocks and thighs cartel. Women know, in
their heads if not their hearts, that buns of steel are not about fitness:
they are about pretending that some anorexic, unnatural, corporate-
constructed ideal is really a norm. Buns of steel are designed to
humiliate women, and to make us complicit in our own degradation, and most women know this too. Silly as they may seem, buns
of steel are worth being angry about because of the eating disorders
they promote among young women and the general sexism
they reinforce in society. So the next time some curled-up rump is
forced into your field of vision, view it not with envy but with contempt. For it doesn't reflect hard work or entitlement so much as
mindless narcissism, unproductive self-absorption, and the media's
ongoing distortion of feminism to further their own misogynistic,
profit-maximizing ends. Buns of steel are just another media Trojan

horse, pretending to advance feminism but harboring antifeminist weaponry.

Narcissism as liberation gutted many of the underlying principles of the women's movement. Instead of group action, we got escapist solitude. Instead of solidarity, we got female competition over men. And, most important, instead of seeing personal disappointments, frustrations, and failures as symptoms of an inequitable and patriarchal society, we saw these, just as in the 1950s, as personal failures, for which we should blame ourselves. Smooth, toned thighs and buttocks obstruct any vision of social change and tell us that, as women, personal change, physical change, is our last, best, and most realistic hope. Women are to take control of their bodies not for political or health reasons but to make them aesthetically pleasing. The "new woman" of the 1980s, then, perpetuated and legitimated the most crass, selfish aspects of consumer capitalism and thus served to distort and deny the most basic and revolutionary principles of feminism. Narcissism as liberation is liberation repackaged, deferred, and denied. Again women felt pinioned, trapped in a web of warring messages. We were supposed to work harder than ever; in fact, the mark of success was having no time for your friends, your family, or yourself. But we were also supposed to indulge ourselves, and to know when and how to kick back, and to do so with style.

Let's take, for example, the politics of the face-lift. Baby boomers with sufficient discretionary income are starting to confront this one, and with the explosion in celebrity journalism, stars' face-lifts and other nips and tucks have become headline news, serving as an enticement and a warning. Cosmetic surgery is being presented as a perfectly natural, affordable, routine procedure, and increasing numbers of women are heeding the call. Cosmetic surgery is growing at a faster rate than any other medical specialty and grosses approximately $300 million a year.[6] The decision to get a face-lift or not is, inescapably, a political decision. Getting one means you're acquiescing to our country's sick norms about beauty, youth, and being "worth it." Not getting one means you're gonna tough it out, be baggy-faced, and take the heat. Actresses and models have no choice. The rest of American women are pulled between these nodes.

But here's what doesn't come out in the war against wrinkles and cellulite: women are as conflicted about aging as they are about other aspects of their lives. For example, when I was twenty and had streaked blond hair, walking down pretty much any street was a nightmare. The incessant yells of "Hey, baby," and other more anatomically graphic remarks, the whistles and other simianlike sounds some men seem to spend an inordinate amount of time perfecting, all these infuriated me and kept me constantly on the defensive. Now that doesn't happen anymore—and I love it. I can walk—no comments; I can jog—no comments; I can walk along the beach—no leers. My eye bags and my "cellulite" are now my friends, my protectors, my armor, and I love them for that. At the same time, part of me will always want to sandpaper them off.

Then there's the love-hate relationship with the eye bags. No woman wants to look like George Shultz after a bad night, but a woman's facial lines are the story of her life. I got mine from pulling too many all-nighters in college, from smoking pot, from drinking tequila with my brother and champagne with my husband, from baking way too long in the sun, from putting in sixty-hour workweeks, from having a child unfamiliar with the concept of sleep, and, of course, from growing older. They've tracked my joys and sorrows, my failures and successes, and I'm supposed to want to chop them off so I can look like an empty vessel, a bimbette? Besides, my husband, who hates it when his favorite actresses get face-lifts and don't look like themselves anymore, likes them. They go with his; they're a team.

So here's the question, girls. And it's one you guys should consider too as Grecian Formula, Clinique, and Soloflex eye your sagging faces and bodies greedily. What if every woman in America woke up tomorrow and simply decided that she was happy with the way she looked? She might exercise to keep herself healthy, and get some Vaseline Intensive Care from CVS to soothe her dry skin, but, basically, that would be the extent of it. Think of the entire multibillion-dollar industries that would crumble. This is one of the reasons lesbians are so vilified—many of them have already made this choice, thereby costing the beauty industry millions. If women decided in the war between feminism and antifeminism being waged in skin-care and diet soda ads that antifeminism had way too big an advantage, women might decide to shift the odds a bit. For example, they might decide to take the $42.50 for skin caviar or skin Spackle and send it, instead, to the Fund for the Feminist Majority, the International Red Cross, the Children's Defense Fund, or some other organization that works for the benefit of women and children.

The reason this won't happen is that advertising, women's magazines, movies, and TV shows have been especially effective in alienating women from their faces and bodies. Women of all ages, who are perfectly capable of denouncing sexist news coverage, or making their own empowering and subversive meanings out of TV shows and films, find it extremely difficult to resist the basic tenet that a face with lines or a thigh with dimples means you are worthless. The media's relentlessly coercive deployment of perfect faces and bodies, and the psychologically, politically, and economically punitive measures taken against women who fail to be young, thin, and beautiful, have intersected seamlessly with age-old American ideals about the work ethic, being productive, and being deserving of rewards. The "I'm Worth It" campaign and all its allies and imitators co-opt the feminist effort to promote female self-esteem to reassure women that, deep down, they aren't worth it at all. The same women who have been able to find feminist empowerment in the most unlikely places—from Harry Reasoner's editorials to Krystle and Alexis's catfights—find nothing but self-hatred and disempowerment here. Of all the disfigurements of feminism, this, perhaps, has been the most effective.

CHAPTER 12

I'm Not a Feminist, But . . .

So here we are, kids. It's the 1990s, a decade I used to think of as science fiction. It's still too soon to tell what the nineties will be remembered for, and whether this decade will produce a fashion fad worse than white go-go boots, music even more odious than heavy metal (or whatever that is that bands like Whitesnake and Metallica play), or TV shows more corrosive to the brain and our nation's social fabric than *Cops, Rescue 911, Inside Edition,* and *Hard Copy.* Certainly any future historian, going through the TV ads of today, will assume there was an outbreak of yeast infections among the young, white, upper-middle-class mothers of America that reached epidemic proportions, and that their doctors happily discussed these infections with them for hours on the telephone.

But for baby boom women, now anywhere between thirty and fifty, and just a tad testy, as well as for their mothers, sisters, and daughters, the 1990s promise to deliver more of the same: a media environment with so many split personalities about the roles and place of women that Sybil seems pretty uncomplicated by comparison. Feminism is still an F word, but having women in the professions—well, a few of them, and in some professions—is OK. Women with lines on their faces are still anathema, unless they're selling denture cream or Pampers for seniors. Opinionated women with big mouths are good for laughs in sitcoms, but keep them the hell out of politics and Hollywood movies—unless they are villains, of course. There's certainly no need for feminism anyway, since we just had

"The Year of the Woman" in 1992 and increased the number of women in the Senate to five, which is plenty. Ads for toilet cleaners, mildew blasters, furniture spray, and food enhancers still emphasize woman's role as the only one in the house who can see dirt or prepare a meal. And the main motto of women today is, supposedly, "I'm not a feminist, but . . ."[1]

As both the news and entertainment media have construed this statement, they emphasize and reinforce what comes before the comma: "I'm not a feminist." They pay much less attention to the "but," and virtually ignore the comma itself. The comma, however, is the fulcrum of the whole statement, which marks the divisions—and, more important, the profound connections—between the disavowal of feminism in the first part of the phrase and its embrace at the end. The comma says that the speaker is ambivalent, that she is torn between a philosophy that seeks to improve her lot in life and a desire not to have to pay too dearly for endorsing that philosophy. Most important, the comma identifies the speaker as someone who both acquiesces to *and* resists media representations of women and of feminism. The speaker has been cowed by stereotypes of the feminist as a hateful, obnoxious, repellent shrew. But the speaker also knows that these women have something to say to her, that some of the feminists she has seen and heard she even likes, and she suspects they might not be as hideous as they're made out to be.

So where are we now, in the era of "I'm not a feminist, but . . ."? We are an overlay of imprints, bearing, in some way or another, the fossilized remains of *Queen for a Day, Sputnik,* the Sexual Revolution, the Chiffons, Beatlemania, perkiness, the women's movement, the catfights, *Charlie's Angels,* and buns of steel. We have learned to be masochistic and narcissistic, feisty and compliant, eager to please and eager to irritate and shock, independent and dependent, assertive and conciliatory. We have learned to wear a hundred masks, and to live with the fact that our inner selves are fragmented, some of the pieces validated by the mass media, others eternally ignored. All our lives, we have watched women from Beatles fans to Anita Hill and Hillary

Rodham Clinton breaching barricades and crossing boundaries they weren't supposed to: we have seen how stepping out of line has been punished and how effective—and utterly futile—such punishments have been. Certain women are demonized, but they, and others emboldened by their actions, come back for more. We have grown up with these ever discrepant representations of women, and related to them all our lives, and while we have shaped them, they have had more power to shape us. We have grown up and continue to live with media images not of our making, so, on some level, we will always feel like outsiders looking in at a culture that regards us as unknowable, mysterious, laughable, other. But we are insiders too, having been formed by this very same culture, our desires researched to the hilt and then sold back to us in a warped, yet still recognizable fashion. We stand on the border, looking out and looking in, feeling simultaneously included and excluded, wooed as consumers yet rejected as people.

One of the major traits that defines womanhood in the 1990s is our daily war with all those media which we love and hate and which, after all these years, don't know what to do about us or for us, although they seem to have a better grip on what to do to us. It is easy for many of us to understand what an advertiser or a TV producer wants us to take away from this ad or that show, but that doesn't mean that women always, in fact, buy into and accept those meanings. We are fed up with ads that tell us we're too old, too fat, and too marked up in some way, but we feel, nonetheless, too old, too fat, and too marked up. We are tired of blockbuster movies that glorify beefy, rippled men who speak monosyllabically and carry extremely well-endowed sticks, but we go to them anyway, nursing our fury and enjoying our catharsis. We get the bends as we escape into the schizophrenic landscape of *Glamour* or *Vogue,* in which editorials, advice columns, and articles urge us to be assertive, strong, no-nonsense feminists while the fashion and beauty layouts insist that we be passive, anorexic spectacles whose only function is to attract men and who should spend our leisure time mastering the art of the pedicure. We throw half-eaten bagels at Saturday morning kids' shows and commercials that train our daughters to be giggling, air-headed Valley Girls, but we go ahead and buy them Glitter Ken and the Fisher-Price toy kitchen on the theory that we played with Barbie and we came out OK—well, sort of. We think that news programs must be getting less sexist because there are now famous women newscasters like Connie Chung, Diane Sawyer, and Nina Totenberg, but we also see how so-called women's issues are either sensationalized (have one more drink and you'll die of breast cancer) or trivialized (so what if a woman has to drive 300 miles to get an abortion, or a sixteen-year-old has to get permission to do so from a father she never sees?), while women's voices about major areas of national policy are ignored. Most of all, the constant erasure of the contradictions that define our lives makes us crazy, since all the media, completely confused and conflicted about what to do about women, subtly acknowledge those contradictions while either pretending they don't exist or insisting they can be resolved, especially with a purchase or two.

It's no wonder that "I'm not a feminist, but . . ." has become an infamous and numbingly overused cliché. It is a statement attributed less to baby boom women than to the "baby bust" generation born between 1965 and 1975, to the much stereotyped and condemned "twentysomething" crowd. As I understand this conversational gambit, it means that the speaker probably supports some combination of equal pay for equal work; reproductive freedom for women; equal access to the same educational, professional, and financial opportunities as men; expanded child-care facilities for working parents; more humane maternity and paternity leave policies; marriages in which husbands cook dinner and empty the diaper pail; and an end to—or even a slowing of—our national epidemic of violence against women of all ages. It also means that the speaker shaves her legs, bathes regularly, does not want to be thought of as a man-hater, a ball-buster, a witch, or a shrew, and maybe even wears mascara, blush-on, and a bra. Most of all, it means that the possibility of having, inside you, a unified, coherent self that always believes the same things at the same time is virtually zero.

This is what it has come to. On the one hand, few women want to take on the baggage of the feminist stereotype. On the other hand, they embrace much of what feminism has made possible for them—which they also learned about, initially, from the media—and are uninterested in returning to the days of woman as doormat. Since the 1960s, legitimation of feminism in the mass media and backlash against it have smacked against each other with the force and chaos of billiard balls colliding. Individual women, too often isolated by the pressures of juggling work, relationships, kids, and trying to see a movie once a year, are left on their own to arrange the balls neatly in some psychic rack that makes sense for them, if only momentarily.

What the mass media don't convey, and can't convey, is that feminism is an ongoing project, a process, undertaken on a daily basis by millions of women of all ages, classes, ethnic and racial backgrounds, and sexual preferences. Feminism is constantly being reinvented, and reinvented through determination and compromise, so that women try, as best they can, to have love and support as well as power and autonomy. As they do so, they have certainly taken note, with Susan Faludi's help, of a backlash filled with wishful thinking pronouncements about the "death" of feminism and the heralding of a new "postfeminist" age.[2] But they have also taken heart in *Roseanne, L.A. Law, Murphy Brown,* Nina Totenberg, and Katie Couric, in the various defiant, funny, smart, and strong women they see on TV.

In the 1980s and early 1990s, we continued to witness the war between feminism and antifeminism in movies, TV shows, popular music, the news, and, especially, Senate confirmation hearings. The first fictional "new woman" we got on TV was Joyce Davenport of *Hill Street Blues,* a no-nonsense, stone-faced, humorless woman in public who was more fun in private but was (no doubt because she was such a bitch) unable to have children. *Remington Steele,* in which a woman used a man as a front for her own detective agency, reaffirmed, as *Charlie's Angels* had, the inevitability of patriarchy while insisting, like *Bewitched,* that women were the brains behind the throne. *L.A. Law* showed us tough, smart, often explicitly feminist female attorneys who won in court yet often lost in real life, and who were in constant competition with each other. *thirtysomething,* one of the best-produced and, hands down, most manipulative and annoying shows of the period, dramatized the struggle for women between family and job, yet Hope, the main, beatific mom, couldn't juggle work and baby so she stayed home and nearly had a psychic breakdown when she had to stop breast feeding. *Cagney & Lacey* was many women's favorite. Here were women who wore guns *and* mascara, who loved each other and fought with each other, who told sexist men where to get off and sued their butts for sexual harassment, and who consciously changed the masks they wore as they changed roles throughout the day. But did the unmarried, childless one really have to be an alcoholic, especially since the mother of three had a lot more reason to drink? And in *Moonlighting,* our sympathies were meant to be with the wisecracking David (Bruce Willis) and not with the frequently unsmiling, more serious-minded Maddie (Cybill Shepherd), although I may have been biased by all those L'Oréal commercials. *Northern Exposure* has finally given us, in Ruth Ann, a feisty, wonderful older woman, but one ongoing joke is how O'Connell, the independent young woman of the show, has a string of previous boyfriends who all died after getting involved with her. Through all this, I see less of a concerted, unified backlash and more of a twisted, constipated, contorted effort to hail women who now have some disposable income and growing aspirations, while also dramatizing that feminism can go a little further, but not too far.

The news media, for their part, are today a schizophrenic mess about feminism, and there is a powerful reverberation between their schizophrenia and our own. They continue to cover feminism and describe feminists as if the movement is monolithic and feminists are all alike. At the same time, in their stories and their hiring practices, we see that in the news media (as elsewhere) feminism is many things to many women; that there is not one feminism but many; and that there are beautiful, amiable women who claim feminism and shrill, mean-spirited ones who condemn it.

Let's take *Time's* cover story for December 4, 1989, "Women Face the '90s." Beneath the headline, the cover asked, "In the '80s they tried to have it all. Now they've just plain had it. Is there a future for feminism?" Inside, the article announced, "Hairy legs haunt the feminist movement, as do images of being strident and lesbian." Hmm, wonder where those specters came from? One college student was quoted as saying, "I picture a feminist as someone who is masculine and who doesn't shave her legs and is doing everything she can to deny that she is feminine." Nothing, apparently, is more disgusting and horrifying than female leg hair. *Time* stated confidently, "Ask a woman under the age of 30 if she is a feminist, and chances are she will shoot back a decisive, and perhaps even a derisive, no." The article cast women my age as "resentful" because "things have not worked out as expected," and whom did we blame? Employers with no flextime plans? Communities with no decent child-care centers? A White House that fought to dismantle affirmative action and thought women were best employed in the Oval Office as astrologers? Husbands who snored peacefully on the couch while we picked up all 708 Lego pieces? Nope, according to *Time,* we blamed the women's movement.

Then, in an especially deft turn, and one the press has gotten quite good at, the article blamed the women's movement for the sins of the media. Women my age now castigated the movement "for not knowing and for emphasizing the wrong issues. The ERA and lesbian rights, while noble causes, seemed to have garnered more attention than the pressing need for childcare and more flexible work schedules." And who spotlighted lesbianism and suggested it should divide women while ignoring feminists' demands for child care, national health insurance, and the like? Why, *quelle surprise,* it was *Time* magazine and the other increasingly sensationalistic media outlets. Then feminism took some more of the usual hits, once again running interference for the media. The women's movement had ignored women of color, poor women, and working-class women, and it had denigrated motherhood and housewives. There was no suggestion, of course, that the media's representation of feminism played any role in these stereotypes.

But after itemizing how younger women couldn't identify with old bags like me, and how old bags like me felt betrayed by the likes of Gloria Steinem and Betty Friedan, the article reviewed how far women had come since the 1950s and how much women credited the women's movement with that progress. Quoting a *Time*/CNN poll, the article reported that 77 percent of women thought the women's movement had made life better, 94 percent said it had helped women become more independent, and 82 percent said it was still improving the lives of women. So why did only 33 percent of women identify themselves as feminists? Because the women's movement had won, and was therefore obsolete. Does this sound like the correct answer to you? Me neither, and apparently it didn't sit so well with the folks at *Time*. Because then the article described how far women still had to go to close the wage gap, to defeminize poverty, and to eliminate women's second shift at home.[3]

As you can see, this article was all over the place. The women's movement allegedly had made many women, especially my age, miserable, yet it had made us happy, by opening up opportunities we treasured and would never give up. Feminists were still caricatured as hairy, humorless bruisers best kept quarantined on some reservation for transsexuals, but it turned out a lot of women who wore panty hose, and knew all too well who Big Bird is, embraced feminist positions and were, therefore, feminists. Equality was a burden; subordination was untenable. Feminism was a curse; feminism was a salvation. Only a few grotesque crones were still feminists; nearly all women were feminists. Feminism was for no one; feminism was for everyone. No wonder young women, who were infants and toddlers at the height of the women's movement, say, "I'm not a feminist, but . . ." They inhabit the only place they can, the place all women know all too well, the site of ambivalence, contradiction, and compromise.

As more women have entered journalism, and so-called women's stories have become headline news, this same schizophrenia percolates throughout the news media and into the representations of feminism we see and hear. In 1970, there were no female anchorwomen on the national news, hardly any at the local level, and very few female TV journalists. Today, the norm is for local newscasts to be cohosted by a male-female team, and national newscasts, morning talk shows, and newsmagazines have made stars out of Barbara Walters, Diane Sawyer, Jane Pauley, Joan Lunden, and Katie Couric. Connie Chung became Dan Rather's coanchor on the *CBS Evening News,* although not without gripes that her presence would trivialize the broadcast (as if Dan's efforts to boost his ratings by sporting, first, red suspenders and then a sweater vest didn't). Some of the sharpest and funniest columnists in the country—Molly Ivins, Katha Pollitt, Barbara Ehrenreich—are women, and in 1992 and 1993, the Pulitzer Prize in commentary went, respectively, to Anna Quindlen and Liz Balmaseda. So it's easy to point to surface appearances and think the revolution has been won.

On the other hand, women's voices are rarely heard on the news. Feminism is still kept in ideological purdah. Female "experts" are interviewed for the nightly news when the topic is abortion, child care, or affirmative action; but when the topic is war, foreign policy, the environment, or national purpose, female voices, and feminist voices in particular, are ignored. A recent study revealed that in 1988 only 10.3 percent of the guests on *Nightline* were female, and of the twenty most frequent guests, none were women. Another study from 1990 found that the ten individuals who appeared most frequently as analysts on the CBS, ABC, and NBC nightly news were all men, and some of them appeared as many as fifty-eight times in a single year.[4] Betty Friedan's Women, Men and Media Project found that the percentage of female correspondents was only 15 percent in 1989, and that there were some nights when you could watch the news and see no women reporters at all. Of the one hundred most frequently seen correspondents on TV, only eight were women. Diane Sawyer and

Connie Chung remain exceptions, and they represent a very small and privileged class of women. More to the point, they are gorgeous.

No woman who looks like Andy Rooney, Charles Kuralt, or Walter Cronkite would ever be allowed to report or comment on the news.[5] Ninety-seven percent of the TV anchors over forty are, you guessed it, male. Christine Craft was canned from her anchor position in Kansas City in 1983 at the wizened age of thirty-six for being "too old, too unattractive and not deferential to men."[6] This kind of agism is really pissing off a lot of women. Why do Clint Eastwood, Robert Redford, Sean Connery, Richard Dreyfuss, and other men in their fifties, sixties, and even seventies continue to work and get great parts while terrific actresses over the age of forty, like Sally Field, Jessica Lange, Meryl Streep, Diane Keaton, Kathleen Turner, Susan Sarandon, and others search in vain for decent roles and have had to set up their own production companies to ensure that they can still work? Movies in which these same aging men kill about fifty-eight people are praised as terrific thrillers while *Thelma and Louise* was denounced as virulent feminism laden with dire social consequences.

The media's unresolved schizophrenia about woman's proper place has taken perhaps its greatest toll on motherhood. It is as mothers today that these contradictions really pull the rug out from under us. After a steady decline in the birthrate that began in 1965, women—and these were primarily baby boom women—began reproducing in greater numbers in the 1980s, leading to a "baby boomlet." I was no exception: in December 1988 I too became a mother. Like many women of my generation, I had postponed having a child until I was in my thirties and felt I had a handle on my work and some sense of how a baby would fit into my husband's and my life. Of course, I knew nothing. Despite some false sense of being "settled" and "ready," I wasn't ready at all. How can you ever be ready for endless crying, constant sleep deprivation, projectile vomiting, or 2:00 A.M. trips to the emergency room? I was in for a lot of shocks, and one of the biggest was this: motherhood challenges every feminist principle you've ever had and, possibly as a result, reinforces them and makes them stronger. At the same time, your need and ability to make compromises reach new highs. Rarely do you oscillate so wildly between feminist ideology and the codes of femininity. While all I heard in the news media was that women, especially young women, were going around prefacing everything they said with "I'm not a feminist, but . . . ," I was saying, "Wait a minute, I *am* a feminist, but . . ." Few things in life are harder than being a feminist and a mother. Even the most egalitarian husband has trouble being an egalitarian parent. As a mother, especially of babies and toddlers, you often find the world stacked against you, with too many responsibilities and expectations falling solely on your shoulders. Yet even as I felt, for the first time, some of the anger, frustration, and resentment my mother had felt thirty years earlier, one thing really was different. It was my consciousness.

Thanks to the women's movement, my consciousness as a woman and as a mother was very different from my mother's. I was aware of our country's pathological schizophrenia about mothers and children: revere them in imagery, revile them in public policy. But this wasn't my own lonely observation; unlike my mother, I could read, hear, and see other women, in a variety of places, articulating these same criticisms. I also had the language, as well as the sense of obligation, to dissect the media's role in sustaining this hypocrisy. Although this new consciousness, like the old, is riddled with chasms, fault lines, and tensions about who I am as a woman and who I can and should be, it provides me with the armor and a few lances against a mass media that, after all these years, still doesn't get it.

As I sat in front of the TV in my husband's sweatpants (the only thing in the house that fit), feeding my baby, I had to confront, in a more personal and immediate way than before, the soft-focus, honey-hued symbolism surrounding moms and babies. I sat there and watched Joan Lunden chirp on cheerfully at 7:15, insisting by her stellar example that we *can* have it all. (This was before the infamous divorce, when we kept being reminded how perfect she and her entire family were.) I saw those Folgers decaf ads in which Dad, supposedly having stayed up all night with the baby sleeping on his chest, puts the baby down and nuzzles happily with his smiling, rested wife while they wake up together and face another fourteen-hour day without caffeine. In contrast to this lovely image, I was finding that being forced to get up hours before the *Today* show even started required the strongest shot of caffeine possible and never, to my recollection, produced a smile. There was no tangerine-hued sunrise making my kitchen look like a dream; hell, it was still pitch black. Anyone attempting to nuzzle would have been shot on sight. And since none of the fathers I knew had breasts (ah, if only they did!), they were relatively worthless during those 1:00 A.M., 3:00 A.M., and 5:00 A.M. nursings the Folgers ad pretended Dad had taken over from Mom. All I felt was that television and advertising had absolutely nothing whatsoever to do with me or my life, except to needle me about how ecstatic I'd be about motherhood if I'd just get over not sleeping. Joan Lunden and Jane Pauley got up at 4:00 A.M. What was the matter with me? Why didn't I have that inner serenity, that sense of peace and fulfillment, that all those Johnson & Johnson ads suggest are part of my maternal DNA?

Nowhere is the gap between image and reality wider than the one separating the smiling, serene, financially comfortable, and perfectly coiffed media mom from her frazzled, exhausted, sputum-covered, real-life counterpart. Everywhere I turned, as I read child-care books, watched TV, or went shopping for baby paraphernalia, I found myself navigating the powerful crosscurrents of middle-class mother-hood. Like all the other messages surrounding us—about sex, about assertiveness, about women in politics, and about independence—the messages about motherhood and babies crash into each other like tidal waves. Shooting these ideological rapids on a daily basis, while also taking care of a baby, can produce a certain astringency in the new mom's worldview. And I found myself getting more astringent as I took inventory of the completely unrealistic images of motherhood we imbibed. Here was my love-hate relationship with the mass media writ large.

In the early months of my daughter's life, I watched more TV than usual, but with a more jaundiced eye. Yet even my old standbys let me down. On *L.A. Law,* Ann Kelsey and Stuart Markowitz, who had been trying unsuccessfully to have a baby, adopted an infant girl. The only difference this baby seemed to make in their lives was that they struggled to find the right mobiles and nanny. In one episode, Ann had to bring the baby to work, and the baby lay in her bassinet while Ann took a deposition. Although the point of the scene was to show how the baby's crying ruined the deposition, I was still completely incredulous. Where were Ann's eye bags? How could she have the presence of mind to do anything, let alone concentrate on legal work, if she had an infant who'd disrupted her sleep several times the night before? Why were there no unsightly milk splotches on the padded shoulders of her $700 outfit? When we saw Ann and Stuart at home with the baby, we didn't see them struggling to complete a brief phone conversation or yelling at each other about whose turn it was to walk the baby around the house until it stopped screaming. No, they were ecstatically rocking a quietly cooing baby who apparently never cried, defecated, or threw up, and who didn't have the poor taste to wreak havoc with her parents' schedules, let alone their previously contented relationship.

Motherhood had virtually no impact on this woman's life or work, while those of us sitting at home in our sputum-covered bathrobes and ratty slippers were wondering how we were going to survive the next day at work on no sleep. This baby, like most media babies, was a trouble-free, ecstasy-producing, attractive little acquisition; if you "get" one, it will make you feel real good, look great in a rocking chair, and make you fall in love with your spouse all over again. Now, while babies are, at times, an indescribable joy, caring for them makes you feel like you've been tortured in an especially sadistic sleep-deprivation experiment. The feel-good images are a complete lie, and you know it. But they burrow into you, forcing you to castigate yourself for not being serene enough, organized enough, or spontaneous enough as a mother.

At the same time that this little fantasy world was beaming out from dramatic television, the concept of the "mommy track" was getting bandied about in the news media, promoted by huge cover stories in the newsmagazines and major stories on TV. According to this proposal, mothers should be on a separate—and unequal—career track that gives them more flexible hours in exchange for no promotions, no challenging assignments, less autonomy, and no raises.

Talk about getting the bends! On the one hand, we had the TV supermoms, size-six women with perfectly applied makeup who could do anything and apparently didn't need any sleep. On the other hand, we got a recognition that motherhood might be just a tad demanding, but acknowledged only in the age-old blame-the-victim solution of the mommy track. Between these two extremes were millions of us, the real mothers of America, with no place to stand. We were either supposed to act as if children don't hamper our ability to be overachieving workaholics and we can do everything we did before plus raise a baby or two or acquiesce to second-class citizenship, acknowledging that being a mother is so debilitating that we're only capable of having dead-end, place-holding jobs while men, including fathers, and women without kids step on our backs to get the next promotion. Either way, the real-life mother is humiliated, especially if she has a job, as opposed to a "career," in which the whole notion of advancement or a "track" is patently absurd. Meanwhile, there is no recognition that fatherhood might be exhausting too, and that new fathers are also operating under a completely different set of circumstances. In the supermom fantasies of TV and the mommy track proposals of corporate America, what remains enshrined is our country's craven, hypercompetitive yuppie work ethic. Babies and parents are supposed to work around these increasingly preposterous norms of what constitutes adequate job performance.

These contradictions surrounding motherhood and children differ from what our mothers confronted, but they have their roots firmly and deeply in the 1950s. For even now, no matter what you do, you can't ever be good enough as a mother. If you don't work, you're a bad mom, and if you do work, you're a bad mom. Then there's all the advice that comes at us from *Working Mother, Parents, Newsweek,* the nightly news, *20/20,* and *Oprah.* Let your baby cry herself to sleep; never let your baby cry. Don't be too rigid, but don't be too permissive. Don't ever spank your child; an occasional swat on the butt is good for a kid. Encourage your child to learn, but don't push her to learn. Be her friend; never be her friend. Rein her in; cut her some slack. The tightrope walks are endless. Once again we find ourselves under surveillance, not only as sex objects, or as workers, but as mothers. And on all sides of us are voices with megaphones, yelling completely opposite things to us as we figure out whether we have time to do a wash or will simply have to turn the kid's underwear inside out tomorrow.

And here, again, we feel the pull between sisterhood and competitive individualism. At 4:00 A.M., when it seemed like everyone in the world except my daughter and I was asleep, I felt myself part of that transhistorical and transcultural group called mothers, the ones who get up, no matter what, listening to the soft snorings of others, while tending to the needs of a child. Now this may sound overly romantic and sentimental, but I didn't expect to feel such a powerful bond with other women across space and time. And I still feel it, whenever I see a mother struggling to get the grocery shopping done with a couple of kids squirming and crying in the cart, or watch her trying to free herself from the frantic grip of a wailing toddler because Mom is late for work and, like it or not, has to leave the day-care center. At any playground, mothers who are complete strangers can enter effortlessly into conversation about kids and child rearing.[7] We smile knowingly at each other in shopping malls, parks, fast-food joints, and toy stores. We connect.

Yet we are divided against each other too. Motherhood, like everything else women do, has been turned into a competition over who's more patient, enterprising, inventive, decisive, hardworking, firm, and loving. Working moms are supposed to overcompensate for their time away from home and the kids by baking cakes in the shape of a triceratops and building marionettes for the weekend puppet show. Out of the media archetype of the supermom came the most revolting application of bureaucratic, human potential double-speak ever to accost mothers: quality time. Stay-at-home moms were hardly exempt from this. The competition across the street with her briefcase and high heels had to institute "quality time" segments in her household, and if you didn't too, your child would lag behind and grow up to hate you. This, at least, was how the news media framed motherhood, with its endless stories about "moms vs. moms."[8] At the same time, we're all supposed to conspire together in yet another grand masquerade that hides those moments when, out of frustration, exhaustion, and desperation, we say truly hateful and juvenile things to our children ("If you don't go to sleep, you'll *never* get to watch Barney again"), refuse to give them what they want or need, and fantasize, most of all, about sending them to Saturn.

This is why Roseanne Barr, now Arnold, became the top female sitcom star in America in the early 1990s. Despite the incredibly hostile treatment she has gotten in the press—because she's four things TV women are not supposed to be, working-class, loudmouthed, overweight, and a feminist—Roseanne became a success because her mission was simple and welcome: to take the schmaltz and hypocrisy out of media images of motherhood. Her famous line from her stand-up routine—"If the kids are alive at five, hey, I've done my job"—spoke to millions of women who love their children more than anything in the world but who also find motherhood wearing, boring, and, at times, infuriating. She spoke to women who had seen through June Cleaver and Donna Reed years ago, and were struggling to see through the supermom image now. Roseanne also took aim at the class biases around media images of motherhood: that good mothers looked like those svelte, smiling, beauty queen moms in Gerber ads or the moms in white muslin on the beach pitching Calvin Klein perfume. Most moms are not corporate attorneys,

Roseanne insisted, nor do they fit into a size six, carry a briefcase, or smile most of the time. They are waitresses, or work in factories, or in tiny office cubicles, or in other dead-end jobs, and they don't have $700 suits or nannies. But the other much more upscale but defiant media mom, Murphy Brown, also gave all the traditional stereotypes about motherhood the raspberries and continued, even after the birth of her child, to be as insensitive, narcissistic, and bossy as before.

In many ways, the media environment that surrounds us is very similar to the one that surrounded our mothers. It is crammed with impossible expectations and oozes with guilt that sticks to every nook and cranny of our psyches. It is dominated by images of upper-middle-class moms, both real and fictional, who "have it all" with little sacrifice, counterposed by upper-middle-class women who have fled the fast track for the comforts of domesticity. These either/or images are our new impossible choices for the 1990s. And we also have, as a holdover from *The Rifleman, Bachelor Father,* and *My Three Sons,* the conceit that the best moms are really dads. This reversal got new life breathed into it by *Kramer vs. Kramer,* in which the selfish bitch wife up and left the cutest, most lovable boy in America to "find herself" while her previously neglectful husband turned into the Albert Schweitzer of dads. The movie never let us see how devoted she had been as a mom—and virtually a single mom, at that—for all those years Dad lived at the office, nor did we see what had provoked her to take the dramatic action she did. In the custody hearing, women viewers were supposed to root for Dustin Hoffman and repudiate Meryl Streep.[9] The "best moms are dads" motif spread through the prime-time schedule like measles, giving us *My Two Dads* and *Full House,* in which Mom is conveniently six feet under and a couple of cool dads move in together to raise the kids.[10]

But *Roseanne* and *Murphy Brown* dramatize the most important difference separating us from our mothers: our stance toward the various mass media. At the same time that media executives tamed the high-spirited Madeline Hayes in *Moonlighting,* or gave us *The Equal-*

izer, a former CIA agent who rescued terminally helpless and perennially stalked female victims in distress, they also brought us *China Beach, Kate & Allie, Designing Women, Cagney & Lacey, Sisters, Sirens,* and *Dr. Quinn, Medicine Woman.* They didn't do this out of altruism; they did it because we're still a big market and, as they are learning, an increasingly jaundiced, pissed-off market that wants to see women on their own, women being brave, women having adventures, and women with mouths on them. Yet this is not enough. Some of us would like to see a lot more women with lines on their faces and a little mileage on them, too.

Women are hardly immune to the svelte images, guilt trips, and all the other normative messages that come at us courtesy of America's media moguls. But we are not putty in their hands either. Our interactions with sitcoms, the news, women's magazines, popular music, and movies are dynamic, a contested push and pull, in which they have most of the power but not all of it. While we can't assume that every woman who saw *Fatal Attraction* or *Pretty Woman* moaned "oh, pleeze" and cursed a lot throughout, neither can we assume that they just got down on their knees at the end and offered to lick their boyfriends' or husbands' boots. And don't think, for a minute, that only upper-middle-class women with Ph.D.'s who study semiotics and discourse analysis can debunk a misogynistic piece of crap like *9½ Weeks.* Some women, of course, are still slaves to the media, buying into liposuction, Ultra Slim-Fast, and the notion that all career women are vipers. But many other women, of all ages, classes, and ethnic backgrounds, have become, as a result of the last twenty years, skeptical viewers who know a lie when they see one.

This is why media women—celebrities as well as public figures—who have deliberately gone against the grain, who have attacked persistent stereotypes about women, have gained notoriety. And the most famous women of our era have dramatized, in their work, their lives, or both, that whatever we might think of as "female identity" is constantly fluid, unstable, contingent. They embody the fact that there is no such thing as *a* female identity for any woman, only many identities and personas, which often resist quick and easy definitions.[11]

Let's take the most famous media woman of them all, Madonna.[12] Madonna hasn't only become one of the richest women in show business, she's also spawned more academic analysis of her work than any celebrity in recent years. Is Madonna a feminist or not a feminist? Is the way she plays with sexist imagery good for women or bad for them? Why were there so many Madonna wanna-bes? And so forth. What has intrigued everyone, academic and nonacademic alike, is whether, and for how long, she'll be able to get away with having it both ways. One of the first signs of what she was up to was her Boy-Toy belt buckle. As she slithered through her early videos and shimmied on stage, Madonna was posing both as a sex object and as someone ridiculing the passivity that usually goes with being a sex object. Drawing from several key predecessors, especially Mae West and Bette Midler, Madonna aggressively took control of her own sexuality and affirmed that it was healthy and liberating for a woman to express her sexual desires, whether they were threatening to men or not. "Boy-Toy" was a joke: this girl wasn't going to do one damn thing to placate anyone's castration anxieties; on the contrary, she was going to elevate them every chance she got. This made critics, especially male critics, insane.

In several of her videos, she pretended to be under masculine control, only to reveal, at the end, that it was all a performance and that she had nothing but contempt for and was completely immune from male sexual power. This was most successfully expressed in her "Open Your Heart" video, designed to display her newly trimmed body after she'd lost fifteen pounds through what the tabloids touted as her popcorn diet. It opens with Madonna as a dancer in a peep show who wears a black bustier and dances suggestively with a chair while pig-faced, slavering men ogle her from their individual cubicles. When the performance is over, she is seen in the kind of baggy pants and jacket Charlie Chaplin used to favor, skipping away from the grip of patriarchy happily, innocently, and androgynously with a young boy. What made feminist critics nuts about Madonna performances like this one was that she got to critique the way women's bodies are reduced to being erotic spectacles for men while still getting the pleasures and rewards of being such a spectacle herself.

But by assuming so many identities—in her video "Express Yourself," a rip-off of Fritz Lang's *Metropolis,* she appears in drag as a corporate CEO and later as a literal sex kitten crawling to a saucer of milk—Madonna offered women viewers a host of masquerades to try on. One of her favorite ploys was to portray a virgin one minute and a whore the next, even suggesting that some virgins were whorelike and some whores virginal. Every performance acknowledged that womanhood was a series of costumes and poses, and shoved in everyone's face how mutually exclusive these roles for women were. In what supposedly constitutes her "real life," she has reinvented herself every year or two with different hairstyles and different acts. While some of her incarnations have been more appealing than others (her recent bare-breasted and highly self-satisfied walk down a fashion runway, for example, crosses over the line she has been so careful to straddle), her fascination comes from the changes themselves, and her insistence that women consist of deeply conflicting identities and personas. It is this kind of woman, unashamed, proud even, of her sexual desires, a woman who steps out of line and won't be pinned down, and who insists that women act out the mutually exclusive roles they're supposed to inhabit, who can't help but inspire admiration, desire, dread, and outrage.

The only other woman in recent years to inspire such extremes of admiration and hatred is Hillary Rodham Clinton. In 1992—which you may recall ruefully was yet another "Year of the Woman"—she got more ink than even Madonna did, and that was the year of Madonna's infamous *Sex* book. In 1993, Hillary was on the cover of nearly every magazine in America, including the "humor" magazine *Spy,* which featured her as a black-lingerie-clad dominatrix. The reference to Madonna was obvious. Hillary became, in the hands of the news media, the lightning rod for people's deepest anxieties and most fervent hopes about the role that women should play in shaping the future of the country. Women watched, with a powerful sense of identification and recognition, whatever their politics, as Hillary put her feminism, her competence, and, most important, her mouth in the closet so her husband could become president of the most conservative industrialized nation on the globe. Once she became first lady—er, excuse me, "copresident"—the male pundits of America clung to their nuts for dear life as they lobbed one verbal projectile after the next at her. Even before her husband's inauguration, the neocons on *The McLaughlin Group* acted as if she were Rasputin in drag, who would do things like hypnotize Bill into appointing "a bunch of wacko leftists to the Supreme Court" instead of "decent people." But she was also "one tough mother," and there were constant references to her learning how to play "hardball." These boys fulminated that she had not been elected, so how dare she stick her nose into public policy issues. Every time she went to Capitol Hill it was a big story because she was doing what no previous first lady had done: in the full light of day, she stepped over the threshold of power, walked into the male sanctum sanctorum; she breached sacred boundaries; she stepped out of line; she went beyond the pale. To arm herself against all that's come her way, and maybe even to keep them all off guard, she's done what any woman would do when she wants perceptions about her to change: she's gotten some new hairdos.

The woman we owe the most to, though, is Anita Hill, who claimed her voice and her past with a dignity many of us found remarkable and thrilling. For testifying against the dumbest and possibly most reactionary and mean-spirited man ever to sit on the Supreme Court, she was labeled a liar, a hysteric, a scorned woman, a hallucinator. For many of us, watching the Republican men go after her like slavering pit bulls, while the Democratic men covered their little weenies and ducked for cover, exposed the lies embedded in *Charlie's Angels* and elsewhere, that there was no such thing as patriarchy, but if there was, it was beneficent and would protect women.

Although the Thomas-Hill hearings were very real, they resonated powerfully with all the accrued media images of women as
victims, women needing to keep their mouths shut, women needing
to stay in their place, women needing to be deferential, compliant,
ever smiling. The sight of this poised, accomplished, well-spoken
woman sitting alone, across from the firing squad of complacent, self-
satisfied white men, who after all this time still didn't get it, hit a
nerve. While Thomas whined about a high-tech lynching, women
saw a high-tech gang rape. Here we watched our daily, private, often
internal conflicts acted out before our eyes, in public. The drama we
witnessed was the intersection between decades of media stereotypes
about women and one woman's shameful treatment by men because
of those stereotypes. We knew how she felt—on some level we had
been there and were still there—trapped by prejudices, expectations,
and norms not of our making. So we knew why she came forward,
why she fought, and why she wanted it all to go away. For the same
media that had told her, as a woman, to shut up and smile had also
told her, as an American, to speak out against injustice and discrimination. Anita Hill dramatized exactly the conflicts each of us has
struggled with since we were little girls.

In the aftermath of the Thomas-Hill hearings, the notion of men
"not getting it," and especially of the mainstream media not getting
it, has coexisted with *Vanity Fair* covers of Sharon Stone half dressed,
busty bimbos advertising beer, the ongoing trashing of sisterhood in
movies like *Single White Female* and *The Hand That Rocks the Cradle,*
and enough douche commercials to choke Moby Dick. It may be the
effects of the lobotomy, but Pat Robertson feels he can still declare
that feminism "encourages women to leave their husbands, kill their
children [and] practice witchcraft."[13] It is still a man's world and a
man's media, but there are also cracks and veins for us to mine, as
there were thirty years ago. And here we are, same as it ever was, on
an ideological yo-yo not unlike the one that raised and lowered our
mothers and their hopes, now raising, now lowering, our own.

So what's a girl to do? First, we should insist that there is nothing inherently superior about Elvis or James Dean in relation to the Shirelles or Natalie Wood. The ridiculing and erasing of our cultural history is nothing less than a ridiculing of our past selves and of who we are today, and while flying nuns and watusi-dancing beach bunnies were pretty revolting, they were also, simultaneously, metaphors for our incipient jailbreak and for efforts to keep us behind bars. Second, we have seen how, over time, the most revolutionary precepts of the women's movement, "Sisterhood Is Powerful" and "The Personal Is Political," have been redramatized and repackaged to convey the opposite: that when you get a bunch of women together all they do is fight, and that the personal is still, in the end, personal.

The American cult of individualism, which urged us to make something of ourselves, and which also helped us become feminists, was retooled in TV shows, women's magazines, and cosmetics ads in the 1970s and '80s to emphasize our isolation from and competition with other women. The political has been collapsed into the personal so that you, the lone individual, are all that matters. When a show like *Charlie's Angels* still stands out as the utopian moment of sisterhood in the mass media, it's obvious that images of female friendship, cooperation, mutuality, and love—you know, like in real life—have been as rare as a day without a male sporting event on TV. No wonder female collective action is so difficult to imagine, while boys operating as a team, patting each other's butts and supporting each other's efforts, is a taken-for-granted image in the media. And the media quarantining of feminists as repulsive, "single-issue" mono-maniacs simply reinforces the notion that we couldn't possibly have anything in common with environmentalists, peace activists, or other groups trying to make the world a better place.

We also have come to realize that, as we have aged, we have not found ourselves hailed the same way by the mass media. We are no longer a generation with clout and with promise, a generation that matters. Some of the collapse in attention is the result of the segmentation of the mass media and the targeting of audiences by age, gender, race, class, income, and locale. One way we do know that we still matter is that advertisers have ripped off all our music, from "Shout" to "Natural Woman" to "My Girl" to "Rescue Me," to sell everything from kitty litter to tampons. But the sense of generational cohesion that the media cultivated in us in the 1960s has dissipated. Instead, what is reinforced is the privatization of American life, the severing of community and atrophying of the public sphere as we shop, attend political rallies, listen to concerts, and hear people talk about current events and cultural trends from the insulated privacy of our sofas. Once this sense of generational collectivity as a market evaporates, so does the sense of political collectivity.

Some right-wing critics condemn the so-called liberal media for shoving godlessness, sexual license, and liberal politics down our throats. Some left-wing critics condemn the media for imposing a narrow, selectively constructed image of the world that benefits elites and keeps the rest of us in our place, stupefied, misled, and deluded. While I believe there is more truth to the latter position than to the former, our cultural history reveals a mass media that *did* present new possibilities to women, that inflated our aspirations like a balloon, then choked them off with a big knot before they got too big, and, at times, exploded them.

The same media that operated the accelerator stepped on the brakes. Because the news media cover what is new, disruptive, and threatening, they also provide publicity for alienated rebels who regard the status quo as something to be destroyed. The coverage such rebels get, however, is a mixed blessing, for it usually seeks to discredit their more extreme positions (even if they're right) while folding into the mainstream what can be carved out and held up as moderate. The entertainment media also look for new, rebellious styles, fads, and language as a way to invigorate old formulas and enliven a pop culture with a rapidly shortening shelf life: hence, the use of rap music, for example, to sell breakfast cereal whose major ingredients are corn syrup and purple dye. Here, too, opposition gets domesticated, processed into fads and fashions, its politics sucked out, its stylistic flourishes pumped up, so that rap isn't about inner-city rage, it's about square-top afros, new dance steps, and harem pants for men.

We have seen the media do this with feminism, first anticipating it, then representing and containing it. Both the news and entertainment media have had enormous power to set the agenda about how people consider, react to, and accept women's changing roles and aspirations. Frequently, and without obvious collusion, the various media have managed to settle on what becomes the prevailing common sense about women's place in the world. Having that common sense repeated and reenacted in sitcoms, movies, and newscasts has a powerful effect on women's self-perceptions and on men's perceptions of them. To point out that these dominant images are perforated with rifts and contradictions that have sometimes emboldened women does not undercut their basic power.[14] The media have helped instigate change for women while using a host of metaphors—women with magical powers, the catfight, the choked-off female voice—to contain and blunt that change.

So, for us, the question about whether the mass media lead social change or lag behind it sets up a false dichotomy, for we have seen and felt them do both at the same time. Yet sometimes the mass media lag much more than they lead, and today we live in an especially conservative media environment, in which ownership of media outlets is increasingly concentrated in the hands of fewer megacorporations and the voices of those not smack dab in the moderate political center are vilified or silenced. Images of scores of women in satin teddies and garter belts hopping in and out of bed with whomever is handy suggest, to some, an overly "liberal" media when such images are, in fact, deeply reactionary. And one of the most persistently conservative elements we women face is the story, the narrative, which continues to be structured around boys taking action, girls waiting for the boys, and girls rescued by the boys. In these stories, someone, usually the girl, is a victim, and someone else, usually the boy, is an actor in the world, while we feel ourselves to be both active agents and ongoing victims of stories we never wrote and images we never drew.

If you look for where the girls are today, you will find fragments of many of them in each of us. We remain shattered into so many pieces, some of them imprinted by femininity, others by feminism. But they don't yet fit together into a coherent whole. One piece might be from *Roseanne,* another from *Thelma and Louise,* another from those noxious Oil of Olay ads. And we still find ourselves riddled through with "on the one hand, on the other hand" responses to Hillary Clinton, reports on date rape, *Glamour,* Cher's face-lifts, and Madonna. We feel our insides to be in a constant state of roiling suspension, our identities as women always contingent.

The only advice I have for women today is to purchase two things: extra slippers, for throwing at the TV set, and extra stationery, for writing letters to soda companies telling them we'll never buy their swill again and will organize boycotts if they keep pitting Cindy Crawford against older women and keep pitting us against one another. We can also reclaim the word *feminist* from the trash heap it's been relegated to by the media and remind them and ourselves that a woman who says, "I'm not a feminist, but . . . ," is, in fact, a feminist. I agree with Susan Faludi, who said, "All women are feminists. It's just a matter of time and encouragement."[15] And despite their best efforts to keep *feminism* a dirty word and women under control, the media will continue, often inadvertently, to play a critical role in providing that encouragement. They are still our worst enemy and our best ally in our ongoing struggle for equality, respect, power, and love.

Epilogue

"Mommy, Mommy, hurry, come quickly, *now!*" implores my daughter at 8:16 A.M. on Saturday. This is the one time of the week she's allowed to watch commercial television, and the price is heavy. I drag my hungover and inadequately caffeinated butt over to the TV set. Her eyes shine like moonstones as I see what's on the screen. "Can I get that, Mommy, can I, puleeze? Please, Mommy." I see before me some hideous plastic doll, or pony, or troll, being pitched by a combination of elated little girls, flashing lights, and rap music. Everything seems to be colored hot pink or lilac. Sometimes it's one of these dolls you can put fake jewels all over, other times it's a troll doll in a wedding dress, or it's something really bad, like Kitty Surprise or Cheerleader Skipper. It is always something specifically targeted to little girls. She is four years old, and she understands, completely, the semiotics of gender differentiation. She never calls me when they're selling Killer Commando Unit, G.I. Joe, and all the other Pentagon-inspired stuff obviously for boys. She knows better. She knows she's a girl, and she knows what's for her. Twenty years of feminist politics and here I am, with a daughter who wants nothing more in the whole wide world than to buy Rollerblade Barbie.

Having grown up with the mass media myself, and considering what that has done for me and to me, I bring all that to bear as I raise my own little girl, who will, in her own way, and with her own generation, have her hopes and fears shaped by the mass media too. Ever since she was old enough to understand books, kids' movies, and *Sesame Street,* I have looked, in vain, for strong and appealing female characters for her to identify with. With a few exceptions, like *The Paperbag Princess,* shrewd, daring girls who outsmart monsters and value their freedom and self-esteem more than marrying some prince are hard to find. There's Maria, who knows how to fix toasters and stereos, on *Sesame Street.* But little kids are, at first, most drawn to the Muppets, and until recently, not one of the main stars—Big Bird, Kermit, the Count, Elmo, Snuffy, or Oscar—was female. Children's books are not much better. Even if they feature animals as the main protagonists, stories for kids too readily assume, automatically, that the main actor is male. Television cartoons, from Winnie the Pooh (no females except Kanga, and she's always doing laundry or cooking), to Garfield to Doug, not to mention the more obnoxious superhero action ones, still treat females either as nonexistent or as ancillary afterthoughts. We have the cartoon *James Bond, Jr.,* but no *Emma Peel, Jr.* And it goes without saying that nearly all the little girls she sees on TV and elsewhere are white.

And then there are the movies. When mothers cling to *The Little Mermaid* as one of the few positive representations of girls, we see how far we have not come. Ariel, the little mermaid in question, is indeed brave, curious, feisty, and defiant. She stands up to her father, saves Prince Eric from drowning, and stares down great white sharks as she hunts for sunken treasure. But her waist is the diameter of a chive, and her salvation comes through her marriage—at the age of sixteen, no less—to Eric. And the sadistic, consummately evil demon in the movie is, you guessed it, an older, overweight woman with too much purple eyeshadow and eyeliner, a female octopus who craves too much power and whose nether regions evoke the dreaded vagina dentate.

Belle, in *Beauty and the Beast,* dreams of escaping from the narrow confines of her small town, of having great adventures, and has nothing but contempt for the local cleft-chinned lout and macho beefcake Gaston. Her dreams of a more interesting, exciting life,

however, are also fulfilled through marriage alone. The most important quality of these characters remains their beauty, followed closely
by their selflessness and the ability to sing. There are gestures to
feminism—Ariel's physical courage, Belle's love of books, and, in
Aladdin, Jasmine's defiance of an arbitrary law that dictates when and
whom she must marry. These are welcome flourishes, and many of
us milk them for all they're worth—"See how *strong* she is,
honey?"—but they are still only flourishes, overwhelmed by the age-
old narrative that selfless, beautiful girls are rewarded by the love of a
prince they barely know. Nonanimated movies for kids are no better.
Hollywood simply takes it for granted that little heroes, like big ones,
are always boys. So little girls get *Home Alone* and who knows how
many sequels, *Cop and a Half, The Karate Kid, Rookie of the Year, Free
Willy,* and *Dennis the Menace,* all with little boy leads, little boy adventures, and little boy heroism, while gutsy, smart, enterprising, and
sassy little girls remain, after all this time, absent, invisible, denied.
Even my daughter, at the age of four, volunteered one day, "Mommy,
there should be more movies with girls."

The one movie that I was happy to have my daughter embrace
was made over fifty years ago, and judging from anecdotal evidence,
it's been enjoying an enormous resurgence among the preschool set.
No narrative has gripped my daughter's imagination more than *The
Wizard of Oz.* And why not? Finally, here's a *girl* who has an adventure and doesn't get married at the end. She runs away from home,
flies to Oz in a cyclone, kills one wicked witch and then another—
although never on purpose—and helps Scarecrow get a brain, Tin
Man get a heart, and Lion get some courage, all of which Dorothy
already has in spades. Throughout the movie, Dorothy is caring,
thoughtful, nurturing, and empathetic, but she's also adventuresome,
determined, and courageous. She tells off Miss Gulch, slaps the lion
while her male friends cower in the bushes, refuses to give the witch
her slippers, and chastises the Wizard himself when she feels he is
bullying her friends. Of course, when she's older, my daughter will
learn the truth about Dorothy: that Judy Garland had to have her

breasts strapped down for the part and was fed bucketfuls of amphetamines so she'd remain as slim as the studio wanted. This, too, I think, will speak to my daughter.

Shortly after seeing a few of the Disney fairy tales, both old and new, my daughter announced, at age three and a half, that she would no longer wear the unisex sweat suits and overalls I'd been dressing her in. It was dresses or nothing. Her favorite pretend games became "wedding" and "family," with her as either the bride or the mom. She loved playing Wizard of Oz—she was always Dorothy, of course—but she also loved playing Snow White, dropping like a sack of onions to the kitchen floor after she'd bitten into the pretend apple. The blocks, the Tinkertoys, and the trucks I had gotten her lay neglected, while the Barbie population began to multiply like fruit flies.

One of the things that feminist moms, and dads, for that matter, confront is the force of genetics. In the 1970s, I was convinced that most of the differences between men and women were the results of socialization. In the nature-nurture debate, I gave nature very little due. But now, as a parent, I have seen my daughter, long before she ever watched television, prefer dolls to trucks, use blocks to build enclosures instead of towers, and focus on interpersonal relationships in her play rather than on hurling projectiles into things. But at the same time, I have seen children's television (which, if anything, is even more retrograde than it was in the 1970s) reinforce and exaggerate these gender differences with a vengeance as if there were no overlap of traits at all between boys and girls.

Back in the 1970s, when Action for Children's Television, under the leadership of Peggy Charren, and feminist activists were pressuring advertisers, the FCC, and the networks to reduce TV violence, eliminate sexism, and stop pushing pink and purple sugar balls as a nutritious breakfast, there seemed to be a few moments when it actually looked like children's television might improve. After all, "Free to Be You and Me" was one of the biggest hit records for kids, and *Sesame Street* was drawing viewers away from commercial television.

But if you turn on Saturday morning TV now, it's as if none of that ever happened. In fact, kids' TV is worse than ever, and certainly more crass, more sexist, and more nutritionally criminal than much of the programming pitched to adults. In addition to all the war toys that train little boys to be cannon fodder and/or gun collectors, and the makeup kits and dolls that train little girls to be sex objects and/or moms, the overall message is about regarding yourself and everyone else you know as a commodity to be bought and sold. Ads geared to each gender encourage kids to dehumanize themselves and one another, to regard people as objects to be acquired or discarded. "Get the right boyfriend! Get the right friends!" commands an ad for a game for girls, Spring Valley High School (or maybe it was called Shop 'Til You Drop). To be a desirable commodity, a little girl must herself consume the right goods so she can make herself pretty and ornament herself properly. Being able to sing and smile admiringly at boys is highly desirable. Being smart, brave, or assertive isn't. On Saturday morning, boys are "cool"; girls are their mirrors, flat, shiny surfaces whose function is to reflect all this coolness back to them and on them. Girls watch boys be "awesome" and do "awesome" things. Girls aren't awesome; they're only spectators.

Already I see my little girl, at the age of four, managing the mixed messages around her. I see her process them, try to control them, and allow them into her sense of her place in the world. She wants to be at the center of the action, and she dictates the precise direction of her pretend games with the authority of a field marshal. In the books she has about rabbits, cats, alligators, and the like, she insists that I change all the pronouns from he to she so the story will be about a girl, not a boy. Already, she is resisting, without yet knowing it, certain sexist presumptions of the media. But she succumbs to them too. For it is also important to her that she be pretty, desired, and the one who beats out the ugly stepsisters for the prince's attention. She wants control and she wants love, and she is growing up in a culture as confused about how much of each a woman can have as it was in the 1950s and '60s. So she will be surrounded by media imagery that holds out promises of female achievement with one hand and slaps her down with the other. Already she knows we have a smart, accomplished first lady, because that's what her mother tells her. What she doesn't know yet, but will soon learn, is the price that first lady has had to pay simply for refusing to sit by the sidelines, cheerlead once in a while, and serve refreshments to the boys. My little girl will have to learn that if she wants nothing more than the same opportunities, access to power, freedom, and autonomy as any little boy in her preschool, sooner or later, she will pay a price never expected of them.

Because of the women's movement, and the ongoing vitality of feminism in the United States, my daughter will also grow up seeing women reporting the nightly news, women on the Supreme Court, women in the House and the Senate. She already has a female doctor, and when we go into town she sees female police officers, shop owners, and mail carriers. She knows women who are lawyers, reproductive rights activists, writers, college professors, corporate vice presidents, filmmakers, and video artists. Some of them are married, and some of them are not, some of them are straight, and some of them are lesbian or bisexual. She has seen women change a flat tire, assemble bookshelves, and operate a power saw. I never knew women like this as a child. When I was her age, all of this was nonexistent, completely unimaginable. As she grows up, she'll get to know these women, my friends whom I regard with awe and pride, and she will learn about the routes they have taken, the many accomplishments they have achieved, and she will learn that it wasn't all easy, but that it was worth the fight. This was something most of our mothers were unable to give us, and it is a precious legacy we can bequeath to their granddaughters.

It is especially important that we protect this legacy because the other lesson our daughters will learn from the mass media is that if they aren't pretty and aren't thin, no matter what their other gifts, they will be thought of as less than they are. If my daughter wants to be a journalist, an actress, a politician, or a tennis champion, looks will matter much more for her than they will for any boy aspiring to the same occupations. It will still make a big difference if she's pretty. It will also make a difference, as it won't for the little boys she plays with now, if she is outspoken, honest about her needs, expectations, and desires, and willing to fight for principles she values. For most of the media images that will surround her as she grows up will equate not just thinness and beauty but also a soft-spoken, deferential voice with her right to be loved, admired, respected. She will learn that to be listened to, she will be expected to speak politely and in a noninflammatory manner, but she will also learn that whether she shouts or whispers (and how many ad campaigns have urged women to whisper?), she'll barely be listened to at all, because she's just a girl.

I see her now, so unself-conscious about her body, so completely happy and comfortable in it, and already I grieve for the time which will come all too soon when she regards that body with self-hate, no matter how fit and healthy it is, and will not get rid of that self-hate for the rest of her life. She and her little girlfriends cavort about nakedly with glee, so beautiful, so free, so unaware of what is to come, of the alienation they will learn to feel against the bodies that now give them so much pleasure and joy. But when they watch *Fern-Gully* together, and see the fairy Crysta's waist, even narrower than Ariel's, or play with their Barbies, the campaign on them has begun. Mothers who intervene—"Isn't her waist really silly and *way* too small? No real person has a waist like that and always walks on her toes"—do so fearing that this is an ideological battle they can't win. We read (with knowing resignation) of the major drop in self-esteem among girls once they reach adolescence, and we know all too well where much of this comes from.[1] And instead of giving our daughters less emaciated heroines, the media moguls just tell us smugly to shut off the TV and don't buy what you don't like, as if it's so easy to insulate your child from the semiotic sea in which she and all her friends swim. Nor do we have the money, technology, or access to fill in the representational blanks in their lives, to give them the heroines they deserve.

One recourse we do have is to teach our daughters how to talk back to and make fun of the mass media. This is especially satisfying since, thanks to Nickelodeon, we sometimes see them watching the same stuff we grew up with. In an episode of *Lassie* my daughter and I watched one morning, a ranger comes to the house to warn the mom that there are some mountain lions in the area. As he tries to show her, on a map, where they'd been spotted, she demurs, confessing that she can't read maps and they just confuse her. Then, on her way to meet Dad and Timmy at a Grange dinner, she gets a flat—which, of course, she hasn't a clue how to change—and then gets caught in one of the traps set for the mountain lions. Lassie—a dog—has more brains than she does and has to save her. Such scenes provide the feminist mom with an opportunity to impart a few words of wisdom about how silly and unrealistic TV can be when it comes to women.

But this was an exception. I don't want to monitor my daughter's TV viewing on Saturday morning, I want to go back to bed. How many mothers have the time or the energy for such interventions? Why should such interventions be so constantly necessary? And even the most conscientious and unharried mom can't compensate for the absences, the erasures, of what their daughters don't see, may never see, about women and bravery, intelligence, and courage. And this is just what little white girls don't see. What of my little girl's best friend, who is Asian? She will confront even more erasures, and more glib stereotypes. Of one thing I am certain. Like us, our daughters will make their own meanings out of much that they see, reading between the lines, absorbing exhortations to be feisty side by side with exhortations to be passive. Like us, they will have to work hard to fend off what cripples them and amplify what empowers them. But why, after all these years, should they still have to work so hard and to resist so much?

What will be dramatically different for my little girl is that she will be less sheltered from images of violence against women than I was. Rape was virtually unheard of in the mainstream media in the

1950s and '60s. Now the actual or threatened violation of women permeates the airwaves and is especially rampant on a channel like MTV, which caters, primarily, to adolescents. The MTV that initially brought us Culture Club, "Beat It," and Cyndi Lauper switched, under the influence of market research, to one of the most relentless showcases of misogyny in America. If MTV is still around in ten years, and if its images don't change much, my daughter will see woman after woman tied up, strapped down, or on her knees in front of some strutting male hominid, begging to service him forever. These women are either garter-belt–clad nymphomaniacs or whip-wielding, castrating bitches: they all have long, red fingernails, huge breasts, buns of steel, and no brains; they adore sunken-chested, sickly looking boys with very big guitars.[2] Worse, they either want to be or deserve to be violated. Anyone who doesn't think such representations matter hasn't read any headlines recently recounting the hostility with which all too many adolescent boys treat girls, or their eagerness to act on such hostilities, especially when they're in groups with names like Spur Posse.

To be fair, in between these little pieces of corporate sewage on MTV, my daughter may also see female performers with guts and talent who defy such imagery. If she is lucky, she'll have her own generation's version of Annie Lennox, En Vogue, Tina Turner, Cyndi Lauper, Salt 'n' Pepa, and Mary-Chapin Carpenter. Her generation may even have girl groups like we did, young women singing together about the ongoing importance of girls sticking together and giving a name to what hurts women.

The other drama my little girl has already witnessed, and has enacted in her own pretend play, is the silencing of the female voice, the amputation of voice from desire. In *The Little Mermaid,* the central story involves Ariel's bargain with the sea witch Ursula: Ariel gets to be a human to meet the prince Eric, but, in exchange, Ursula takes away her voice. Feeling voiceless, and experiencing a severing between their true feelings and their own voices, is also, it turns out, a central psychological drama for adolescent girls in America.[3] But the culprits are hardly individual women. Rather, they are an entire system, buttressed by media imagery, that urges young girls to learn how to mute themselves. It is therefore especially incumbent on my generation to help our daughters claim their voices. This is why music for women continues to be so important. Thirty years after "Will You Love Me Tomorrow," I remain convinced that singing certain songs with a group of friends at the top of your lungs sometimes helps you say things, later, at the top of your heart. I want to introduce my daughter to the music that got me through, because it is through this music that female resilience, camaraderie, and wisdom are often most powerfully and genuinely expressed. For every time she hears "Someday My Prince Will Come" I want her to hear "Sisters Are Doing It for Themselves."

I want my daughter to listen to Martha and the Vandellas, the Chiffons, and the Marvelettes, and I want her to know that girl talk didn't die out when the Shirelles stopped making hits. The early and mid-1970s (and beyond) would have been a lot bleaker and lonelier for me if it hadn't been for Laura Nyro, Joni Mitchell, Aretha Franklin, Bonnie Raitt, Bette Midler, the Pointer Sisters, LaBelle, Melissa Manchester, and Carole King. When I got totally fed up with news stories documenting women's "fear of success," or the endless rapes on prime time, or the ads that used the words *freedom* and *liberation* to sell douches, I could listen to women sing about the sexual passions, political outrage, strength, and defiance we shared like a secret pledge. All these singers were acknowledging that with the women's movement, girl talk mattered more than ever. Some of these women wrote their own music and played their own instruments; their music was more knowing, more sexually frank, and more politically inflected than girl group music had been. But it shared that same sense of irrepressible optimism that, no matter what, women would endure and prevail, and this is a powerful tradition to pass on to little girls who all too soon will be awash in the misogyny of heavy metal and rap.

This music will do nothing less than help my daughter survive. Women's music has acknowledged that we would indeed bob below the surface from time to time, sometimes feeling as if we wouldn't rise again, but then up we'd come, resurfaced, renewed. Melissa Manchester insisted, in songs like "This Lady's Not Home," "Home to Myself," and "Talkin' to Myself (And Feelin' Fine)," that certain women (and a lot more women than men thought) craved solitude and that they needed to be alone as much as, and sometimes more than, they needed or wanted to be with any man. The Divine Miss M exuded a totally confident, authoritative sexuality, not just in her music but also in her costumes, stage talk, and infamous retelling of those bawdy Sophie Tucker jokes. Long before Madonna, Bette Midler trashed the notion that women had to be or should be sexually innocent and demure. Bonnie Raitt, by covering the Sippie Wallace songs "Women Be Wise (Don't Advertise Your Man)," "Mighty Tight Woman," and "You Got to Know How," reintroduced us to a female blues tradition that demanded recognition and preservation because of its exuberant assertion of female sexual desire. In songs like "Give It Up or Let Me Go" and "Ain't Nobody Home," she made it clear that women like her expected men to cut the bullshit or take a hike. In "I'm a Radio," Joni Mitchell indicated that women like her were just as comfortable with casual, nonbinding relationships as men were. These were take-control women, at least in their music, reinforcing in positive terms what the rest of the mass media were castigating as negative.

The most poetic of these women was Laura Nyro, and already one of my daughter's favorite songs is what she calls "Wash You Up and Down," her title for Nyro's feminist call to arms, "Save the Country." Nyro's songs affirmed that women usually found themselves in the grip of forces beyond their control but that women also shared a form of knowledge, a wisdom combined of fatalism and feistiness, that helped them assume an ironic stance toward fate and helped them triumph over its cruelties. The exuberance of her piano playing and the unyielding survivalism of her lyrics insisted that women, despite the odds, were simply too resilient, too dogged, too optimistic, to be kept down. Twenty years later, Mary-Chapin Carpenter makes the same claims for women in "I Feel Lucky," "I Take My Chances," and "The Hard Way." Women do have to struggle and put up with suffocating stereotypes, but we often get lucky as well, usually because of our spirit, our willingness to try again, and our capacity for love.

These are the voices I want my daughter to sing along with. This is what I want her to know about the women who came before her. These are women who claimed their voices, and sang about what too many of us have felt we couldn't say in regular speech: our pride in ourselves, our anger, our sexual desires, our weariness of always having to compromise. I hope that she will relate this music to real women she knows, to her grandmothers who never quit, to her mother's friends who gamely dance around the living room with her to this music, and to her mother, who periodically turns this music up to house-shaking levels to blow out the self-doubt, the guilt, and the fear.

I don't believe I can insulate my daughter from the mass media, nor do I want to. There are pleasures there for her, ones she already knows and ones she will learn. The sitcoms, records, magazines, and movies she grows up with will form, for better and for worse, the culture she will share with other people she barely knows. Yet there is much in this culture I find pernicious, revolting, and, increasingly, dangerous, especially since she is a girl. She will be treated a certain way precisely because of how boys—and even other girls—apply their media lessons to everyday life. I will try to teach her to be a resistant, back-talking, bullshit-detecting media consumer, and to treasure the strong, funny, subversive women she does get to see. I will also remind her that any time a performer or a cultural form especially loved by young girls is ridiculed and dismissed, she and her friends should not be embarrassed. Instead, they should be suspicious about just who is feeling threatened, or superior, and why.

Yet despite my interventions—and, given how kids are, probably because of them—I fear that she will experience the same amputations I have experienced, between my mind and my body, my desires and my voice, my past and my present, my old self and my current self. And I know that what she sees and hears on television, on the radio, in magazines, newspapers, and movies, will reinforce and justify the political, economic, and social realities she will live with when she becomes a woman. But I also suspect that she and her generation may get wiser to all this sooner than we did—look at what she knows already, and she's only four—and that they will be less patient and less willing to compromise. This, at least, is my hope. For she will see with her eyes and feel in her spirit that despite all this, women are not helpless victims, they are fighters. And she will want to be a fighter too.

Acknowledgments

I really was minding my own business when Paul Golob of Times Books called to talk about a book project on women and the media. I had been working on such a project, in various incarnations, for an embarrassingly long time, and with decidedly mixed results. It was Paul who envisioned this book, in its current form and tone, and who helped me envision it too. Without his initial support, and faith, this book simply would not have been written in this way. And then, once he got me going, he turned out to be one of the finest editors I've ever met, or even heard of: tough, critical, astute, fun, and always in your corner. I am deeply grateful to him. I also want to thank my agent, Lizzie Grossman, who stuck with me through thick and thin, and whose advice and enthusiasm have been invaluable.

This book is, in part, an attempt at translation, an effort to relay some of the very important thinking about the mass media and women that has circulated in the academic community. With translations there are always slippages and gaps, when one form of language simply fails to capture the ideas and nuances of another. So my apologies to those whose elegant theoretical work I have plundered, distilled, and reworked. The writings of several people have been indispensable to me and to the field: Janice Radway, George Lipsitz, Linda Williams, Mary Ann Doane, Judith Mayne, Sut Jhally, Justin Lewis, Todd Gitlin, Susan McClary, John Fiske, Barbara Bradby, Larry Grossberg, and Chantal Mouffe.

During the years that I spent letting this book gestate, I incurred many debts. Mari Jo Buhle guided my first tentative studies of the representation of women in the media, and Paul Buhle encouraged my journalistic writing on this topic. Two grants from the National Endowment for the Humanities provided time and money for initial research. Susan Bell helped shape this research and got me thinking in more visual terms. Jeff Reid and Sheryl Larson at *In These Times* gave me my first opportunity to do more journalistic writing, and their encouragement and sense of play allowed me to experiment with different styles and topics. I have been blessed by this same spirit of generosity at *The Progressive,* where Matthew Rothschild, Erwin Knoll, and Linda Rocawich have encouraged media criticism from a feminist perspective. I am also grateful to the staffs of the Museum of Radio and Television, the Vanderbilt Television News Archive, the Library of Congress, the National Archives, the Johnson Library at Hampshire College, and the Frost Library at Amherst College.

Teaching at Hampshire College has introduced me to hundreds of smart and energetic students whose ideas, questions, and enthusiasm have kept me on my toes and inspired my work. Several of these students served as research assistants on this project, and I thank Jane Gerhard, Jill Pierce, Colin Loggins, Kara Knott, and Lisa Davis for their endless trips to the library and the Xerox machine, as well as for their suggestions and their company.

I would also like to thank Wendy Wolf, whom I met when she was an editor at Pantheon. Wendy saw an early version of a proposal for a book on the representation of women in the media, and she grilled me somewhat mercilessly about its focus and analytical purpose. Because of that grilling, I came to realize what I did—and did not—want to write about; I threw out the old proposal and wrote a new one, which became the basis for this book. That kind of honest and time-consuming criticism is hard to come by, and I am grateful to her for providing it in the midst of a very busy schedule. I am also indebted to Leslie Mason and Mary Ellen Burns, who provided detailed and invaluable readings of the manuscript that focused my thinking and boosted my spirits. And my daughter, Ella, with her decapitated Barbies strewn about the house, her insistence that all the personal pronouns in her books be changed to *she,* and her refusal to be passive about anything, has profoundly fortified me and my faith in female defiance.

Three women in particular have had a powerful impact on my thinking and writing, serving as much as mentors as they have as friends. The fact that all three of them are my colleagues at Hampshire College is one of life's small miracles. It was Joan Braderman who dragged me, kicking and screaming, into the world of feminist film criticism and who opened me up to a whole new way of thinking about images and our love-hate relationship to them. By teaching with her, having her read my work, and watching her various video pieces, I was pulled into an intellectual and artistic realm that demanded, simultaneously, more sophisticated and more playful thinking. Mary Russo opened up cultural theory for me, and her widely cited essay on female grotesques, as well as our many conversations and her intellectual generosity, transformed my ideas about gender and representation. Meredith Michaels, probably the most principled and gutsy woman I know, helped my understanding of narrative theory and theories of subjectivity, and dissected my work as only a trained philosopher can. Joan, Mary, and Meredith have been constant sources of support, insight, and refreshingly honest criticism. I never could have written this book without them, so I dedicate it to these three extraordinary women, with gratitude and love.

I also dedicate this book to my husband, T. R. Durham. It was T.R. who found the topic for the first journalistic piece I ever got published; T.R. who gave me the confidence to find, and use, my voice; T.R. who did the grocery shopping, the day-care drop-off, and the endless runs to the office supply store so I could write. And it was T.R. who listened when no one else could or would, who sustained me when I got discouraged, and who has tolerated living in a house overrun by teetering stacks of videotapes of *Charlie's Angels* and *Bewitched, Glamour* magazines from 1967, and alluvial fields of note cards, pads, Post-it notes, and computer printouts. His unbridled enthusiasm for this project, especially in the face of other losses and challenges, has meant the world to me.

*N*otes

INTRODUCTION

1. Claudia Wallis, "Women Face the '90s," *Time,* December 4, 1989, p. 81.

2. Wini Breines explores these contradictions as well, and focuses on the roots of feminism in the 1950s. See *Young, White and Miserable: Growing Up Female in the Fifties* (Boston: Beacon Press, 1992).

3. Various feminist scholars have studied and documented women's contradictory responses to the mass media. See Janice Radway, *Reading the Romance* (Chapel Hill: University of North Carolina Press, 1984); Linda Williams, " 'Something Else Besides a Mother': *Stella Dallas* and the Maternal Melodrama," in Christine Gledhill, ed., *Home Is Where the Heart Is* (London: British Film Institute, 1987); Judith Mayne, "The Woman at the Keyhole: Women's Cinema and Feminist Film Criticism," in Mary Ann Doane et al., eds., *Re-Vision: Essays in Feminist Film Criticism* (Frederick, MD: University Publications of America, 1984); Susan McClary, *Feminine Endings: Music, Gender and Sexuality* (Minneapolis: University of Minnesota Press, 1991). Feminist video artists also were some of the first to explore these contradictory relationships to the media. See Joan Braderman, *Natalie Didn't Drown,* ©1983, distributed by Video Data Bank, Chicago.

4. For a summary of the media's power, and of viewers' resistance to that power, see Justin Lewis, *The Ideological Octopus* (New York: Routledge, 1991).

5. Chantal Mouffe, "Hegemony and New Political Subjects: Toward a New Concept of Democracy," in Cary Nelson and Lawrence Grossberg, eds., *Marxism and the Interpretation of Culture* (Urbana: University of Illinois Press, 1988), pp. 94–95.

6. For scholarly analysis and documentation of the biases and impact of the news media, see Herbert Gans, *Deciding What's News* (New York: Vintage, 1980); Todd Gitlin, *The Whole World Is Watching* (Berkeley: University of California Press, 1980); Michael Parenti, *Inventing Reality* (New York: St. Martin's Press, 1986); and Noam Chomsky and Edward Hermann, *Manufacturing Consent: The Political Economy of the Mass Media* (New York: Pantheon, 1988).

7. Landon Jones, *Great Expectations: America and the Baby Boom Generation* (New York: Coward, McCann & Geoghegan, 1980), p. 73.

8. This point has been emphasized by Barbara Ehrenreich, Elizabeth Hess, and Gloria Jacobs in *Re-Making Love: The Feminization of Sex* (Garden City, NY: Anchor Press, Doubleday, 1986), p. 29.

9. Carroll Smith Rosenberg, *Disorderly Conduct: Visions of Gender in Victorian America* (New York: Alfred A. Knopf, 1985). See Wini Breines's discussion of the contradictions surrounding girls in the 1950s in *Young, White and Miserable*.

10. Gitlin, *The Whole World Is Watching*, p. 29.

11. John Fiske has been one of the most important advocates of viewer resistance to mass media images. See "Television: Polysemy and Popularity," in *Critical Studies in Mass Communication*, vol. 3, December 1986, pp. 391–408; *Television Culture* (London: Methuen, 1987); and "British Cultural Studies," in Robert Allen, ed., *Channels of Discourse* (Chapel Hill: University of North Carolina Press, 1987).

12. Laura Mulvey, "Visual Pleasure and Narrative Cinema," *Screen*, Autumn 1975, pp. 6–18.

13. John Berger, *Ways of Seeing* (New York: Penguin, 1977), pp. 46–47.

14. Mirra Komarovsky, "Cultural Contradictions and Sex Roles," *American Journal of Sociology*, vol. 52, 1946, pp. 184–189; Maren Lockwood Carden, *The New Feminist Movement* (New York: Russell Sage Foundation, 1974), p. 23.

15. Much of this work on cultural contradictions within the media was inspired by Jürgen Habermas, *Legitimation Crisis* (Boston: Beacon Press, 1975). For an impressive application of these ideas to popular culture see George Lipsitz, "The Meaning of Memory: Family, Class and Ethnicity in Early Network Television," in Lipsitz, *Time Passages* (Minneapolis: University of Minnesota Press, 1990); and T. J. Jackson Lears, "From Salvation to Realization: Advertising and the Therapeutic Roots of the Consumer Culture, 1880–1930," in Richard Wightman Fox and T. J. Jackson Lears, eds., *The Culture of Consumption* (New York: Pantheon, 1983).

CHAPTER 1: FRACTURED FAIRY TALES

1. Walter Lippman quoted in *Webster's Guide to American History* (Springfield, MA: G. & C. Merriam, 1971), p. 555; "Sputnik II: The Surge of Soviet Science," *Newsweek*, November 11, 1957, p. 73.

2. "Walt Disney: Imagineer of Fun," *Newsweek*, December 26, 1966, p. 69.

3. For a discussion of the notion of "the surveyor" and "the surveyed" as installed in the heads of women by advertisers, see John Berger, *Ways of Seeing* (New York: Penguin, 1977).

4. Rita Lang Kleinfelder, *When We Were Young: A Baby-Boomer Yearbook* (New York: Prentice Hall, 1993), p. 175.

5. Les Brown, *Les Brown's Encyclopedia of Television* (New York: New York Zoetrope, 1982), p. 344.

6. "Jackie," *Time,* January 20, 1961, p. 20.

7. "First Lady Puts on a Water-Skiing 'Show,' " *U.S. News and World Report,* January 15, 1962, p. 12.

8. "Stunning Egghead," *Newsweek,* February 22, 1960, p. 29.

9. "Jackie," *Time,* January 20, 1961, p. 25.

10. "First Lady Gives a Lesson in Diplomacy," *U.S. News and World Report,* January 1, 1962, p. 52.

11. Cited in Ralph G. Martin, *A Hero for Our Time: An Intimate Story of the Kennedy Years* (New York: Macmillan, 1983), p. 354.

12. Cited in Paul F. Boller, Jr., *Presidential Wives: An Anecdotal History* (New York: Oxford University Press, 1988), p. 363.

13. "How the Public Rates the Nation's First Lady," *U.S. News and World Report,* October 8, 1962, p. 28.

14. "Queen of America," *Time,* March 23, 1962, p. 13.

CHAPTER 2: MAMA SAID

1. For a history of women during this period see Susan Ware, *Holding Their Own: American Women in the 1930s* (Boston: Twayne Publishers, 1982); Susan Hartmann, *The Homefront and Beyond: American Women in the 1940s* (Boston: Twayne, 1982); William H. Chafe, *The American Woman: Her Changing Social, Economic and Political Roles, 1920–1970* (New York: Oxford University Press, 1972); and Sara M. Evans, *Born for Liberty* (New York: Free Press, 1989).

2. Carol Hymowitz and Michaele Weissman, *A History of Women in America* (New York: Bantam, 1978), p. 306.

3. For an excellent presentation of this material see the film by Connie Field, *The Life and Times of Rosie the Riveter,* ©1980, distributed by Clarity Educational Productions.

4. Ginette Castro, *American Feminism: A Contemporary History* (New York: New York University Press, 1990), p. 7.

5. For an excellent discussion of this film see Linda Williams, "Feminist Film Theory: *Mildred Pierce* and the Second World War," in E. Deidre Pribam, ed., *Female Spectators: Looking at Film and Television* (New York: Verso, 1988), pp. 12–30.

6. See E. Ann Kaplan, ed., *Women in Film Noir* (London: British Film Institute, 1980).

7. Susan Faludi makes this point in *Backlash: The Undeclared War Against American Women* (New York: Crown, 1991), p. 54.

8. For a discussion of these 1950s sitcoms, see Mary Beth Haralovich, "Suburban Family Sitcoms and Consumer Product Design: Addressing the Social Sub-

jectivity of Homemakers in the 50s," in Phillip Drummond and Richard Paterson, *Television and Its Audience* (London: BFI, British Film Institute, 1988), pp. 38–58.

9. Eleanor Roosevelt, "If You Ask Me," *Ladies' Home Journal,* January 1946.

10. E. Sager, "Profile of Success," *Ladies' Home Journal,* April 1946, pp. 32–33.

11. B. H. Hoffman, "How Much Should They Earn?," *Ladies' Home Journal,* July 1946, p. 22.

12. Richard Coudenhove-Kalergi, "Queens Did Better Than Kings," *Ladies' Home Journal,* July 1946, pp. 115–16.

13. See Elaine Tyler May, *Homeward Bound: American Families in the Cold War Era* (New York: Basic Books, 1988), pp. 20–22.

14. George Lawton, "Proof That She Is the Stronger Sex," *New York Times Magazine,* December 12, 1948, pp. 67–68; "Women May Control U.S.," *Science Digest,* August 1947, p. 29.

15. Clifford R. Adams, "Making Marriage Work," *Ladies' Home Journal,* April 1948, p. 26, and September 1948, p. 26.

16. James F. Bender, "What Sends People to Reno," *Ladies' Home Journal,* April 1948, p. 26.

17. Letters to the editor, *Ladies' Home Journal,* March 1948, p. 4.

18. Leland Stowe, "What's Wrong with American Women?," *Reader's Digest,* October 1949, pp. 49–51.

19. Fred Schwed, Jr., "Woman—Foibles of, Etc.," *Reader's Digest,* August 1951, p. 54.

20. Agnes E. Meyer, "Women Aren't Men," *Reader's Digest,* November 1950, pp. 80–84.

21. The two classic studies of women and housework are Ruth Schwartz Cowan, *More Work for Mother: The Ironies of Household Technology from the Open Hearth to the Microwave* (New York: Basic Books, 1983); and Susan Strasser, *Never Done: A History of American Housework* (New York: Pantheon, 1982).

22. "Employment of Women Reaches All-Time High in 1955," *Personnel Guidance Journal,* February 1956, p. 339.

23. Arlie Hochschild, *The Second Shift* (New York: Avon, 1989).

CHAPTER 3: SEX AND THE SINGLE TEENAGER

1. William I. Nichols, "Let's Not Panic at the 'New Morality,' " *Reader's Digest,* July 1966, p. 75.

2. On sexual mores for women in the 1950s and 1960s see Elaine Tyler May, *Homeward Bound: American Families in the Cold War Era* (New York: Basic Books, 1988); and Rickie Solinger, *Wake Up Little Susie: Single Pregnancy and Race Before Roe v. Wade* (New York: Routledge, 1992). For changes in dating practices see Beth L. Bailey, *From Front Porch to Back Seat: Courtship in Twentieth Century America* (Balti-

more: Johns Hopkins University Press, 1988). For an overview of changing sexual mores see John D'Emilio and Estelle Freedman, *Intimate Matters: A History of Sexuality in America* (New York: Harper & Row, 1988).

3. Ann Landers, "Straight Talk on Sex and Growing Up," *Life,* August 1961, pp. 74ff.

4. One example was Arnold Maremont, the director of Illinois's Public Assistance Program. See "Birth Control Devices and Debates Engross the U.S.," *Life,* May 10, 1963, pp. 37–45.

5. "The Second Sexual Revolution," *Time,* January 24, 1964, pp. 54–59; "Sexual Behavior of College Girls," *School and Society,* April 3, 1965, p. 208; "No Moral Revolution Discovered, Yet," *Science News,* January 20, 1968, pp. 60–61.

6. Pearl S. Buck, "The Sexual Revolution," *Ladies' Home Journal,* September 1964, p. 43.

7. "Second Sexual Revolution," p. 55.

8. Virgil G. Damon and Isabella Taves, "My Daughter Is in Trouble," *Look,* August 14, 1962, pp. 26–8ff.

9. "Unstructured Relations," *Newsweek,* July 4, 1966, p. 78.

10. David Boroff, "Among the Fallen Idols, Virginity, Chastity and Repression," *Esquire,* July 1961, p. 98.

11. "The Free Sex Movement," *Time,* March 11, 1966, p. 66.

12. Donald A. Eldridge, "More on Campus Mores," *Saturday Review,* June 20, 1964, p. 58.

13. "If They Had Only Waited," *Reader's Digest,* January 1965, p. 87.

14. "Second Sexual Revolution," p. 54.

15. Boroff, p. 98.

16. D. Wharton, "How to Stop the Movies' Sickening Exploitation of Sex," *Reader's Digest,* March 1961, pp. 37–40; J. Crosby, "Speaking Out: Movies Are Too Dirty," *Saturday Evening Post,* November 10, 1962, pp. 8ff.; O. K. Armstrong, "Must Our Movies Be Obscene?" *Reader's Digest,* November 1965, pp. 54–56.

17. A reconsideration of Brown also appears in Barbara Ehrenreich, Elizabeth Hess, and Gloria Jacobs, *Re-Making Love: The Feminization of Sex* (Garden City: Anchor Press, Doubleday, 1986).

18. Helen Gurley Brown, *Sex and the Single Girl* (London: Frederick Muller Ltd, 1962), p. 98.

19. Ibid., p. 15.

20. Ibid., p. 13.

21. Gloria Steinem, "The Moral Disarmament of Betty Coed," *Esquire,* September 1962, p. 97ff.

22. Gael Greene, *Sex and the College Girl* (New York: Dial Press, 1964); Greene interviewed 614 students, 538 girls and 76 boys from 102 colleges and universities in America. Quotations on pp. 39–41.

23. Thomas Doherty, *Teenagers and Teenpics: The Juvenilization of American Movies in the 1950s* (Boston: Unwin Hyman, 1988), p. 54.

24. Rita Lang Kleinfelder, *When We Were Young: A Baby-Boomer Yearbook* (New York: Prentice Hall, 1993), p. 408.

25. Ibid., p. 432.

26. See Laura Mulvey, "Visual Pleasure and Narrative Cinema," *Screen,* Autumn 1975, pp. 6–18.

27. Here I draw from Linda Williams's arguments in " 'Something Else Besides a Mother': *Stella Dallas* and the Maternal Melodrama," in Christine Gledhill, ed., *Home Is Where the Heart Is* (London: British Film Institute, 1987).

28. The phrase describing woman as having the quality "to-be-looked-at" in films was coined by feminist film critic Laura Mulvey in "Visual Pleasure and Narrative Cinema."

29. Janice Radway argues that this fantasy about the feminization of patriarchy is central to the success of romance novels. See *Reading the Romance* (Chapel Hill: University of North Carolina Press, 1984).

30. A study done in 1964–65 by Mervin Freedman at Stanford established that three-fourths or more of America's unmarried college women were virgins and that premarital intercourse among college women was usually restricted to their future husbands. A later study also established that the Sexual Revolution really began in the 1970s. See "Sexual Behavior of College Girls," *School and Society,* April 3, 1965, p. 208; Sandra L. Hofferth, Joan R. Kahn, and Wendy Baldwin, "Pre-marital Sexual Activity Among U.S. Teenage Women over the Past Three Decades," *Family Planning Perspectives,* vol. 19, March–April 1987, pp. 46–53.

CHAPTER 4: WHY THE SHIRELLES MATTERED

1. See the chart listings in Norm N. Nite, *Rock On Almanac* (New York: Harper & Row, 1989).

2. Charlotte Greig, *Will You Still Love Me Tomorrow?* (London: Virago Press, 1989), p. 33.

3. Cited in Ed Ward et al., *Rock of Ages: The Rolling Stone History of Rock & Roll* (New York: Summit, 1986), p. 275.

4. My thinking has been greatly influenced by Barbara Bradby, "Do Talk and Don't Talk: The Division of the Subject in Girl Group Music," in Simon Frith and Andrew Goodwin, *On Record: Rock, Pop, & the Written Word* (New York: Pantheon, 1990); Susan McClary, *Feminine Endings: Music, Gender and Sexuality* (Minneapolis: University of Minnesota Press, 1991); and Greig, *Will You Still Love Me Tomorrow?*

5. The power of music, primarily classical, is explored in Anthony Storr, *Music and the Mind* (New York: Free Press, 1992), p. 7.

6. Greig, *Will You Still Love Me Tomorrow?*, p. 121.

7. This point is emphasized by Barbara Bradby.

CHAPTER 5: SHE'S GOT THE DEVIL IN HER HEART

1. "It's All Jake," *Glamour,* March 1963.

2. "Teens Grow as Top Target for Many Products," *Printer's Ink,* February 15, 1963, p. 3.

3. See *Glamour's* "Back to School" issue, August 1966.

4. "George, Paul, Ringo and John," *Newsweek,* February 24, 1964, p. 54.

5. Ibid.

6. "Beatlemania," *Newsweek,* November 18, 1963, p. 104.

7. David Dempsey, "Why the Girls Scream, Weep, Flip," *New York Times Magazine,* February 23, 1964, p. 15+.

8. The other major feminist rereading of Beatlemania is in Barbara Ehrenreich, Elizabeth Hess, and Gloria Jacobs, *Re-Making Love: The Feminization of Sex* (Garden City: Anchor Press, Doubleday, 1986).

9. Ibid., p. 35.

10. David Reisman, "What the Beatles Prove About Teenagers," *U.S. News & World Report,* February 24, 1964, p. 88.

11. "George, Paul, Ringo and John," p. 54.

12. Cited in Ehrenreich et al., *Re-Making Love,* p. 36; see also Anna Quindlen, "A Paul Girl," in *Living Out Loud* (New York: Random House), pp. 6–9.

13. Ehrenreich et al., *Re-Making Love,* p. 11.

CHAPTER 6: GENIES AND WITCHES

1. "The American Female," *Harper's,* October 1962, p. 117.

2. Marjorie Hunter, "U.S. Panel Urges Women to Sue for Equal Rights," *New York Times,* October 12, 1963, p. 1.

3. *Publisher's Weekly,* January 18, 1965, pp. 68, 72.

4. Paul Foley, "Whatever Happened to Women's Rights," *Atlantic Monthly,* March 1964, pp. 63–65; Foley, "Women's Rights—and What They Don't Do About Them," *Reader's Digest,* May 1964, pp. 22–23.

5. "How Women's Role in U.S. Is Changing," *U.S. News & World Report,* May 30, 1966, pp. 58–60.

6. For a discussion of the monstrosity of female sexuality see Linda Williams, "When the Woman Looks," in Mary Ann Doane et al., eds., *Re-Vision: Essays in Feminist Film Criticism* (Frederick, MD: University Publications of America, 1984).

7. Tim Brooks and Earle Marsh, *The Complete Directory to Prime Time Network TV Shows* (New York: Ballantine, 1979), pp. 62, 806–808.

8. The term and concept of the female grotesque comes from Mary Russo, "Female Grotesques: Carnival and Theory," in Teresa de Lauretis, ed., *Feminist Studies/Critical Studies* (Bloomington: University of Indiana Press, 1986).

9. Brooks and Marsh, *Complete Directory,* p. 205.

CHAPTER 7: THROWING OUT OUR BRAS

1. Alice Echols, *Daring to Be Bad: Radical Feminism in America, 1967–1975* (Minneapolis: University of Minnesota Press, 1989), p. 93.

2. Ibid., p. 105.

3. Valerie Solanas, "Excerpts from the SCUM Manifesto," in Robin Morgan, ed., *Sisterhood Is Powerful* (New York: Vintage, 1970), pp. 514–519.

4. U.S. Department of Commerce, *Historical Statistics of the United States* (Washington, DC: Government Printing Office, 1975), p. 385.

5. Erik Barnouw, *Tube of Plenty* (New York: Oxford University Press, 1975), p. 170; Daniel Boorstin termed such news stories "pseudo-events" in *The Image: A Guide to Pseudo-events in America* (New York: Harper & Row, 1961).

6. Ed Ward et al., *Rock of Ages: The Rolling Stone History of Rock & Roll* (New York: Summit, 1986), p. 256.

7. "Sibyl with Guitar," *Time,* November 23, 1962, pp. 54–60.

8. Ward et al., *Rock of Ages,* p. 256.

9. For accounts of the emergence of feminism out of the civil rights and anti-war movements, see Sara Evans, *Personal Politics* (New York: Vintage, 1979); Judith Hole and Ellen Levine, *Rebirth of Feminism* (New York: Quadrangle, 1971); and Echols, *Daring to Be Bad.*

10. For the importance of such communications networks to the success of social movements see Jo Freeman, "On the Origins of Social Movements" and "A Model for Analyzing the Strategic Options of Social Movement Organizations," in Jo Freeman, ed., *Social Movements of the Sixties and Seventies* (New York: Longman, 1983).

11. Rita Lang Kleinfelder, *When We Were Young: A Baby-Boomer Yearbook* (New York: Prentice Hall, 1993), p. 472.

12. Todd Gitlin, *The Whole World Is Watching* (Berkeley: University of California Press, 1980), p. 121.

13. See ibid., pp. 47–52 and pp. 90–94.

14. Ibid., p. 6.

15. "No More Miss America!" in Robin Morgan, ed., *Sisterhood is Powerful* (New York: Vintage, 1970), pp. 521–524.

16. Charlotte Curtis, "Miss America Pageant Is Picketed by 100 Women," *New York Times,* September 8, 1968, p. 81. Kathie Amatniek, a radical feminist, changed her named to Kathie Sarachild.

17. Echols, *Daring to Be Bad,* pp. 98–99.

18. "The Big Letdown," *Newsweek,* September 1, 1969, pp. 49–50.

CHAPTER 8: I AM WOMAN, HEAR ME ROAR

1. Maren Lockwood Carden, *The New Feminist Movement* (New York: Russell Sage Foundation, 1974), pp. 32–33.

2. Judith Hole and Ellen Levine, *Rebirth of Feminism* (New York: Quadrangle, 1971), p. 266.

3. Ibid., pp. 397–398. See also the various writings in Robin Morgan, ed., *Sisterhood Is Powerful* (New York: Vintage, 1970).

4. For accounts of the politics and history of the women's movement see Hole and Levine's *Rebirth of Feminism;* Carden's *New Feminist Movement;* Ginette Castro, *American Feminism: A Contemporary History* (New York: New York University Press, 1990); Alice Echols, *Daring to Be Bad: Radical Feminism in America, 1967–1975* (Minneapolis: University of Minnesota Press, 1989); and Marcia Cohen, *The Sisterhood: The Inside Story of the Women's Movement and the Leaders Who Made It Happen* (New York: Fawcett Columbine, 1989).

5. "The New Feminists: Revolt Against 'Sexism,' " *Time,* November 21, 1969, pp. 53–56.

6. Susan Brownmiller, "Sisterhood Is Powerful," *New York Times Magazine,* March 15, 1970, p. 27.

7. Sandie North, "Reporting the Movement," *Atlantic,* March 1970, p. 106.

8. "Other Voices: How Social Scientists See Women's Lib," *Newsweek,* March 23, 1970, p. 75.

9. "Reporting the Movement," p. 106.

10. "Very Volcanic," *Newsweek,* August 31, 1970, p. 47.

11. "Who's Come a Long Way, Baby?," *Time,* August 31, 1970, pp. 16–21.

12. Linda Charlton, "Women March Down Fifth in Equality Drive," *New York Times,* August 27, 1970, p. 1, p. 30.

13. "Leading Feminist Puts Hairdo Before Strike," *New York Times,* August 27, 1970, p. 30.

14. Grace Lichtenstein, "For Most Women, 'Strike' Day Was Just a Topic of Conversation," *New York Times,* August 27, 1970, p. 30.

15. Lacey Fosburgh, "Traditional Groups Prefer to Ignore Women's Lib," *New York Times,* August 26, 1970, p. 44.

16. "The Liberated Woman," *New York Times,* August 27, 1970, p. 34.

17. "Women on the March," *Time,* September 7, 1970, pp. 12–13.

18. "The Women Who Know Their Place," *Newsweek,* September 7, 1970, pp. 16–17.

CHAPTER 9: THE RISE OF THE BIONIC BIMBO

1. See Todd Gitlin, *Inside Prime Time* (New York: Pantheon, 1983); and Horace Newcomb and Robert S. Alley, *The Producer's Medium* (New York: Oxford University Press, 1983).

2. Joreen, "The 51 Percent Minority Group: A Statistical Essay," in Robin Morgan, ed., *Sisterhood Is Powerful* (New York: Vintage, 1970), pp. 39–43.

3. Marcia Cohen, *The Sisterhood: The Inside Story of the Women's Movement and the Leaders Who Made It Happen* (New York: Fawcett Columbine, 1989), p. 329.

4. Philippe Perebinossoff, "What Does a Kiss Mean? The Love Comic Formula and the Creation of the Ideal Teen-age Girl," *Journal of Popular Culture,* vol. 8, Spring 1975, pp. 826–827.

5. Caroline Bird, "What's TV Doing for 50.9 Percent of Americans?," *TV Guide,* February 27, 1971, pp. 5–8; Leonard Gross, "Why Can't a Woman Be More Like a Man?," *TV Guide,* August 11, 1973, pp. 6ff.

6. Judy Klemesrud, "TV's Women Are Dingbats," *New York Times,* May 27, 1973, p. D-5; Stephanie Harrington, "Women Get the Short End of the Shtick," *New York Times,* November 18, 1973, p. D-21; Gail Rock, "Same Time, Same Station, Same Sexism," *Ms.,* December 1973, pp. 24–28.

7. See Gaye Tuchman et al., *Hearth and Home: Images of Women in the Mass Media* (New York: Oxford University Press, 1978); Jean McNeil, "Feminism, Femininity, and the Television Series: A Content Analysis," *Journal of Broadcasting,* vol. 19, 1975, pp. 259–269; Nancy Tedesco, "Patterns in Prime Time," *Journal of Communication,* vol. 24, Spring 1974, pp. 119–124.

8. Alice E. Courtney and Thomas W. Whipple, "Women in TV Commercials," *Journal of Communication,* vol. 24, Spring 1974, pp. 111–113.

9. Erving Goffman, *Gender Advertisements* (Cambridge: Harvard University Press, 1979).

10. Carol Tavris and Toby Jayaratne, "What 120,000 Young Women Can Tell You About Sex, Motherhood, Menstruation, Housework—and Men," *Redbook,* January 1973, pp. 67ff.

11. "Big Bea," *Time,* October 1, 1973, p. 66.

12. For an account of interviewees' responses to the show see Andrea L. Press, *Women Watching Television* (Philadelphia: University of Pennsylvania Press, 1991), pp. 77–79.

13. Gerard Jones, *Honey, I'm Home* (New York: Grove Press, 1992), p. 194.

14. Ibid., pp. 230–231.

15. George Gerbner, "The Dynamics of Cultural Resistance," in Tuchman et al., *Hearth and Home,* pp. 48–50.

16. Sue Cameron, "Police Drama: Women Are on the Case," *Ms.,* October 1974, p. 104.

17. "TV's Super Women," *Time,* November 22, 1976, p. 69.

18. Ibid.

19. For a discussion of masculinity as masquerade see Carole-Anne Tyler, "Boys Will Be Girls: The Politics of Gay Drag," in Diana Fuss, ed., *Inside/Out: Lesbian Theories, Gay Theories* (New York: Routledge, 1991).

CHAPTER 10: THE ERA AS CATFIGHT

1. For a provocative and hilarious feminist analysis of *Dynasty,* including the catfight, see Joan Braderman's videotape *Joan Does Dynasty,* ©1986, distributed by Video Data Bank, Chicago, and Women Make Movies, New York.

2. Amy Erdman Farrell, "Self-help and Sisterhood: The Limits to Feminist Discourse in *Ms.* Magazine, 1972–1989," paper delivered at the Berkshire Conference on the History of Women, June 12, 1993.

3. See Jane J. Mansbridge, *Why We Lost the ERA* (Chicago: University of Chicago Press, 1986), pp. 201–218.

4. Herbert Gans, *Deciding What's News* (New York: Vintage, 1980), pp. 50–51.

5. Mary Russo, "Female Grotesques: Carnival and Theory," in Teresa de Lauretis, ed., *Feminist Studies/Critical Studies* (Bloomington: Indiana University Press, 1986), p. 213.

6. Alice Echols, *Daring to Be Bad: Radical Feminism in America, 1967–1975* (Minneapolis: University of Minnesota Press, 1989), p. 210.

7. "Gloria Steinem," *Newsweek,* August 16, 1971, p. 51.

8. Marcia Cohen, *The Sisterhood: The Inside Story of the Women's Movement and the Leaders Who Made It Happen* (New York: Fawcett Columbine, 1989), pp. 235–238.

9. "Women's Lib: A Second Look," *Time,* December 14, 1970, p. 50.

10. Millett wrote about her encounters with fame and the media in *Flying* (New York: Alfred A. Knopf, 1974).

11. Paul Wilkes, "Mother Superior to Women's Lib," *New York Times Magazine,* November 29, 1970, pp. 27ff.

12. "Bellacose Abzug," *Time,* August 16, 1971, pp. 14–15.

13. Sheila Tobias points this out in Cohen, *The Sisterhood,* p. 321.

14. Ibid., p. 320.

15. For a more in-depth analysis of why the amendment failed see Mary Frances Berry, *Why ERA Failed* (Indianapolis: University of Indiana Press, 1986); and Mansbridge, *Why We Lost the ERA.*

16. "Is Equal Rights Amendment Dead?" *U.S. News & World Report,* December 1, 1975, p. 39.

17. Joseph Lelyveld, "Should Women Be Nicer Than Men?," *New York Times Magazine,* April 17, 1977, p. 126.

18. Mansbridge, *Why We Lost the ERA,* p. 224; Berry, *Why ERA Failed,* p. 82.

19. "Anti-ERA Evangelist Wins Again," p. 20; Lelyveld, "Should Women Be Nicer?" p. 126.

20. The most notable example is Joan Braderman's videotape, *Joan Does Dynasty,* ©1986.

21. My discussion draws from Ien Ang's *Watching Dallas* (New York: Methuen, 1985); for quotations from these episodes see pp. 126–128.

22. Kim Schroder, "The Pleasure of *Dynasty:* The Weekly Reconstruction of Self-confidence," in Phillip Drummond and Richard Paterson, eds., *Television and Its Audience* (London: British Film Institute, 1988), p. 73.

CHAPTER 11: NARCISSISM AS LIBERATION

1. For a funny and very smart discussion of elite culture in the 1980s see Debora Silverman, *Selling Culture: Bloomingdale's, Diana Vreeland and the New Aristocracy of Taste in Reagan's America* (New York: Pantheon, 1986).

2. Naomi Wolf, *The Beauty Myth* (New York: Doubleday, 1991), p. 109.

3. Ibid., p. 99.

4. Melissa Stanton, "Looking After Your Looks," *Glamour,* August 1993, p. 233.

5. "A Better Butt, Fast!" and "Why 15 Million Women Own Guns" in *Glamour,* May, 1993, p. 270ff and p. 260ff.

6. Wolf, *The Beauty Myth,* p. 232.

CHAPTER 12: I'M NOT A FEMINIST, BUT . . .

1. For recent overviews of the status of feminism in America see Johanna Brenner, "U.S. Feminism in the Nineties," *New Left Review,* July–August 1993, pp. 101–159; and Wendy Kaminer, "Feminism's Identity Crisis," *Atlantic,* October 1993, pp. 51 ff.

2. Susan Faludi, *Backlash: The Undeclared War Against American Women* (New York: Crown, 1991), pp. 76–77.

3. Claudia Wallis, "Onward, Women!," *Time,* December 4, 1989, pp. 81–89.

4. Susan Douglas, "The Representation of Women in the News Media," *EXTRA!,* March–April 1991, p. 2.

5. As Marion Goldin, former producer of *60 Minutes,* quipped, "What woman [on TV] looks like Morley Safer?" Quoted in Judy Southworth, "Women Media Workers: No Room at the Top," *EXTRA!,* March–April 1991, p. 16.

6. Naomi Wolf, *The Beauty Myth* (New York: Doubleday, 1991), p. 35.

7. On the "sisterhood of motherhood" see Anna Quindlen, "The Days of Gilded Rigatoni," in *Thinking Out Loud* (New York: Random House, 1993), p. 83.

8. Faludi, *Backlash,* pp. 81–82.

9. See Judith Mayne's analysis of *Kramer vs. Kramer* in "The Woman at the Keyhole: Women's Cinema and Feminist Film Criticism," in Mary Ann Doane et al., eds., *Re-Vision: Essays in Feminist Film Criticism* (Frederick, MD: University Publications of America, 1984), pp. 61–62.

10. Faludi, *Backlash,* p. 143.

11. Susan McClary, *Feminine Endings: Music, Gender and Sexuality* (Minneapolis: University of Minnesota Press, 1991), p. 150.

12. My discussion of Madonna draws heavily from Susan McClary's excellent analysis in *Feminine Endings.*

13. "Robertson Depicts Witches and Killers in a Feminist Effort," *New York Times,* August 26, 1993.

14. Justin Lewis, *The Ideological Octopus* (New York: Routledge, 1991), pp. 203–205.

15. Ruth Conniff, "An Interview with Susan Faludi," *Progressive,* June 1993, p. 35.

EPILOGUE

1. Lyn Mikel Brown and Carol Gilligan, *Meeting at the Crossroads: Women's Psychology and Girls' Development* (Cambridge: Harvard University Press, 1993).

2. For a critique of MTV that argues that many of these videos promote a rape culture in America see Sut Jhally's videotape *Dreamworlds,* ©1990, distributed by Mediated, Northampton, MA.

3. Brown and Gilligan, *Meeting at the Crossroads,* pp. 4–7.

Index